Connecting with Kids Through Stories

of related interest

Big Steps for Little People
Parenting Your Adopted Child
Celia Foster
Forewords by David Howe and Daniel A. Hughes
ISBN 978 1 84310 620 3

A Safe Place for Caleb
An Interactive Book for Kids, Teens and Adults with Issues of Attachment, Grief, Loss or Early Trauma
Kathleen A. Chara and Paul J. Chara, Jr.
Illustrated by J.M. Berns
ISBN 978 1 84310 799 6

Nurturing Attachments
Supporting Children who are Fostered or Adopted
Kim S. Golding
ISBN 978 1 84310 614 2

Life Story Books for Adopted Children
A Family Friendly Approach
Joy Rees
Illustrated by Jamie Goldberg
ISBN 978 1 84310 953 2

The Child's Own Story
Life Story Work with Traumatized Children
Richard Rose and Terry Philpot
Foreword by Mary Walsh, co-founder and Chief Executive of SACCS
ISBN 978 1 84310 287 8

Delivering Recovery Series
A Short Introduction to Attachment and Attachment Disorder
Colby Pearce
ISBN 978 1 84310 957 0

A Practical Guide to Caring for Children and Teenagers with Attachment Difficulties
Chris Taylor
ISBN 978 1 84905 081 4

New Families, Old Scripts
A Guide to the Language of Trauma and Attachment in Adoptive Families
Caroline Archer and Christine Gordon
ISBN 978 1 84310 258 8

Connecting with Kids Through Stories

Using Narratives to Facilitate Attachment in Adopted Children

Second Edition

*Denise B. Lacher, Todd Nichols,
Melissa Nichols and Joanne C. May*

Jessica Kingsley *Publishers*
London and Philadelphia

Front cover image: Shutterstock. The cover image is for illustrative
purposes only, and any person featuring is a model.

First published in 2012
by Jessica Kingsley Publishers
116 Pentonville Road
London N1 9JB, UK
and
400 Market Street, Suite 400
Philadelphia, PA 19106, USA

www.jkp.com

Library of Congress Cataloging in Publication Data
Connecting with kids through stories : using narratives to facilitate
attachment in adopted children / Denise B. Lacher ... [et al.]. -- 2nd ed.
p. cm.
Includes bibliographical references and index.
ISBN 978-1-84905-869-8 (alk. paper)
1. Adopted children. 2. Narrative therapy. 3. Adopted children--Family
relationships. I. Lacher, Denise B., 1959-
HV875.L14 2012
362.734--dc23
2011027481

British Library Cataloguing in Publication Data
A CIP catalogue record for this book is available from the British Library

ISBN 978 1 84905 869 8
eISBN 978 0 85700 454 3

Printed and bound in Great Britain

Contents

Legacy of an Adopted Child   9

ACKNOWLEDGEMENTS   11

Introduction   13

Note   16

Chapter 1 The Internal Working Model   17

...and so it begins...the formation of the internal working
        model   18

Attachment relationships   20

The development of attachment   20

The importance of attachment relationships   24

The transmission of attachment   25

Life events   27

Complex trauma   29

The effects of trauma   30

Development   33

Meanings (or "peanut butter and a crib")   36

Summary   39

Chapter 2 Putting the Pieces Together: Discovering
           the Child's Model   40

The search   43

Discovery   55

Summary   56

Chapter 3 Narratives That Bond, Heal, and Teach   57

Section 1: How Narratives Work   58

Neuroscience of narratives   59

How stories can be therapy   60

Summary   62

Section 2: Constructing and Telling Stories   63

The setting for Family Attachment Narrative Therapy   63

The perspective   65

The hero   66
The message   67
Incorporating props in the telling   69
Additional thoughts   70
Summary   71

Chapter 4   Parental Attunement and Regulation   73
How attunement and regulation enhance or alter development 75
Section 1: How to Attune to your Child   **76**
Components of attunement   79
Factors affecting attunement   81
**Section 2: Regulation—Helping your Child to
    Calm**   **85**
Factors affecting regulation   86
Techniques to enhance attachment and increase regulation   90
Summary   95

Chapter 5   Claiming Narratives   96
Section 1: The purpose of Claiming Narratives   **97**
When parents find it difficult to bond   97
When the child finds it difficult to trust   98
Shifting the child's internal working model   99
Establishing birth order   100
Claiming the extended family   101
Passing on the family traditions, history, and rituals   102
Other issues   102
Summary   103
Section 2: Telling Claiming Narratives   **104**
If you had been…   104
Problem-solving tips   109
Summary   112

Chapter 6   Trauma Narratives   113
Section 1: The purpose of Trauma Narratives   **113**
Healing the pain of trauma   114
Shifting the child's internal working model   115
Creating understanding and empathy   115
Summary   117
Section 2: Telling Trauma Narratives   **117**
When to seek professional help   125
Problem-solving tips   128
Summary   130

Chapter 7   Developmental Narratives   131
    Section 1: The Purpose of Developmental
        Narratives   131
    Facilitating cognitive development   132
    Facilitating emotional development   134
    Building relationships   135
    Remedial skill building   136
    Enhancing development   138
    Summary   138
    Section 2: Telling Developmental Narratives   139
    When you were a two-year-old you would have...   140
    Problem-solving tips   146
    Summary   147

Chapter 8   Successful Child Narratives   149
    Section 1: The Purpose of Successful Child
        Narratives   150
    Teaching children values   150
    Reinforcing cause and effect thinking   151
    Presenting alternative behaviors   151
    Explaining the basics of how to do life   153
    Summary   154
    Section 2: Telling Successful Child Narratives   154
    The meaning of behavior   155
    Changing behaviors with narratives   158
    Teaching behavior with narratives   161
    Problem-solving tips   165
    Summary   166

Chapter 9   Stories, Stories, and More Stories   167
    Claiming narrative example   168
    Trauma narrative example   172
    Another trauma narrative   175
    Trauma narrative example: For older adopted children   178
    Trauma narrative example: For an internationally adopted
        child   181
    Developmental narrative example: How children learn secure
        base behaviors   187
    Developmental narrative example: How children learn to
        regulate anger and frustration   188
    Successful child narrative example   190
    Successful child narrative: Telling the truth   192

Trauma/successful child narrative: How to move forward 194
"*Rosebud,*" by Gaye Guyton 194
Trauma/successful child narrative: Lying and stealing 201
Developmental/successful child narrative: Learning how to
    be a friend 202
Successful child narrative: Learning to trust 204
"*Mistfire,*" by Donna Oehrig 204
Summary 208

Conclusion 209
A final word 210

APPENDIX A: EMDR 212

APPENDIX B: STORY CONSTRUCTION GUIDE 213

REFERENCES 215

RESOURCES AND FURTHER READING 223

SUBJECT INDEX 232

AUTHOR INDEX 237

Legacy of an Adopted Child

Once there were two women, who never knew each other.
One you do not remember, the other you call mother.
Two different lives shaped to make you one.
One became your guiding star, the other became your sun.
The first one gave you life. The second one taught you to live it.
The first gave you a need for love, the second was there to give it.
One gave you a nationality, the other gave you a name.
One gave you a talent, the other gave you aim.
One gave you emotions, the other calmed your fears.
One saw your first sweet smile, the other dried your tears.
One sought for you a home she could not provide.
The other prayed for a child and her hope was not denied.
And now you ask me through your tears,
The age-old question unanswered through the years.
Heredity or environment, which are you a product of?
Neither my darling, neither,
Just two different kinds of love.

Author unknown

Acknowledgements

We would like to thank Joanne May, the founder of the Family Attachment and Counseling Center, for her vision in developing Family Attachment Narrative Therapy. Her belief in the innate ability of parents to help their children was a driving force behind the work. Her support and encouragement in writing this book was much appreciated. Our colleagues at the Family Attachment and Counseling Center contributed valuable and honest feedback, nurturing, and lots of chocolate.

Most of all we would like to thank the parents and children who have shared their experiences of hurt, pain, and anger as well as success and joy with us. Our lives have been blessed and changed by them. Each and every narrative inspired and challenged the methodology, taking it places we had not yet imagined. We really could not have done this without them. The second edition contains stories written by Gaye Guyton and Donna Oehrig, parents who generously shared their narrative journey with us. We hope you enjoy reading them as much as we enjoyed listening to them.

Denise

My parents, family, and friends have not only shaped who I am but have been blessings in my life. Mom, thanks for being my secure base—I know I can count on you to be there. Thank you, Scott, for picking up the slack; and the groceries, and the dishes, and the laundry…when there were not enough hours in the day. Holly and Anne, sharing your journey through life has taught me so much about parenting and playing. Thanks for not giving up on this "less than perfect" mom. Thanks Holly and Jeff for giving me the opportunity for more practice on the most beautiful grandbaby ever born! A special thank you to my daughter, Anne Lacher, without whom the new resource and recommended reading section would not exist. And Todd and Melissa, it's been a longer road than we thought, but made much easier by your friendship.

Todd

Melissa, Jeremy, Anna, and Grace—what a wonderful family with which I've been blessed! You continue to add so much to my life. Thank you all for your constant support and teaching. Mom, the older I get, the more I appreciate your wisdom. Denise, your work ethic is legendary. Thank you for spearheading the second edition project.

Melissa

It is hard to find the words to express accurately my gratitude to those who have offered their inspiration, encouragement, and support through the rewriting process of this manuscript. I am greatly blessed by my family—Todd, Jeremy, Anna, and Grace. Todd, you have been a strong support with wise, loving words. Mom, thank you for your leadership, aid, and counsel. Denise, I so appreciate your thoughtful, tireless work on this project. Lastly, many thanks to the countless families that I have had the privilege to encounter in my work. You are an inspiration to me. Your courage, fortitude, and wisdom are truly amazing.

Introduction

Just two different kinds of love.

There is a growing awareness that early environment and experience are as important to growth and development as a child's genetic makeup. Children who experience sensitive loving care, not perfect but good enough care, experience the world in a different way than children whose early care was inconsistent, neglectful, or abusive. Our earliest experiences have been shown to shape how our genes are expressed and influence later development. Those experiences, whether positive or negative, create a working model or template of life, relationships, and behaviors. This core set of beliefs is the foundation of our ever developing and changing personality.

Life is full of challenges. If a foundation is stable and secure individuals face adversity with hope, using whatever skills they have, knowing that they have the support and help of family and friends. When a foundation is shaky, the world seems a dangerous place where survival of the fittest is the rule. In 1995, realizing the need to rebuild the foundations of these individuals, we began using stories to challenge mistaken beliefs and restructure the working model in order to help parents and children live a connected life. We called this process Family Attachment Narrative Therapy. At first we got incredulous looks and eye rolls, but since *Connecting with Kids Through Stories* was first published a growing number of parents have approached our clinic *because* we use stories. Already using narratives at home, they wanted to augment their techniques to better help their child.

When we began researching and writing the first edition of this book ten years ago, our children were young and our lives were busy. We had collectively worked with hundreds of families, equipping them to connect with their children. But our need to share this narrative technique beyond the walls of our offices and tell the stories of the struggles and successes of the families we work with day in and day out made us crazy enough to force ourselves to sit down and write. Ten years later our children are older, we are older, and our lives are no less busy but here we are again, wanting to share more stories. This second edition provides more tools to help parents to engage with their children in new and joyful ways. Family Attachment Narrative Therapy is easy to learn and easy to use. "Claiming," "trauma," "developmental," and "successful child" narratives are tailored to the child's individual situation and grounded in a parent's understanding of his or her child's characteristics and nuances. There are many books out there containing therapeutic stories to use with children, classrooms, groups, and adults. We still believe the best stories are created by parents to address the unique needs of their child. Parents have an ability to assess their child's model and create a one of a kind story that begins to chip away at mistaken beliefs and mend the cracks in that shaky foundation.

Foster and adoptive parents provide thousands of attuned, caring, corrective experiences to their new children. They reassure them time and time again that they are safe and loved no matter what. They talk, lecture, teach, and preach until they have nothing left to say; but the old model stubbornly endures. Traditional parenting techniques may cause a rupture in the parent and child relationship and may reinforce a child's existing beliefs about self and others. Stories and story time help to repair the daily disconnections that occur and help the child heal from his past and teach him new ways of behaving at home, in the school, and in the community.

Although the book is written in a "how to" format it is not designed to present a "one size fits all" answer to parenting. We have found that the meaning of the behavior is unique to each child, and proper and effective solutions require piecing together this meaning. This is the work of the parent—someone who knows and desires a lasting relationship with a child. *Connecting with Kids Through Stories* looks at the possible causes of difficult behavior and provides a way to understand and work with a child who is troubled.

Chapter 1 describes the formation of the child's internal working model in response to attachment experiences, life events, and course of development. How to discover the child's unique model and piece together the meaning of behavior is the focus of Chapter 2. Understanding the meaning of behavior guides the formation of narratives and the selection of parenting techniques. Case examples are used to demonstrate this principle. Chapter 3 examines the neuroscience of narrative therapy: changing the internal working model through metaphor and neural integration. Family Attachment Narrative Therapy as a comprehensive treatment is compared with other therapies that use narrative techniques. The process of telling narratives that bond, heal, and teach is introduced. Clinical examples illustrate the impact and effectiveness of various setting choices, props, perspective, and protagonists. Chapter 4 defines parental attunement and regulation as critical factors in fostering attachment. It presents factors affecting attunement and techniques to help children regulate in the face of challenges. Narratives also play a role in enhancing attunement and developing coping strategies. Chapters 5, 6, 7, and 8 explain each category of parent narrative: "Claiming," "trauma," "developmental," and "successful child." Chapter 9 includes full length samples of all four narrative types. As parents master the four basic types of narratives, many find stories that combine components of each narrative type useful. Examples of these combination stories are also provided. Several narrative examples designed to address the most common behavior problems and social and developmental needs of children are also included in this chapter.

We have made extensive use of examples throughout the book which we hope will illustrate the variety and richness of the approach. The story of fictional parents (Bill and Karen) and their adopted child (Robert), born to a 15-year-old chemically dependent mother, is developed throughout the book and placed at opportune locations in the text to illustrate the methodology. Readers explore the impact of maltreatment on Robert's development and the formation of his internal working model. The story continues as Karen and Bill, frustrated by Robert's behaviors, work with a therapist to piece together the complex internal working model behind Robert's behavior and develop narratives to help him heal. Additional vignettes of other children are used to illustrate the technique, and are sprinkled throughout the text. Many of the examples are based on real clients, but in all cases identifying information has been altered to protect confidentiality.

It should be noted that the examples given are intended to help readers understand how to construct narratives for children. The examples are not intended to be used to help a child. The best stories for each child will be different from the examples. Attuned parents who understand the meaning of their child's behavior will be able to develop unique and fun stories that help and teach their child. This is the underlying basis for this book. Throughout the book, the pronouns "he" and "she" are alternately used for ease of reading.

Connecting with Kids Through Stories is intended to help families struggling with very difficult and complex issues. Insecure attachment, traumatic life experiences, and developmental issues may cause behavior problems in children that challenge even the most experienced parents. Our hope is that Family Attachment Narrative Therapy will be a powerful tool. When used to address the issues underlying the behavior, the child's negative internal working model is transformed. A new, healthy model changes the child's view of himself, of the adults around him, and of the world. Stories do have the power to change a life.

Note

In light of the controversy surrounding attachment therapy, we feel that it is important to draw a distinction between Family Attachment Narrative Therapy and some other approaches. Attachment therapy is often considered to be coercive holding therapy or some form of therapy which uses controlling, confrontational techniques. Family Attachment Narrative Therapy is a gentle, nonprovocative, nonintrusive methodology in which parents are the primary agents of healing their hurt child.

Chapter 1

The Internal Working Model

Two different lives shaped to make you one.
One became your guiding star, the other became your sun.

Robert was not a wanted child. Tanya was 15. She didn't want to be a mother. She smoked—sometimes a pack a day. She liked to hang out and party with her friends. Someone always managed to get some weed and a bottle. When the nurse at the clinic asked about drug and alcohol use she always denied it. She didn't want trouble, and what difference would it make anyway? Tanya had been placed in a group home with other teenagers after running away from her house. She said her mother's boyfriend hit her and she couldn't stay there one more minute. She would be moving back home after the baby was born. Her mother promised that the boyfriend would be gone by then.

When the baby was born, Tanya was terrified. The pain was bad. She didn't want to hold him after she gave birth, she just wanted to curl up and sleep. She watched the nurses fuss and coo at him. "Let them," she thought. When she arrived home with Robert, the boyfriend was there, drunk and mean as ever. He yelled every time the baby cried. Tanya's mom told her to feed him; she tried but he just kept crying. So she left and found her friends. When she got back, Robert was sleeping on her bed. She slept too.

Robert felt uncomfortable, hungry, wet, and alone most of the time. He cried a lot. Sometimes someone came and other times he fell asleep exhausted. Sometimes someone came and his head exploded in hurt and he cried harder. As the weeks passed, he stopped crying much. His bottom was raw and sore, but he didn't cry. When he was fed, he ate as fast as he could. There were lots of people, lots of noise, and nothing made sense. He rubbed his cheek on the mattress and held his bottle tight. When he learned to crawl, and then walk, he discovered that he could get what he wanted all by himself. He learned that sometimes when he toddled up to the big people, they smiled, offered treats, and played with him. At other times when he would do the same thing, he would be pushed or shoved away. He couldn't figure out what he had done wrong. He still tried to get what he wanted, he was just more careful. The big people left him alone most of the time. Sometimes they yelled at him and said he was bad, ugly, and stupid. He didn't know what that meant but it hurt; it was kind of like the other sort of hurt, but this hurt didn't go away. Sometimes they played with him but he never let his guard down. He expected more hurt.

...and so it begins...the formation of the internal working model

The meaning a child makes of his early life experiences, coupled with the behaviors he develops in response to those events, has an impact on his future and on his family, neighbors, and community. A child draws conclusions about himself and his world in relation to early experiences. He is more likely to draw positive conclusions in response to early relationships that are characterized by nurturing and consistency. In the case of a child with hurtful experiences, such as Robert, he is at higher risk of developing negative conclusions. A child in this situation is more likely to manifest behaviors that make him a greater challenge to parent. In many cases the child is finally removed from his birth family. Nonetheless, the conclusions formed in early life may stick with him and inhibit his ability to lead a productive, cooperative, connected life with others, particularly his new caretakers. Some children possess a capacity for resilience to overcome a beginning such as Robert's. But for many other children these experiences will engender social, emotional, and behavioral problems throughout their lifespan.

The power of a parent's smile, touch, and loving interactions is enormous. Unfortunately, traumatic early life experiences are far too common in our society. Prenatal exposure to alcohol and drugs, abuse and neglect, and inconsistent caregivers influence the child's development. The child's experience of attachment relationships and life events affect his process of development. In the course of thousands of parent–child interactions, the child forms a representational map or internal working model (Bowlby 1969/1982). This model is a template of expectations and beliefs about self, others, and relationships. Understanding the internal working model is the key to doing Family Attachment Narrative Therapy. The internal working model develops in early childhood. Like snowflakes, no two are alike. And, like snowflakes, the complexity and beauty can only be seen if closely examined one at a time. The model is unique to the individual. Shaped by experience, it informs interpretation of events and is continually modified and updated by new behaviors and experiences: "expectations and representation are the 'carriers' of experience. They are the connection between behavior–experience at one age and behavior–experience at the next" (Sroufe *et al.* 2009, p.231). We explore each of these concepts below. Figure 1.1 depicts a child's working model. The circles represent three spheres—attachment and relationship experiences, life events and trauma, and development—are interconnected. Each sphere influences the meaning a child draws from early experiences.

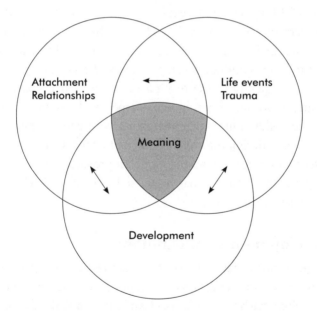

Figure 1.1: The internal working model. Loving or terrifying attachment experiences influence numerous aspects of the developmental process. Life events influence brain development and the child's ability to relate to others. A child's growth and development along an adaptive, normal pathway can be altered by early experiences such as abuse or neglect.

Attachment relationships

Attachment is about connections between people. John Bowlby (1969/1982, 1973, 1980) introduced *attachment theory* to describe behaviors he had observed between parents and children. In infants, these behaviors are designed to maintain closeness with an attachment figure who provides support and security. The level of attachment security depends partly on whether the parent is emotionally and physically available and responsive to the infant's needs. When an infant is under stress he makes noises, cries, and moves to get the attention of the caregiver. Such attachment behaviors stop when the primary caretaker comforts and relieves the infant's stress.

Although most evident in infancy and early childhood, attachment behaviors—ways of moving closer and connecting with the parent and other significant people in life—are present in adolescence and adulthood. As the child grows, the attachment figure is utilized as a secure base from which the child moves out to explore and socialize (Ainsworth 1967). When the caretaker is nearby and watching he has the confidence to move away, pick up an interesting toy, or join another child in the sandbox. By one year of age children develop patterns of attachment behaviors in response to the quality of the relationship with their primary caregiver. These patterns are an enduring set of specific behaviors that infants, toddlers, and children use when interacting with parents, caregivers, and other adults. Identifying the child's dominant attachment pattern is useful in discovering his internal working model. It provides clues to what might have happened back then, what he missed out on, and what he might need from current caregivers.

The development of attachment

Attachment behavior patterns may be organized or disorganized. When a child displays purposeful behavior designed to elicit a response from the parent, his attachment style is classified as organized. Smiling and approaching the parent with outstretched arms is an example of organized behavior. So is screaming, throwing toys, and moving away from a parent who is entering the room. Organized patterns include three types: secure, anxious-resistant (ambivalent), and anxious-avoidant (Ainsworth *et al.* 1978).

Secure attachments flourish when the caregiver is attuned and responsive to the child. Attunement (Siegel 1999, 2001) is a highly sensitive state in which parents are able to respond to the individual needs of the child. A sensitive parent recognizes the child's physical and mental state, whether the child is bored, lonely, uncomfortable, content, and so on. A sensitive parent responds to the child's needs by providing comfort, nurturing, or stimulation. The child is confident. He perceives the caregiver as loving and available when he is stressed. A securely attached infant clearly recognizes and prefers the attachment figure. He may even calm down when the parent enters the room, anticipating that his need will be satisfied. A securely attached toddler will boldly explore his environment under the parent's watchful eye. He frequently checks in with the parent by seeking eye contact or a quick hug, showing her his toy, or presenting her with the picture he has just created. Securely attached children may protest when the parent leaves; however, they are able to tolerate increasingly longer periods of separation without being overwhelmed with feelings of distress. They look forward to the parents' return and happily greet them, initiating physical contact.

When the parent lacks such attunement and responsiveness and is inconsistent in responding to the child's attachment behaviors, an ambivalent or resistant style of attachment may develop. In this relationship the parent's own needs and feelings seem to impair her ability to tune into her child's needs. Excitedly bouncing a tired, sleepy baby, or angrily feeding a fussy but full infant are examples of a mismatch between the parent and child's states. Because the child is unsure that his needs will be satisfied he may be preoccupied with any discomfort he experiences and discontent with the parent's attempt to attend to him. In this behavior pattern the child may cling, resist separations, be angry, and difficult to soothe. Children with a resistant attachment are susceptible to anxiety and depression (Sroufe *et al.* 2009).

We witnessed this style of attachment working with Frank and his new foster family. Frank was raised in a crack house where life was uncertain and chaotic. Now anything and everything could make him angry. He clutched his foster mother's leg with every ounce of strength he had while screaming, "Get away from me! Leave me alone! I hate you!" He hit when he was mad and then immediately kissed the spot saying, "Are you OK?"

The situation seems laughable, but parents living with a child who has an ambivalent attachment feel drained and exhausted by the never ending demands for attention and the constant anger and attacks. A child who demonstrates a resistant style of attachment focuses all of his attention and energy on the parent or substitute caregiver, never trusting that she will be available every time he has needs. "I can't trust you!" seems to be one of his underlying beliefs.

When a parent is insensitive to the child's state or ineffective at meeting his needs, the child becomes frustrated. A child who experiences such neglect may develop an anxious-avoidant attachment pattern. An avoidantly attached child did not experience his parent as available. His signals for attention, nurturing, and comfort were largely ignored. The parent may have even rejected or punished him for being distressed. The child with an avoidant pattern of attachment does not expect the parent to be responsive. He avoids the frustration of those interactions by over-controlling and suppressing normal attachment behaviors. He withdraws, refuses to ask for help, or actively ignores the parent (Sroufe *et al.* 2009). Outwardly he appears independent and self-sufficient, yet he may be vulnerable to depression and externalizing conduct problems.

Ellen was a child with an avoidant style of relating to her parents. She had been placed with them for three years and her parents felt stuck. They felt no closer emotionally to her than the day she came. She was not aggressive or destroying property like some of their friends' adopted children, so they felt lucky in some ways. Sometimes they wondered if they even needed help; maybe they were expecting too much. Ellen simply would not allow them to be her parents. Largely ignored unless she needed something, they felt used and manipulated. They were certain that as soon as Ellen turned 18 she would take off and never look back. "I don't need anyone!" seemed to be her motto.

Some children do not fit into one of the attachment categories that feature a somewhat organized way of interacting with the caregiver. Main and Solomon (1986, 1990) labeled the absence of a planned strategy in approaching the attachment figure as disorganized or disoriented. Disorganized attachment is often found in children who have been maltreated. The child is confused, trapped in the dilemma that the source of stress is the person from whom he is driven to seek comfort. He both needs and fears his parent. Disorganized attachment may also be evident in families where there is no abuse taking place. Instead, parents may have unresolved trauma or loss in their own past. As a result, they experience rapid changes in mood and behavior, or the child's behavior and needs trigger memories related to experiences in their family of origin. The parent's moods and resulting actions are unrelated to the child's signals. Consequently, the child is frightened. The child fears the parent yet has no other alternative if he is hungry or hurt. When a child is displaying disorganized attachment during a separation and reunion with his parent, his behavior seems to make no sense. He may display a mixture of approach and avoidance behaviors when in the presence of the caregiver. He may freeze as if in a trance, fall down, walk in circles, or walk toward the parent while looking in the opposite direction (Main and Solomon 1986, 1990). These children may eventually discover a way of dealing with their parent as they near school age (Main and Cassidy 1988). The child learns to manage the anxiety of interactions by controlling the parent.

Evan was bossy and mouthy to his mother. In response she threatened punishment but seldom followed through. He ignored the threats and his mother, until eventually she gave in to keep the peace. If that did not work, he blew up. By the time he had calmed down neither of them could remember what he had been asked to do.

Heather was scared of her mother's anger and threats but could still control what she did by carefully manipulating her mother with kindness. Attuned to every nuance of her mother's moods, she stayed close by to comfort, soothe, and calm her. She danced silly dances to make her laugh, made her a cup of tea when she looked tired, and reminded her to take her medicine when she had a hard time getting out of bed in the morning.

Both Evan and Heather had finally found a way to stay close to their mothers, remain safe, and get what they wanted.

The importance of attachment relationships

A strong, secure attachment promotes the child's social and emotional development. A child's expectations of how the parent will respond tend to become enduring beliefs that he applies to other relationships (Main, Kaplan, and Cassidy 1985). Several studies suggest that attachment patterns in infancy may be related to the older child's behavior in relationships with others. Securely attached children who expect parents and others to respond positively to them are typically regarded as socially competent within peer and, eventually, romantic relationships. Securely attached children are self-confident and rate higher on measures of self-esteem (Sroufe et al. 2009). They are perceived by others as empathetic, compliant, less dependent, and as having better self-control.

Insecurely attached children display maladaptive behaviors with others. (For the purposes of this book, an insecure attachment refers to the attachment classifications of ambivalent, avoidant, and disorganized.) A child with an anxious-avoidant pattern of attachment is often described as angry, hostile, and withdrawn. As the child gets older parents frequently seek help for severe conduct problems. He may lack the basic social skills necessary to find acceptance by his peers. Impulsive and demanding or withdrawn and fearful patterns of behavior are observed in anxious-resistant children. They are uncertain what kind of response, if any, they may get from a parent or peer. Observations of ambivalently attached children also revealed a lack of confidence in how to approach their environment. They are frequently treated for anxiety related disorders.

A child with a disorganized pattern of attachment seems to be at risk of lifelong cognitive, emotional, and social problems. He may alternate between aggressively defending himself from peers to withdrawing from any social situations that could be stressful. Anxiety and lack of experience result in responses that appear odd to their peers. Examples of the disorganized child's behavior in groups may be screaming and dashing in to grab a toy or lying down in the middle of a group of children playing house (Belsky and Cassidy 1994; Bretherton 1985; Elicker, Englund, and Sroufe 1992; Erickson, Sroufe, and Egeland 1985; Sroufe et al. 2009).

Adopted children receive outpatient and inpatient mental health services at higher rates than their non-adopted peers (Palacios and Brodzinsky 2010). Those who experienced abuse and neglect prior to placement were at higher risk for adjustment issues. Adoptive parents commonly report conduct problems, defiance, difficulties with attention and hyperactivity, and a propensity for substance abuse. A significant number of children adopted internationally also exhibit persistent problems after placement with a nurturing family (Rutter *et al.* 2009; Rutter and O'Connor 2004). In most cases, children who experienced foster care fared better than those who received institutional care. Childcare practices in large group settings may lack the necessary personalized care (attuned interactions, reflective conversations, and playful exchanges) for optimal development. Outcome is related to age at adoption. Those who are adopted at younger ages show the largest gains. Improvement in brain growth, cognitive and psychological development, and attachment security has been reported in the first three years after placement. However, some older children, perhaps because of prolonged exposure to deprivation, continued to display social disinhibition, learning difficulties, and emotional and behavioral problems.

The transmission of attachment

Few would argue that genes and environment (including early interactions with caregivers) affect a child's process of development. But just how do those attachment experiences translate into the child's future model for relationships? Sensitivity and attunement are important factors influencing the development of the child's internal working model. But these two factors alone do not explain the pattern of attachment demonstrated by the child within the parent–child dyad. Furthermore, the parent's own attachment pattern (secure, avoidant/dismissing, resistant/preoccupied, or disorganized/unresolved), while an important influence, is not necessarily predictive of the child's attachment classification (Fonagy 1999). Bowlby (1988) noted that the communication between parent and child, not just the acts of caretaking, were important to the child's development. What seems to matter most is the parents' ability to talk about their own childhood experiences in a coherent, organized way (Bretherton and Munholland 1999). This capacity to think about one's own emotions and behavior in conjunction with another's behavior and mental state promotes secure attachment in children. As the parent observes, verbally reflects, and elaborates on the child's emotions, the child understands what he is feeling and may begin to interpret and consider what others might be thinking and feeling. In essence the parent is teaching the child to "read the minds" of others. Not only can he attribute meaning to the actions of those around him, but he can begin to think about his own behavior—his own mind. Mentalizing is an extremely important skill when a child lives in adverse circumstances including poverty, domestic violence, neglect, and abuse. Unfortunately, the parents of a maltreated child are unlikely to transmit this skill to their child. A child raised in this setting may not be able to understand and control his emotions and behavior. He may also misinterpret the actions of others. He cannot read his parent's mind and instead, makes attributions based only on what he can see. Moreover, he may avoid the mental world altogether in order to survive (Fonagy and Target 1997).

Children with insecure patterns of relating to others express these negative expectations in their day-to-day behavior with parents, teachers, coaches, neighbors, and peers. Regrettably, an inaccurate model may hinder attachment to a new foster or adoptive parent after the child has been placed in the home. The child still expects parents to ignore, frustrate, or hurt him. Undeserving parents find themselves the target of behaviors that range from annoying chatter to aggressive assaults. A child with an insecure attachment develops defenses to protect himself from a world he believes is unsafe and unpredictable. Although necessary, those same defenses make changing inaccurate models more difficult. Information that contradicts his current internal working model is screened from conscious thought. It seems as if he only notices and remembers negative events and dismisses anything positive that happens to him. Such a child's memory of Disney World may be "You didn't buy me anything." A perfect day at the lake is reduced to "I never get to drive the boat!"

The effect of past experiences cannot be erased but models can be updated. New positive experiences with adoptive parents can modify existing expectations and create new ones (Palacios and Brodzinsky 2010). As the child's capacity for memory and thinking develops, he is able to reassess experiences (Carlson and Sroufe 1995). Changes in the interactions and communications between parent and child can shift working models (Bowlby 1988; Bretherton 1987; Bretherton and Munholland 1999). In a supportive environment in which parents co-construct narratives about past, present, and future, a child can understand and cope with the past

(Oppenheim 2006). That is what Family Attachment Narrative Therapy is all about. Time after time, we have seen narratives shift beliefs, change behaviors, and transform families.

> Tanya's relationship with her mother had always been a stormy one. Her mother's love and attention had been sporadic. When a boyfriend moved in and the parties began, it meant trouble. There would be fights, yelling, and hitting. She hated the times when her mom didn't get up in the morning. She would wake up to get ready for school but she never knew if she was early or late. There were never clean clothes and she knew the kids and teachers would whisper. She was scared to walk the six blocks alone. Things were better when there was no boyfriend around. Sometimes Tanya and her mom played or went to the park.
>
> When Tanya got older she yelled and fought back. She ran away from the chaos. She hung out with friends and stopped going to school. Tanya's experiences made it hard for her to feel anything toward her son. Immature and focused on her own needs, she was unable to read his cues. She responded in a random way to his cries or failed to respond at all.
>
> Hungry, uncomfortable, frightened, and angry, Robert's heart raced. He startled easily. Every sensation increased his distress. His eyes, arms, and legs moved and he fussed constantly. Some infants give up at this point; not Robert. But the continuous stress changed the way his brain developed. The world didn't make sense to Robert. He was never sure what would happen. His home seemed dangerous and unpredictable. He learned to avoid contact with anything or anyone.

Life events

Life is full of stress. Even positive and pleasant experiences cause stress. Children are better able to handle stress and strong emotions if they have developed a relationship with someone they can count on when they need help. The working model of a securely attached child anticipates comfort and reassurance from the attachment figure. This model may serve to protect the child from developing posttraumatic stress in response to experiences the child perceives as terrifying (Liotti 1999; van der Kolk and Fisler 1994). In contrast, the working model of an insecurely attached child may create a vulnerability to stress.

Beginning with Bowlby, theorists and researchers have hypothesized that attachment is more than an emotional bond of trust (Schore 2001a; Sroufe 1996). Attachment can also be viewed as a regulatory system vital to the infant's social-emotional development. Secure attachment relationships help children develop the capacity to regulate or manage emotional responses to everyday life experiences. Attachment relationships that provide security and safety seem to protect children from the effects of stress, even severe stress or traumatic life events. In contrast, early trauma, especially trauma that occurs within the parent–child relationship, may put the child at risk for developing psychological problems (Schore 2001b; Siegel 1999).

Advances in brain-imaging technology have led to an explosion of research on the role of traumatic experiences on the developing brain (Perry 1997; Perry *et al.* 1995; Schore 1994; Siegel 1999). From the moment of conception, the brain is under constant change in response to life events. The environment, particularly the social relationship between an infant and caretaker, influences genetic expression (Schore 2005). Secure attachment relationships nourish the brain and may serve to buffer the child from genetic risk factors. Trauma that takes place in those important relationships may be toxic to the developing brain of a child (Perry 1997; Siegel 1999, 2001).

Dan Siegel's book *The Developing Mind: How Relationships and the Brain Interact to Shape Who We Are* (1999) is an excellent resource for readers seeking additional information. In a genetically driven process, infants are born with an excess of neurons which organize and reorganize into networks based both on experience and genetic code. Over time, neurons not included in regularly used networks are pruned away.

The genes contained in our DNA are the blueprint for development, but environment and experience play a role in how each gene is interpreted and ultimately expressed (Stiles 2008). For example, if an individual has a genetic predisposition towards depression, his early experience of care and support may serve to suppress this tendency. In contrast, neglect and abuse may result in its expression. External environmental factors may modify genetic material and those changes are immediately transmittable to the next generation. Neural networks also interconnect and communicate with each other horizontally between left and right hemispheres and vertically, from the cortex through the midbrain to the brain stem.

Early experiences of deprivation have been found to affect brain structure and function. Areas involved in memory formation, emotional regulation, and the interconnectivity of the right and left hemisphere appear particularly sensitive to environmental conditions (Mehta *et al.* 2009). While there are sensitive periods in which specific stimuli result in optimal neural development, the brain also evidences plasticity, or the ability to change and grow in response to new experiences, throughout the lifespan. "The human brain is an 'organ of adaption' to the physical and social world" (Cozolino 2002, p.16). The brain has the ability to change for better or worse based on our experiences and interactions with others and the environment.

Complex trauma

The term complex trauma refers to the two-fold concept of repeated exposure to trauma (e.g., all forms of abuse and neglect, including witnessing domestic violence) that begins early in life, and the long-term effects on the developmental process (National Child Traumatic Stress Network 2003). Such exposure to trauma affects multiple domains of functioning: attachment, biology, affect regulation and behavioral control, dissociation, cognition, and self-concept. In this useful conceptualization, attachment and the child's behavioral functioning are not viewed separately, but holistically, as one of several important domains.

Just as reactive attachment disorder fails to adequately describe many children with insecure attachments, the mental health diagnosis of posttraumatic stress disorder does not fully encapsulate the impairment trauma causes in children. The complex trauma framework is useful to place the child's traumatic experiences in a larger context and to help parents better understand the complexity of the child and his multi-domain adaptation to trauma. This reminds us that the best treatment for such children will address multiple domains of impairment. Parents often come to treatment with a focus on behavior, but the complex trauma concept helps them to understand that effective therapy will have a holistic and multi-faceted approach.

The effects of trauma

In the US, child protection agencies received over three million referrals related to child maltreatment (US Department of Health and Human Services *et al.* 2010). While not all of these reports were substantiated, child abuse is a major source of trauma for children. A large percentage of childhood abuse victims are under the age of one. Even infants and very young children exposed to trauma may display a complex web of symptoms that affects attachment and development. The research evidence is overwhelming. The issue of child maltreatment cannot be disregarded. We can no longer go on thinking that because a child was young he does not remember the trauma and will get over it.

During the first months of life, an infant is developing the biological structures to regulate arousal. Maltreatment at this time may result in long-term over-reactivity to stress. In early childhood, the individual gradually begins to filter sensory stimuli and evaluate information based on context and past experience, instead of responding reflexively. Trauma alters right brain development and integration of the left and right hemisphere functions (Schore 2001b). Traumatized children have difficulty regulating strong feelings such as anger, fear, excitement, shame, hopelessness, and despair; their capacity for thinking is blocked and the emotional right brain takes over (National Child Traumatic Stress Network 2003).

The capacity for regulation is believed to be a function of the right hemisphere of the brain; its development dominates the child's first three years of life (Schore 2001a, 2005). In these first years, the mother or primary caregiver is responsible for the external regulation of the child's level of arousal and emotional states. When the child is uncomfortable, upset, angry, or afraid, soothing actions by the parent help him return to a calm and quiet state. Internally the mechanisms for self-regulation are forming. Attuned, sensitive responses to the child's cues help the child learn to regulate his emotions under stress. At the same time, relational trauma contributes to the development of negative internal working models, fosters negative feelings of self-worth, and impairs basic trust (van der Kolk 1996).

In middle childhood and adolescence the brain areas responsible for executive function are developing. Executive function refers to a set of cognitive skills that coordinate thoughts and actions in order to achieve purposeful, goal-directed behaviors (Riggs *et al.* 2006). Executive function is commonly associated with planning, organizing, working memory, and inhibiting one response in favor of another. Deficits in these areas lead to problems with attention, aggression, self-concept, peer relationships, learning, and decision making. Trauma and related disruptions in attachment may affect development of executive function. For example, executive function deficits are one important factor underlying adverse outcomes associated with profound early deprivation, such as that experienced by some Romanian adoptees (Colvert *et al.* 2008).

Each child's stress reaction will be different. Generally it falls into three categories of problems: identification of emotion, expression of emotion, and emotional modulation (National Child Traumatic Stress Network 2003). Unable to interpret internal experiences, children may try to cope by dissociating from their emotions and experiences. They may begin to avoid any experience, positive or stressful, that may evoke strong emotions. Dissociation and avoidance may take many forms. Some children withdraw physically in response to a perceived threat (flight). Other children may remain physically present but withdraw or numb themselves emotionally (another form of flight), thus avoiding psychological contact with what is stressful to them. Others remain chronically dysregulated. They react aggressively when their stress level begins to rise and verbally or physically fight back.

When the experiences of a child are overwhelmingly stressful, the brain tends to function in a continuous survival mode. Hyper-arousal (fight) and dissociation (flight) are normal responses that enable children to survive a neglectful and abusive environment (Perry *et al.* 1995). Ever watchful and wary of danger, the child is constantly on the verge of a state of fight or flight. These strategies may well serve the child while enmeshed in the trauma, but problems occur when the child is removed from the dangerous environment and placed in a new home. For a parent this means that minor matters can cause major reactions. Asking a child to empty the dishwasher may not seem like a life-threatening situation to an adoptive or foster parent, but to a child sensitized to stress it could cause a flight/fight response. Remember, even pleasant experiences cause some stress. Peering through the glass at zoo animals, being jostled in line for ice cream, or riding the zoo train all cause stress and could lead to a meltdown or a shut down. Despite the new parents' efforts to love, comfort, nurture, and keep the child safe the child's learned responses to stress can frustrate all attempts.

Contributing to the negative impact of trauma on the developing child is the child's inability to attribute the responsibility for the maltreatment appropriately. Only humans have the ability to judge and even personalize the traumatic experience and under stress children may fail to assess the event correctly (van der Kolk 1996). Children are great observers but lousy interpreters of the world around them (Dreikurs with Soltz 1990). Maltreated children have difficulty reflecting or thinking about their own internal world or the mental state of others and may be less empathetic than peers. Unable to take the perspective of the other person (Mom had a bad day) or see themselves realistically (I can beat anyone!), their decisions and actions may be unwise (Burack et al. 2006). In addition, younger children still believe they are the center of the world around them. If they have not progressed through this egocentric stage, they may fail to see the role others play in the traumatic life events.

The meaning children assign to their early experiences is critical to their ability to resolve traumatic experiences. We have worked with siblings who went through the same trauma, yet formed different conclusions about the events. The younger sibling was in an earlier stage of development and attributed responsibility for the neglect and eventual abandonment at an orphanage to himself. He believed that if he had behaved better, he would not have been rejected by his birth family. His internal working model reflected those beliefs. He expected to be rejected by his adoptive parents. His feelings of shame and worry that his "badness" would be discovered contributed to the development of depression and anxiety. In contrast, the older sibling concluded that her birth parents' alcoholism was not her fault. She was old enough to recognize that alcoholism, drug use, and poverty were pervasive in her country. While sad and angry that her family could not overcome their difficulties and keep the family intact, she did not take responsibility for the disruption.

The meaning a child makes of his early experiences contributes to his developing internal working model. Clients with posttraumatic stress and the professionals who work with them know that the effects of trauma are difficult but not impossible to treat. Beliefs and behaviors can change. Research is now suggesting that the brain remains open to change throughout life. Reading a book, learning to dance, and conversing with an old friend all provide experiences that cause subtle changes in the brain. New experiences in a child's life may influence attachment patterns of behavior and the brain's regulatory systems (Siegel 2001; Sroufe *et al.* 2009). Family Attachment Narrative Therapy is a way parents can provide their children with new experiences, reshaping their working model and eventually their behavior.

> Robert experienced ongoing abuse and neglect that injured his developing brain. He was left alone for long periods of time without caring human interactions and sensory stimulation. Without loving touch, the sight of his mother's face, interesting toys to look at, sounds that aroused his curiosity, essential neurological connections were not made. Unable to regulate his responses to stress, he seemed inconsolable and Tanya often gave up trying to soothe him.
>
> Robert was easily overwhelmed when his senses were stimulated. Loud unexplained sounds caused terror. Touch that should have been pleasant was uncomfortable. Robert learned that some stress could be avoided if he just ignored what was happening around him. He didn't look at anyone or anything. Rubbing his cheek against the mattress, his eyes stared unfocused at the wall.
>
> Getting what he wanted also relieved the stress he felt. He became obsessed with getting what he wanted. Limits and restrictions by the adults around him intensified the emotions he was experiencing. Eventually a "no" triggered a full "fight/flight" response. Robert alternated between striking out aggressively and retreating to the safety of his mattress.

Development

Development is a lifelong process. Heredity in combination with environment and experience continuously interact. The individual and environment are mutually transforming (Sroufe *et al.* 2009). Development is not something that happens to a child. The child creates, interprets, and plays an active role in the process. Emotional and behavioral problems arise when the child experiences overwhelming stress without parental support. He adapts but the developmental pathway deviates from normal. As early as the nineteenth century Janet (1889, cited in Schore 2001b) observed that trauma impaired an individual's ability to "assimilate new experiences...as if their personality development has stopped at a certain point" (p.210). In addition, other changes in development may occur due to prenatal exposure to chemicals, malnutrition, or other medical conditions such as chromosomal and structural abnormalities of the central nervous system.

Infancy appears to be a sensitive period for attachment. Healthy growth and development depends on feeling safe and secure in the environment. Securely attached children develop skills that prepare them for increasingly independent functioning as they grow up (Erickson *et al.* 1985). Conversely, lack of a secure attachment increases the probability of a qualitative change in the normal developmental pathway. Without responsive care the capacity for attachment may be compromised (Sroufe *et al.* 2009). Due to successive attempts to adapt to stress the child may follow a deviant pathway leading to antisocial and delinquent behavior (Egeland *et al.* 2002). As discussed above, trauma results in a dysregulated emotional state in the infant or child. In this constant state of anxiety, the child focuses his energy on relieving the discomfort of stress. Some constantly seek the attention of caregivers at the expense of exploration, play, and social behaviors (Bowlby 1969/1982). Others shut down, escaping the source of stress. In both cases, the child's resources are focused on avoiding stress rather than mastering important developmental tasks.

Change is possible but it is constrained by past history (Bowlby 1988; Sroufe *et al.* 2009). Early experiences cannot be eradicated but patterns of adaptation can change if stress is relieved and the child and his family receive additional support. It is common to see children who were raised in orphanages blossom once adopted. In a safe environment, their development leaps ahead. In many cases, however, the catch-up process is not a smooth, steady progression. The result is children who act much younger than their actual age.

Mark and his mother had lived with relatives or on the streets of a village in India most of his life. It was a dangerous and unpredictable life. She found a job in a city but could not work and care for him. He was left at the door of an orphanage at age three and never saw his mother again. His new parents adopted him when he was seven. Despite a year of consistent attention and love, he seemed so much younger than his peers in school.

The parents we work with often observe that the child's development seems to have changed or slowed down at the point in his life where he lost his safety and security. Mark's parents believe he was stuck at a three-year-old level when they adopted him. He was making some progress but they wonder if he will always lag behind.

Maltreated children may have difficulty with common cognitive concepts such as object permanence, causality, and symbolic function. They struggle with feelings of anxiety when parents leave for work, when a teacher takes maternity leave, or when their toys and belongings are out of sight. In the world that they came from, nothing was constant. And now, "out of sight" truly means "out of mind." Such a child resists separations from those closest to him and from beloved possessions. In addition, many children do not appear to have mastered cause and effect thinking. They repeat the same mistakes over and over, seldom learning from the consequences of their actions. Even after suffering injuries, one child persisted in climbing to the top of furniture and jumping.

Altered development is also revealed in a child's play. We have seen children who do not know how to play at a developmentally appropriate level. Toys are touched, dumped, lined up, and then put away without the child actually playing. Imagination and pretend play are conspicuously absent.

Most troubling to adoptive and foster parents is the apparent lack of conscience in children. Parents commonly report that their child shows no remorse or guilt. He laughs when others are hurt or angry. Unable to understand how someone else might feel, he seems puzzled and frustrated when he is given consequences. When a child's emotional functioning is impaired he may become easily overwhelmed by strong feelings. Parents cannot reason with him. His behavior may have little organization and seems to be an unintentional reaction to feelings of anxiety or anger. Although children who suffered trauma in their early relationships struggle to master necessary tasks and stages, physical deficits, emotional and social delays, and negative beliefs hinder their progress.

Robert didn't play with toys the way other children did. He wandered around the house and neighborhood watching, always watching. He would sometimes stand in front of the TV staring at the constantly changing images. He seldom spoke. Robert had lots of feelings, but no way to name or express his emotion. He was focused on getting and doing what he wanted even if it resulted in being yelled at or hurt. Deprived of normal interactions with a caregiver, Robert's development detoured in a dangerous direction. He could not sit still, constantly misbehaved, and then fell apart when he was upset. To an outsider he may appear like a "spoiled brat"; however, his early experiences and lack of nurturing care have impeded his development of self-regulation, speech, attention, and conscience.

Meanings (or "peanut butter and a crib")

As shown in Figure 1.1, (p.19) attachment, life events, and development are interconnected. Stress affects the nature and quality of attachment, attachment affects how events are perceived, and both affect development. The shaded middle area is the meaning a person draws from the three spheres. It is the meaning that drives the child's behavior. If the faulty, negative beliefs are challenged and shifted to something more positive and healthy, healing takes place in all three spheres. If the meaning is not revised it may become entrenched, expanding as the person grows older. At some point the meaning gets so enlarged that the individual may no longer see the underlying influences. He believes that he is bad or worthless but can no longer see that these beliefs may be related to early attachment or trauma. The meaning becomes who he is. This model has applications for many psychological disorders, not just attachment.

Family Attachment Narrative Therapy targets each of the three spheres with parent narratives (see Figure 1.2). Claiming narratives target disruptions in attachment and relationships. Trauma narratives assist children to process life events and the negative conclusions that are drawn about these experiences. Developmental and successful child narratives teach children and help them grow up. The importance of narratives and how they affect the internal working model is discussed in more detail in later chapters.

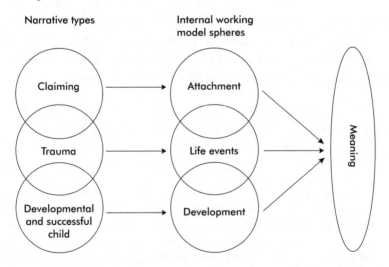

Figure 1.2: The influence of narratives. Parent narratives have an impact on each of the three spheres that make up the working model, ultimately facilitating change in the meaning a child has made of his life experiences.

The internal working model is a mental model of self and others. It has the potential to affect a child's future experiences and relationships. This model begins to develop before the child's first birthday and is made up of emotions, sensations, and perceptions (Siegel 1999). During this implicit stage of memory development, attunement with the parent is primarily nonverbal and physical in nature. Parents connect and communicate with children through sight, sound, and touch. As the child begins to use language to communicate with the parent, a more explicit form of memory is possible, containing facts and events as well as emotions and conclusions. The parent's words provide the framework for the child's experiences and memories. Narrative memory refers to the way experiences are stored and recalled in story form. In simple words, he can now tell someone who is he is and talk about what he did, is doing, and wants to do in the future.

It is by the use of narratives between parent and child that children learn cultural roles and expectations, the reasons for behavior, and the consequences of deviating from the cultural norm. This process is crucial for the development of conscience. The child must have internalized the beliefs and values of his parents in order to judge whether a particular action is acceptable. Siegel (2001) suggests that this co-construction of narratives between parent and child creates understanding and gives meaning. It helps the child to make sense of his internal (thoughts and feelings) and external (environment and others) world. We believe parent narratives can provide the verbal meaning necessary for the child to internalize a different life perspective, a new internal working model.

So what does this have to do with peanut butter and a crib? The child's internal working model influences perceptions, thoughts, feelings, and actions. It defines who the child is. The story of Emily illustrates the importance of accurate, healthy internal working models. Emily was left at the hospital after her birth. She experienced the loss of her mother and the trauma of separation. She spent a short time in an institution where she had multiple caregivers who were not attuned to her unique needs. Traumatized and confused, she was moved to a foster family to prepare her for an adoptive family. Her experiences in this family are not known. At the age of eight months, she was escorted to the US to join her new family. Again she experienced loss and trauma.

Emily's new family joyfully greeted her. At last, she had consistent, nurturing care by parents who were attuned to her cues. She laughed and smiled. She liked to be rocked to sleep and cuddled.

When she was older, it got harder for her parents to put her to sleep. They would rock her to sleep but when they tried to put her down she would wake up and cry. Well-meaning family, friends, and a pediatrician told Emily's parents that she would never learn to fall asleep on her own unless they let her cry it out. Her parents took all the advice and did what they were told was best for their little girl. For a week they rocked her, read her stories, and then put her in her crib to sleep. She screamed and cried. They talked to her from the door of the room but did not pick her up. She eventually fell asleep sobbing.

This little girl had survived many stressful, even traumatic, life events in the past. Once in her new family, she and her parents began to reconstruct a life narrative that was positive and coherent. She began to believe she was loveable, valuable, and her parents would always be there to take care of her. The events of the crib changed that belief.

Now, for those parents reading this thinking, "Oh no, I did that when my child was a toddler," relax. Emily's previous experiences and course of development combined with her prenatal experience, genetics, and temperament all merged to form her belief system. This belief system shaped her interpretation of being left in the crib. It was the culminating event that came to define who she is. The frame of her internal working model was set. Each time she heard "no," was not given what she wanted, or was frustrated by failure, her model became more firmly entrenched. She started screaming in the crib, but now she screams in the car, the kitchen, the school, the bathtub and everywhere. "No" means "I don't love you, I won't take care of you." At the age of 13 she stands screaming in the kitchen for her mom to put peanut butter on her toast. When mom is busy and asks Emily to do it herself, she collapses on the floor crying, "You don't love me! You never take care of me!" The anxious, frightened toddler in the crib screaming to be rocked becomes the anxious, frightened teen screaming for peanut butter.

Robert believed that the world was unpredictable and dangerous. When the police took him away from the house he didn't protest. With his heart racing, he silently watched out the car window and kept an eye on the men in the front seat. The teddy bear they had handed him as they carried him to the car lay unnoticed on the floor. After they arrived at the hospital he spent two hours in a room with lots of people bustling around. Some stopped to talk to him, or examine him; one gave him food which he shoved quickly into his mouth before it could be taken away. Eventually, he was back in the car. It was dark. This time they stopped at a house. It wasn't his house. A woman put him in the bath and then dressed him. He lay in bed with his eyes closed until the house seemed quiet. He slipped out of bed to explore. He would not sleep until he had figured out where stuff was.

Summary

The roots of difficult behavior in children can often be traced back to maladaptive responses to stress that changed their course of development. Children deprived of a nurturing, attuned relationship with a caregiver tend not only to construct a chaotic life narrative but also form mistaken, destructive conclusions about personal value and the meaning of experiences. Fortunately, children also possess the ability to embrace an alternative or the deserved ideal, and construct new narratives. The key to constructing adaptive life narratives is discovering the child's internal working model.

Chapter 2

Putting the Pieces Together

Discovering the Child's Model

And now you ask me through your tears,
The age-old question unanswered through the years.
Heredity or environment, which are you a product of?

Robert's adoptive parents are at the end of their rope. Bill and Karen are committed to being his parents but lately feel like they should be "committed." After successfully raising biological, foster, and adoptive children, they believed that they could help Robert, now four years old. They have parented many challenging children, but he seems to thwart every effort. The screaming, hitting, kicking, and spitting don't faze these parents. Their primary concern is his almost obsessive focus on getting what he wants, when he wants it.

Bill and Karen describe how Robert sneaks out of his room at night to play and to get food. When confronted he denies it. When put back in his room he begins screaming and chanting to get what he wants, keeping the whole house awake. They give in to restore peace but feel angry and resentful. Their home is being run by a four-year-old. He behaves like the perfect child when anyone else is around but as soon as they leave, he starts manipulating to get what he wants. "How can he be so good at it? He's just four! What's he going to be like when he's 13?"

Karen, who works at home, is the most discouraged. Despite her best efforts to love and nurture him, nothing has changed in the 14 months he has been with them. No consequence or punishment seems to matter and they have tried them all. Bill and Karen end their story by asking, "Why does he do this? How can we help him?"

The success of Family Attachment Narrative Therapy rests on discovering the meaning the child has drawn from early life events and evaluating the effect of those experiences on the child's development. Although children usually enter our program with multiple mental health diagnoses based on their behavior, the "why?" of the behaviors is different for each child. Many parents contact our clinic stating that they have seen a symptoms checklist for reactive attachment disorder on a website and that their child has every behavior. For many parents it is a relief to find out that there might be a name for what is going on with the child. It is also comforting to know that there are other families out there struggling with the same issues. However, a child with attachment difficulties may not exhibit these typical problem behaviors. We have evaluated children who have few or none of the "symptoms," yet displayed distortions of age appropriate attachment behaviors with parents, patterns that might be categorized as insecure. We have also assessed children who displayed every one of these symptoms and yet do not meet diagnostic criteria for reactive attachment disorder. An evaluation must include an assessment of the child's early life history and of the quality and strength of the child's current relationships. A history of abuse, neglect or multiple caregivers is not enough for a diagnosis and not all children who experience adverse parenting early in life have problems developing meaningful, stable relationships.

A 12-year-old girl was referred for treatment after being evaluated by another professional and given diagnoses of oppositional defiant disorder and reactive attachment disorder. During the process of determining the meaning of her behavior the team discovered that an older brother had told her she was adopted, which was untrue. Subsequently a series of events took place within her family that indicated to her that she was being treated differently and unfairly. Her behaviors matched those from the list of symptoms commonly associated with attachment disorders. But her early history did not match the criteria for reactive attachment disorder. Her behavior appeared to be a deliberate attempt to break the emotional connection between herself and her family. When her mistaken beliefs were discovered, loving narratives along with actual videos of her birth shifted her internal working model, restoring the relationship between her parents and herself.

Interestingly, some of these checklist behaviors may be closely related to disorganized/disoriented attachment (Gurganus 2002). However, caution must be used when comparing a child's behavior to a symptom checklist. The pattern of interaction between the child and others reveals the nature of attachment relationships and the internal working model, not just behavior alone.

There has recently been much discussion in the literature about the appropriate terminology to describe attachment problems. There seems to be a consensus that the diagnostic label of reactive attachment disorder and its diagnostic criteria, as stated in the Diagnostic and Statistical Manual of Mental Disorders—Fourth Edition (DSM-IV-TR), are insufficient to describe the clinical manifestations of insecure attachments observed by parents and professionals. Other labels commonly used include attachment disorder, disinhibited attachment disorder, secure base distortions, insecure attachment, no discriminated attachment figure, disrupted attachment disorder, and problems in attachment style or pattern. All of these terms are used to describe a spectrum of problems in emotional development, arising from a failure to form secure attachments to primary caregiving figures in early childhood. The official diagnostic labels of posttraumatic stress disorder or reactive attachment disorder do not adequately address the developmental sequelae of problems arising from insecure attachment patterns and childhood trauma (Sroufe *et al.* 2009).

The goal of discovering the internal working model does not rest on searching for the correct diagnosis. Diagnostic labels in children are generally descriptive of behavior and tend to be unstable, changing frequently depending on the current situation and the diagnostician's bias. There is a place for diagnoses. A diagnosis may suggest a particular type of treatment. A mental health diagnosis is often necessary to receive financial, therapeutic or educational support. But the label itself is less relevant than the information that leads to it, data that helps in understanding the child.

Applying a diagnosis to Robert's behavior may be the first step in developing a treatment plan in many traditional therapies. He might meet criteria for reactive attachment disorder and oppositional defiant disorder (ODD). Some might classify his symptoms as childhood bipolar disorder. He is also displaying behavior that could be related to attention deficit hyperactivity disorder (ADHD) and has some obsessive-compulsive features (OCD) as well. It's quite an alphabet soup.

Unfortunately, these diagnoses reveal little about the meaning of the behavior. The key is to focus on the underlying issues—what happened to Robert in the spheres of attachment experiences and life events and at what developmental level is he functioning? This information along with discovering Robert's beliefs about his experiences will shape the stories that lead to healing.

Family Attachment Narrative Therapy assumes that behavior is symptomatic of deeper underlying issues. Without addressing these issues the behavior cannot be permanently changed. Discerning the meaning of behavior in children with attachment problems is a crucial step in the healing process. The child's history and current behavior will provide many clues to the internal working model, and discovering the meaning of this information is vital to address the child's problems effectively. The following section discusses how to discover the child's internal working model.

The search

Managing behavior and establishing emotional bonds isn't enough. Effective treatment for children requires discovering the child's internal working model. Bowlby (1973) suggested that the internal working model could be understood by knowing the detail of the events in the life of the child. The single most important source of information about children's attachment patterns is the parents. By living with the child and observing her behavior, moods, preferences, and all the individual peculiarities, parents possess the specific knowledge needed to make sense of her behavior. Parents may further their understanding by researching her early history, noticing behavior in the home, school, and community, and seeking out psychological testing if necessary.

At this point, many parents may be thinking, "If I knew my child so well, I wouldn't be reading this book! I don't understand her at all anymore." Living with children or adolescents with attachment issues is not easy. Previous parenting experience does not explain her behavior and many normal parenting techniques do not work. It is complex and messy.

But parents really do have clues and information that can help them piece it together.

Discovering the internal working model of a child usually takes time. While a simple "I'm bad" may characterize some children's beliefs about themselves, other children present with a many faceted belief system. Somewhat like Sherlock Holmes, parents go down many dark alleys to collect clues and evidence, unsure of what the final solution to the mystery may be. But, like any good mystery, part of the intrigue is in the endless possibilities. It is sometimes challenging and always fascinating.

History

Our first consideration is the child's early history. The question of "What happened to this child in his/her early years?" is asked of all parents and professionals involved. What kind of care and nurturing did the child receive? Were there multiple caregivers? Were the child and caregiver separated? For how long? Was the child in daycare? Were there any significant events that could have caused the child to conclude that caregivers cannot be trusted? Parents and professionals should seek out available background and history. Records that might be helpful include birth records, medical records, police and child protection reports, social histories, placement and transfer summaries, and court documents. Previous psychological testing, school assessments, language, sensory, and neurological evaluations all provide pieces to the puzzle. For some children volumes of records must be waded through; for others there is a paltry amount of information. As we look ahead, collecting history on the child not only provides information about the development of her internal working model, but also structures the content of stories which will be used in Family Attachment Narrative Therapy.

Bill and Karen have very little documented history on Robert. Social services became involved when he was two years old after a neighbor called stating there was a child wandering around in the dark. When the police determined where he lived they found the home full of garbage and animal feces. The toilet was overflowing and there was moldy food on the counters and in the refrigerator. The only adult present was his grandmother's boyfriend, who had been drinking.

Robert was transported to the hospital for an examination and then to a foster home. Both Tanya and her mother said they wanted him back. A reunification plan was set up but they did not follow through, and the social worker began the process to terminate Tanya's parental rights. Robert was in foster care for five months before being placed with Bill and Karen, who hope to adopt him. He displayed many of his current behaviors in the previous foster home. Bill and Karen have additional information about his birth family and home from the foster parents, who supervised visits with his birth mother, Tanya, and sometimes picked him up at the home. Tanya reportedly paid little attention to Robert during the visits. He watched TV or wandered outside by himself. He was typically returned wearing a wet, soiled diaper. Robert didn't have much of a medical history. Tanya had not followed through with check-ups. He had been seen in the emergency room for a head injury. The note said he had fallen down the stairs. He also had scars on his arms that looked like teeth marks.

Standardized testing

Testing may help parents describe their child's behavior, personality, and development. Testing can also provide important insights on how well children are functioning; how they learn and process information; and how they perceive themselves, others, and the world around them. Behavior rating scales help to expose patterns including the frequency and intensity of behaviors. Parents who consult professionals find that each usually has his or her favorite instrument. We currently use the Achenbach Child Behavior Checklist (CBCL; Achenbach and Rescorla 2001) and the Child Behavior Rating Scale (CBRS; May and Nichols 1997). These checklists provide descriptive data in a standardized format. In the CBCL behavioral characteristics as reported by the child, a parent, and teacher are compared to normative samples of peers. Again these descriptions are helpful but not necessarily diagnostic. Other behavior scales that may be helpful are the Conners Rating Scales or the Behavior Assessment System for Children. Posttraumatic stress disorder symptom checklists for preschool and young children such as the Trauma Symptom Checklist (Briere 1996) may also be useful in assessing whether or not behavior problems are related to past life experiences.

The CBCL provides information on a wide range of behaviors related to anxiety, depression, social problems, thought problems, attention problems, withdrawn behaviors, somatic complaints, and delinquent and aggressive behavior. This checklist may suggest underlying feelings related to the child's maladaptive behavior. For example, many children with an anxious attachment have a strong need to be in control. They attempt to control adults, peers, and all aspects of the environment, and may quickly blow up when that control seems threatened. A high score on the anxiety scale suggests that insecurity and fear may be driving the controlling behavior. So trying to show kids "who's boss" may actually increase their fears and intensify their demands and anger. Why is the child anxious? What events could have caused the anxiety to develop? How is that anxiety manifested in her behavior with her parents? These are some of the questions that might lead to a hypothesis about the internal working model.

The CBRS is designed to assess the presence of behaviors that meet diagnostic criteria for Conduct Disorder, Oppositional Defiant Disorder (ODD), Attention Deficit Hyperactivity Disorder (ADHD), as well as behaviors that have been reported in children exhibiting insecure attachment patterns. These behaviors are commonly reported by parents and professionals who work with children with attachment disorders. The CBRS yields sufficient information to compare a child's functioning with diagnostic categories of mental health disorders. The CBRS also assesses the frequency and intensity of problem behaviors. As such, the CBRS is a useful intake instrument that can be used to screen children for potential admission into a treatment program. The CBRS can also document functioning prior to treatment and at various stages during the therapeutic process to gather data on treatment outcomes.

Children deprived of parental encouragement and support may have delays in gross and fine motor skills, speech, and cognitive and emotional development. These deviations from normal developmental abilities may be uneven. The child may be operating at her chronological age in verbal expression (she can talk the talk); however, when stressed, her ability to solve problems plummets to a level that is incongruent with her age (she can't walk the walk). The Vineland Adaptive Behavior Scales assess personal and social functioning of individuals from birth to late adulthood (Sparrow, Balla, and Cicchetti 2005). This instrument is available in survey form, interview form, and teacher form and assesses behavior in four domains: communication (receptive, expressive, written); daily living skills (personal, domestic, community); socialization (interpersonal, play and leisure, coping skills); and motor skills (gross and fine). It gives both standard and age equivalent scores. Age equivalents are helpful as parents attempt to understand their child's difficult behaviors. An age equivalent of two years and eight months in the area of coping skills explains much to parents who are dealing with the tantrums of a 12-year-old. The Vineland typically reveals delays in one or more domains of functioning for our child clinical population. They often display developmental difficulties related to early life experiences, and current stress related to everyday circumstances.

To avoid a court-ordered out-of-home placement after breaking and entering charges, a ten-year-old was referred for intensive therapy. The court was determined to send him to a juvenile correctional facility to deter future criminal activity. The Vineland revealed that Zach was operating at an 11- to 13-year-old level in the daily living skills area. To those who did not know him well, he appeared competent, as if he knew exactly what he was doing. However, his expressive and receptive communication scores were in the five- to seven- year range, and his socialization scores were in the three- to five- year range. Zach's silence, interpreted as defiance by the judge, may have been due to his inability to comprehend what the legal official was saying.

His problem behaviors were partially due to low coping skills. He handled frustration and problems like a preschooler. When he lost his temper, he hit others and destroyed property. If he wanted something, he took it. Being sent to a juvenile facility would most likely contribute to Zach's existing problems, and probably not deter him from the same behavior in the future. The Vineland revealed that he lacked many of the skills necessary to control his own impulses.

Other measures that may be helpful in figuring out why children behave the way they do include projective drawings, sentence completions, and projective assessments such as the Thematic Apperception Test (TAT), the Children's Apperception Test (CAT), and the Rorschach Inkblot Test. Narrative assessments such as the MacArthur Story Stem Battery (Bretherton *et al.* 1990), the Attachment Story Completion Task (Bretherton,

Ridgeway, and Cassidy 1990) or the Manchester Child Attachment Story Task (Green *et al.* 2000) are useful to assess attachment patterns. Elements such as narrative coherence, ability to talk about emotions, whether the child expects adults to be available and helpful, and whether the child brings the story to completion bring to light specific issues in attachment (Oppenheim and Waters 1995). Cognitive testing such as the Wechsler Intelligence Scale for Children and Stanford-Binet Intelligence Scales may provide information about the child's strengths and unique challenges. If prenatal exposure to alcohol or drugs is suspected, an evaluation for Fetal Alcohol Spectrum Disorder may be indicated.

Children who have experienced deprivation in the early years of life may have sensory processing problems that contribute to their behavior problems. For example, if a child seems unwilling to accept affection from parents, it is important to determine if this is due to an avoidant attachment style or tactile defensiveness. Excessive running, jumping, climbing, talking, and noise is frequently attributed to ADHD in children. However, anxiety or sensory difficulties often mimic symptoms associated with ADHD and should be considered.

Alex was going to get kicked off the bus. He was out of his seat, bugging other kids, pushing, and tripping his friends in the aisles. When he arrived at school he was usually out of control. He raced around the room, touching and handling everything, and would not join his classmates for morning circle time. He laughed loudly and distracted others with body noises and animal sounds such as barks, meows, and cock-a-doodle-doos. Parents asked teachers to track Alex's behavior over the course of the day and week.

It turned out that the behaviors happened most mornings after getting off the bus. An evaluation revealed that his behavior was consistent with a sensory processing disorder. Armed with this information, Alex's parents were able to work with the transportation company and school to develop a sensory plan for Alex. He was moved to a smaller bus where seat belts were available and allowed to chew gum and listen to music during the ride to school. He was also given time in the gym to satisfy his craving for stimulation before entering the classroom. Such interventions worked better to calm Alex and achieve the results adults desired than giving him consequences.

Assessments to rule out sensory integration dysfunction may provide additional information about the "why" of certain behaviors. The knowledge gathered through assessment is valuable to parents and professionals when there are pieces missing from the puzzle.

Bill and Karen hoped that an evaluation would help them figure out what was going on with Robert. He was so different from any other child they had parented before. The results of some of the testing forms they filled out confirmed that he was indeed not just an active child. The Vineland ranked Robert low on the communication domain. He had difficulty understanding what was said to him and telling others what he wanted. His social skills were low too. He was not able to consider anyone else's needs, share with others, or give instead of just take. With this information it now made sense that Robert resorted to tantrums when he was frustrated. Bill and Karen also realized that their expectations for Robert were too high. Robert, however, was very independent and insisted on taking care of himself. He had a high score in daily living skills. It was easy to understand why Bill and Karen and his preschool teacher had treated him like other four year olds.

Observational methods

Observations of the child in play with the parent or with a therapist also provide information about the child's internal working model. Unstructured play time permits observation of the quality and content of play without imposition of outside limits. Following the child's lead, playing the way she plays, while watching and listening can be fascinating. The emotional content and themes of the play may reveal aspects of the child's internal working model. A child hiding under furniture, disguising herself, and burying figures in the sand may indicate anxiety and fear. It may even provide clues to how she handled her traumatic past and currently responds to stress. Noting general themes of symbolic play may hint at the conclusions the child has drawn about her life experiences. For example, constant battles in which opponents are overcome by brute force may reveal a belief in the need to be violent in order to survive. Keep in mind that there might be many reasons the child is fighting battles during play time. If it is a clue to her model, it will fit with the other pieces of the puzzle parents are collecting. Parents with intimate knowledge of their child's day-to-day activities often understand the meaning of play before professionals. One 12-year-old repeatedly stuffed dolls into the trunk of a car. Was she reenacting a past experience? In this case, the parent supplied the necessary information. The child had been listening to an older sibling's rap music and acting out the lyrics.

Day after day in the play session Nicholas cooked, filling pots, pans, plates, and bowls with "food" (play sand) and pouring drinks for everyone. Then he "ate" and cleaned up the mess while telling the dolls and animals surrounding him that if they behaved tomorrow they would get to eat too. Next he roughly grabbed the hungry, crying dolls and threw them in bed. His parents related that the scenario had not changed much in the two years since he was adopted. After several claiming narratives, Nicholas's parents were encouraged when he lovingly fed and rocked a baby doll to sleep just as they had described how they would have taken care of him. Perhaps his working model was beginning to change.

Play clearly exposes developmental delays. A 17-year-old who plays dress up, an eight-year-old who lines up cars, moving them back and forth without an imaginative narrative, a six-year-old playing alongside someone else without interacting or sharing are all illustrations of play that might be considered developmentally inappropriate. For experienced parents, comparing the child to other children they have parented in the past may help to determine the child's level of functioning.

Observations of the parent and child interacting may also be useful. Structured observations such as the Marschak Interaction Method (Booth and Jernberg 2009), the Strange Situation (Ainsworth *et al.* 1978) or another separation-reunion task may be helpful in determining issues within the dyad. The nature and quality of the attachment relationship between the parent and child is often revealed in their play and interactions together. The separation-reunion procedures can be useful in determining attachment behavior patterns in the child. Securely attached children confidently explore the playroom, checking in and making frequent eye contact with the parent. In addition, there is a mutual enjoyment of the play and of each other. Attuned parents are attentive to the child's actions and emotions during the play and have age appropriate expectations. Conversely, children who perceive that their parent is not physically or emotionally available may loudly object to separations and cling to the parent even in a room with inviting toys. Others avoid direct contact, disobey the parents' requests, refuse help or nurturing, and ignore the parents' comings and goings. The Marschak Interaction Method allows clinicians to assess how the caregiver structures activities for the child and whether he or she encourages engagement and completion of the tasks at an appropriate level for the child's development. They also reveal how playful, nurturing, and attuned the parent is to the child's emotional state and level of frustration.

Bill and Karen had lots of toys in the house and in Robert's room. He dumped them out, carried them around the house, and even threw them when he was mad, but he did not play with any of them. He didn't seem to care if a toy was lost or broken. During Robert's evaluation he was observed both with Bill and Karen and with a therapist. Robert always separated easily from Bill and Karen to go with the therapist. He did not talk much during play observations. Robert randomly picked toys off the shelves, played briefly with them, and dropped them to move on to the next. When the floor became cluttered he just walked on top of the toys. He did not look like he was having fun. During the parent–child observations he avoided eye contact and physical touch unless Karen offered food. He did not protest when Bill and Karen left the room or react when they reentered. He was oppositional to Karen's requests but would comply if Bill restated the request more firmly. Robert allowed a story to be read to him but immediately slid off their laps and stepped on Karen's feet. Bill and Karen reported that if they had attempted this at home he would have been much more aggressive and loud.

What the parents know

Each child is unique. No therapist can ever understand a child's nuances at the same level as a parent, and this is precisely the type of intimate knowledge that is necessary to create effective narratives. Parents are able to describe in great detail the child's behavior and mood shifts—what makes the child tick. More importantly, the parent knows, or at least is in the best position to guess at, the underlying feelings and meaning of the child's behavior.

Parents often possess stories, undocumented history that has been passed by word of mouth from previous foster parents or social workers, and information from the child that no professional knows. The child may recall memories of traumatic events and tell her own narratives as she becomes more comfortable in the new family. She may also spin stories to shock or test them ("Will you still love me if you know the worst about me?"). A young child's implicit memories of trauma may be revealed through behavior instead of words. Children who have experienced abuse may flinch and raise their arms to protect themselves when parents move too quickly. They may fear baths, the dark, going to bed, or physical touch. Everyday stress or parental requests may result in flashbacks, hysterics, tantrums or nightmares. Many experiences may remind them of where, when, and how they were abused. A child's action or reactions can provide information about possible traumatic events.

One four-year-old girl screamed hysterically when her foster mother ran water for the bathtub or backyard pool. Once it stopped running she happily played in the water. It was a mystery why. One day when talking about water, the little girl mentioned "deep water." With a little encouragement other words and phrases were added including "shower," "door shut," and "grandpa." Her mother and a social worker who had known the birth family for years were able to piece together that she had once been in a glass shower stall with a man while the running water got deeper and deeper. The mother now had a better picture of a traumatic life event that had happened to her little girl and was able to craft a healing story to help her overcome her fears.

Internal working models are based on our life experiences. These expectations guide interpretation of subsequent life events and behavior within relationships. But what if a child's circumstances change? Adoption is a dramatic intervention in a child's life. In a new safe environment, adopted children may "catch up" to non-adopted peers in the areas of physical growth, attachment, and cognition (IJzendoorn and Juffer 2006). But despite gains, there are a significant number of adoptees still receiving mental health and educational services. It seems that even with a change in environment, past experience continues to affect a child's reactions to others, often provoking negative responses in her parents (Sroufe *et al.* 2009; Steele *et al.* 2003). Parents often report that it feels as if their child is purposefully trying to get them to yell at her, hit her, or send her away. If the child is successful, her working model is confirmed.

> Bill noticed that if he moved too quickly, Robert flinched and ducked. When their older children had friends over to play, Robert usually retreated from the noise and activity. He watched but seldom joined in. When Robert first came to live with them, he could fall asleep anywhere. He would just drop off in the middle of bright lights and noise. He wandered out of the yard despite repeated consequences. Robert would wander into the rooms of Bill and Karen's older children and go through their things, taking what he wanted. Sometimes he took money, but sometimes he just took junk that he couldn't possibly need. It didn't seem to matter what they said or did; he just kept doing it until they finally put locks on their doors. When Bill and Karen considered Robert's history in relation to these actions his behavior began to make sense to them. All of these behaviors served a purpose in his previous family.

Relating behavior to the child's history can be a painful process, especially if the parents have been reacting to difficult behaviors with anger and consequences. Once they understand the behavior, many parents feel guilty about the "less than perfect" techniques they previously employed. Placing the behavior in the context of the past touches the parents' empathy for the child. It may also stir up anger at who and what caused their child's pain. Instead of just reacting to the behavior, parents have an opportunity to become an understanding champion of the child. As they begin to understand why the child is doing what she is doing, hope is renewed. Now they have a way to help the child heal and give themselves relief from problem behaviors.

Embarrassed by frequent phone calls from her daughter's school, one mom worked hard to shape up the out of control behavior. As she dug deeper and discovered the meaning of the behavior, however, her approach changed. The school provided services to special needs children, including her daughter. Kids were pulled from the classroom by professionals in white lab coats for occupational, physical or speech therapy. In the orphanage where her daughter was raised the medical director wore a white coat and took sick children out of the group. Some never came back. Her daughter's "out of control behavior" was due to her traumatic memories being constantly triggered by the professionals in white coats taking kids from the room. Now the mom's goal was to help the school understand why her daughter behaved the way that she did and what the school could do to avoid triggering her behavior.

One of the most common problems parents seek help with is tantrums. Robert has loud and sometimes violent tantrums that disrupt the family and limit their activities in the community. They never know when he is going to "go off." Bill and Karen have heard that sometimes the child is taking out all his or her past anger on the new, "safe" parents. That may be true, but it doesn't make them feel any better. When asked what usually triggers the tantrums, Karen reports that usually it's when Robert doesn't get what he wants at the moment he wants it.

What is underneath Robert's powerful drive to get what he wants? How did that need develop? How is it related to his prenatal environment and his early history? Have his early attachment and trauma experiences affected his development? How do these delays affect his ability to learn and to handle stress? Bill and Karen, along with the professionals assisting them, were not able to answer these questions outright. However, they had some hunches. They were able to make educated guesses based on what they did know and using their intuition. Many of the answers were contained in the stories they told about Robert.

Karen states that last week she put Robert in his room to cool off during a tantrum. He kicked and beat on the door as usual. She can see his room from the kitchen and keeps an eye on him as he will sneak out and try to get whatever it is that he is mad about. Surprisingly, he stayed in his room this time—maybe because it was close to naptime. Karen walked by his room occasionally, listening to make sure he wasn't destroying something. It was too quiet. She peeked into the room. He had pulled all of the covers off the bed onto the floor and was lying on top of the bare mattress rubbing his face against it. She notes that he seems to like rubbing things on his cheeks. Looking for the "why" of his behavior, Karen speculated that he might have been left alone a lot and rubbed his cheek to comfort himself. She reflected on this as she comforted him. She now had information that might be helpful in a narrative.

Discovery

There are key questions that lead parents and professionals away from behavior to the "why" and the "how." Why is the child behaving this way? How is it related to her early attachment experiences? How is it related to trauma in her past? Is it a developmental adaptation that has outlived its usefulness in the child's survival? The collection of stories and observations about a child contains pieces of the internal working model and may lead to healing narratives. The focus must always be on what is underneath the behavior.

After gathering sufficient information the pieces can be put together to form a working hypothesis of the child's internal working model. The hypothesis should be constantly updated as new information is available. Narratives that target and shift the mistaken beliefs of the model are then possible. Often the child's internal working model can be characterized as "I am bad or evil, I deserved to be abused, I deserve to be hated, and my bad behavior is who I am." The model may be blatantly obvious. Hearing the beginning of a claiming narrative "When you were a tiny baby you deserved to be loved," one child immediately protested "No! I'm not! I'm bad!" But for other children, the meaning they have constructed for their life and future is deeply buried under layers of hurt, shame, and anxiety. The thoughts and feelings are unspeakable. Those around the child may only see difficult behavior. An interpretation solely based on the external behaviors may obstruct the construction of potential healing narratives. How hypotheses are used to construct stories that help children connect, heal, and learn is discussed in the following chapters.

The formation of Robert's unique internal working model was profoundly affected by prenatal events. Unwanted and uncared for, his development was affected by his birth mother's alcohol and drug use. As an infant he was frequently left alone and had few loving interactions with the adults around him. Anger changed to despair. Some infants might have died, but not Robert. He had determination. He was a survivor and once Robert was mobile he found ways to get his own needs met, to comfort and soothe himself. Unrestricted, needs merged with wants. Developmentally delayed, he had few words to express himself, poor impulse control, and limited cause and effect thinking. Robert was four yet Bill believed that Robert thought he was an adult, free to do as he pleased.

Bill and Karen's stories about Robert provided pieces of information that helped them make sense of Robert's tantrums and other behaviors. He seemed to believe that he did not need anyone. He used adults to get what he wanted, but they were not to be trusted. He felt safer if adults just left him alone. As their understanding of Robert's internal working model grew, their frustration with him decreased. Bill and Karen intuitively knew that they would need to make a connection with Robert before they could use narratives to shift mistaken beliefs.

Summary

Behavior cannot be permanently changed without addressing underlying attachment, trauma, and developmental issues. The "why" of behavior is different for each child. Parents are the primary resource for information about the child. Testing and observation may also be helpful. The goal is not to find a diagnostic category, but to discover the child's internal working model. The search is for the meaning of behavior. Parents and professionals seek to understand the relationship between the behavior and the child's early attachment experiences, life events, and developmental pathway. Once a hypothesis is formed, narratives are constructed to target the negative and erroneous conclusions formed in early childhood. New beliefs develop that can change the child's internal working model and, consequently, her behavior.

Chapter 3

Narratives That Bond, Heal, and Teach

The first one gave you life. The second taught you to live it.

The flames of a warm fire gently light the faces of a father and daughter cuddled under a faded star quilt. Entranced, the child listens attentively. She turns the pages as her father reads the story that has become their nighttime ritual. She wants the same story to be read over and over again, eventually memorizing the words and "reading" to Dad. It's one of those moments that you hope the child will treasure forever.

Story time is a perfect bonding activity. Bonding activities are any actions that increase physical proximity and facilitate feelings of safety, security, affection, and trust. It is a time when emotional connections are formed between two people. The parent of a child with attachment disturbances and behavioral disorders may have a different experience of these activities. The child complains, interrupts, wriggles, and fidgets before hopping off to go and play with something else. So much for the moment to treasure. Some parents have compared it to cuddling with eight pairs of elbows and knees. They are left with feelings of frustration and disappointment rather than closeness and intimacy.

Family Attachment Narrative Therapy can be an effective tool to help children develop trust, heal from past experiences, and learn new behaviors. The key is discovering the child's internal working model and meaning of the behavior (Nichols, Lacher, and May 2002). Narratives are then constructed to address the negative belief system that drives the behavior. Generally parents begin with *claiming* narratives, stories which assist the parent and child in developing an emotional bond and a feeling of belonging to the family. Eventually *trauma* narratives are introduced, telling the child's trauma story, bringing it coherence, and helping the child to make sense of it. *Developmental* narratives are designed to help a child learn and master the tasks and stages he may have missed out on while growing up in a neglectful, abusive environment. Learning new ways to adapt to stress and environmental circumstances allows a child to move back toward a healthier developmental pathway (Sroufe *et al.* 2009). *Successful child* narratives teach and present alternatives to the challenging behaviors of a child with a negative working model. Parents also use narratives to impart family values, faith, history, and rituals. As we evaluate the narratives we have heard over the years some common themes emerge, which will be presented later in this chapter. Narratives represent the ideal in parenting—what it could have been like for both the parent and child had they been together. Narratives never attempt to alter the child's actual history. Instead the child is introduced to new possibilities for positive beliefs about himself and others. The narratives convey the parents' unconditional love for the child. Stories work. Parents can help their children to heal through this powerful medium.

Section 1: How Narratives Work

Any lover of the fine arts is familiar with the capacity of a story to affect an individual's thoughts, feelings, and subsequent actions as vividly as if that person were actually involved in the experience. For example, after an encounter with two children whose mother had got rid of the family pet as a punishment, composer Paul Schoenfield wrote a piece of music to lessen the children's pain. Called *Dog Heaven*, the piece tells the story about a jazz club in canine afterlife, a place where the streets are lined with bones and there is a fire hydrant on every corner (Schoenfield, undated).

Some authors and therapists use the power of metaphor in their work to alter conceptions, feelings, and, ultimately, behaviors. Defined as literally using one object or idea in order to suggest a resemblance to another, a metaphor may be a symbol, analogy, figure of speech, parable, or story. On the surface the listener attends to the content, facts, and details about the character, and the problem and possibilities for resolution. But hidden symbols, meanings, and suggestions embedded in the story indirectly communicate to the child at a deeper level. The best stories are those based on the listener's personal experience. An absorbed client or child may even project meanings beyond those that the teller hoped for (Yapko 1990). The indirect nature of metaphor decreases resistance. It's just a story. The oral language of the story combined with nonverbal communication such as voice, facial expressions, and gestures create a meta-message that has the potential to bypass cognitive defenses. If just talking to a child worked, most parents would not be reading this book and countless other parenting-related publications.

Stories are universal and timeless. In every culture and throughout history people have told stories to each other. Stories convey social and family history, pass on traditions and beliefs, and transmit moral standards, guidelines, and the rules governing a community. Jerome Bruner (1987) suggests that narratives have the ability to organize memory and perceptions and give purpose to life. The everyday chatter between family members enables a child to make sense of his experiences. Our stories become who we are. That life story creates our first mental model, telling us who we are and how we fit into the world around us. Narratives also may allow for the "continuing interpretation and reinterpretation of our experience" (Bruner 1987, p.12). If the story is changed, the perception and understanding of self can be changed. When a client is presented with new information he must choose between excluding that new information from conscious awareness or accepting and integrating it into his self-identity. It is not uncommon for parents to analyze and edit their own life narratives while in therapy sessions for their child. One father discovered while reminiscing with his mother that his parents divorced after his mother left his father. He was shocked. Throughout his childhood, adolescence, and adult years he believed that his dad left him. This belief shaped the person he thought he was and even fueled a period of rebellion as a teenager. Now confronted with new information he was able to edit his life story, update his mental model, and eventually change his own relationship with his son.

Neuroscience of narratives

Communication and language in the context of a relationship appear to be major factors in brain development (Cozolino 2002; Siegel 1999). Words have the ability to shape our thoughts, feelings, beliefs, actions, and relationships. When placed together in a cohesive form such as a story the effect can be more powerful. Listening to a story is a strenuous workout for the brain. Narratives seem to play a role in top-down neural integration, activating conscious thoughts, emotions, and body. Listening to a story requires both linear interpretive functions (primarily left hemisphere) and the processing of emotion and sensation (right hemisphere). The audience must remember and pay attention to characters and their personalities, thoughts and emotions, the setting details, the sequence of events and at the same time notice the storyteller's expression, voice, gestures, and movement.

Current attachment theory recognizes the importance of parent–infant reciprocal, attuned interactions for the development of a healthy working model and a coherent life narrative. In the sharing of emotions and language the parent and child co-construct stories about the past, present, and future. An autobiographical, narrative self emerges (Siegel 1999). Such interactions form the foundation for the capacity for reflective function or mentalization (Bretherton 2006; Fonagy 1999; Oppenheim and Waters 1995). This ability to understand the mind of another—to think about the parent's intentions, thoughts and feelings—is vital if the child has experienced maltreatment. Without it, the child develops negative beliefs about himself, the parent, and other adults. This negative model, as described in the previous chapters, frames later experiences and has a direct impact on how individuals interpret life events. Children with an insecure attachment may have difficulty integrating life experiences into a meaningful story. In short, anxiously attached children struggle to make sense of the actions of others and the events going on around them (Fonagy 2000). Within a supportive relationship, conversational co-construction allows children to explore the past in safety and consider different perspectives (Oppenheim and Waters 1995).

How stories can be therapy

On a warm spring morning, Todd and Melissa were walking through a park to meet a colleague for breakfast. She is a child psychiatrist who has worked in the field of attachment and bonding for many years. Over granola and a large latte, she asked about our work with maltreated children. After a brief explanation of what we do, she leaned forward and asked incredulously, "So parents tell the kids stories and they get better?"

Again and again, professionals and parents ask us some version of this question. Yes, it sounds too easy, too good to be true. But stories indeed make a difference. Our life story changes over time. Stories instruct us and help us make sense of our experience of the world. By telling our story and listening to our story told by others we discover ourselves. Reflecting on our history allows us to connect to the past, present, and future (Reese *et al.* 2010; Siegel and Hartzell 2003).

We believe that parent narratives can help the child internalize a new life perspective, a different internal working model. An individualized story told by parents who intuitively know their child's needs and emotions offers a way to renew their child's mind. Negative and faulty meanings in the child's ongoing life story can be challenged and edited, thus recreating his self-identity (Cozolino 2002).

Many therapeutic approaches use the concept of creating a new story about the self as a component of therapy. Psychodynamic therapies such as psychoanalysis, object relations, and self-psychology recognize the existence of the conscious and unconscious minds and the importance of early childhood experiences. By analyzing the past and an individual's interpretation of events, unconscious beliefs are brought into awareness, leaving the client free to adjust his assumptions about himself and change his behavior. Cognitive therapies seek to alter emotion and behavior by encouraging clients to identify dysfunctional ways of thinking and then challenge and rewrite those convictions (Beck and Weishaar 1989). In Narrative Therapy (White and Epston 1990) the therapist collaborates with the client to re-author a problem-filled story that has shaped the client's identity. In the process of questioning and externalizing the problem, new ways of thinking about the difficulty emerge, and the client's life story and beliefs about himself change. Dyadic Developmental Psychotherapy (Becker-Weidman 2005) is an experiential approach in which the child's trauma narrative is revised by reading and reenacting the trauma experience within the context of an attuned relationship. This allows the child to understand those traumatic events and their associated thoughts, feelings, and behavior. The developers postulate that greater emotional and behavioral regulation results from the new life story created in the process. Similarly, in Trauma-Focused Cognitive Behavioral Therapy, trauma narration is an important part of the treatment (Cohen, Mannarino, and Deblinger 2006). The child describes his experience(s) by telling the story verbally, in writing, or through art. In the telling, the child is assisted in processing related thoughts and feelings. Things these therapies seem to have in common include first, the recognition that both emotion and thinking are vital to the process of change and second, that a person's life narrative is examined and reworked within a safe, collaborative relationship with the therapist.

The core belief of Family Attachment Narrative Therapy is that *parents* are the key to helping children heal from past negative attachment relationships, traumatic life events, and the resulting developmental issues. Family Attachment Narrative Therapy is a comprehensive treatment approach designed for children who are struggling with issues related to trauma, disruptions in attachment, grief, and loss. Many children with negative beliefs about self and parents have problems regulating strong emotions and controlling behavior. Narratives told by parents restructure or redo these models and teach more adaptive ways of coping. In addition, empathetic and attuned interactions during story time correct existing beliefs about parents and adults. Our methodology has been challenged, extended, and refined by the parents we have worked with over the years. Creatively utilizing narratives in ways we had not imagined, we as professionals have found ourselves following their lead and expertise in helping their children.

Summary

Story times are moments to connect—sometimes. Connecting with children who had traumatic early histories can be hard. Parents struggle to get them to sit still, let alone listen to a story. A child's first stories told by a sensitive and loving caregiver lay the foundation for what will become his narrative self. Parents tell their child what just happened, what he is feeling in that moment, and how it connects to both his past and future. A parent's capacity to accurately reflect that information to her child creates and updates his mental model and, eventually, his ability to reflect on himself and those he cares about. Stories are often used in psychotherapy and are the primary feature of Family Attachment Narrative Therapy. A key distinction between Family Attachment Narrative Therapy and other methodologies is that parents, not therapists, create and tell the stories. Narratives are a powerful medium by which experience is defined. Telling and retelling our story permits us to consider alternate perspectives, endings, and conclusions.

Section 2: Constructing and Telling Stories

Some readers might be thinking, "I can't tell stories; this isn't going to work." We would argue that even just answering the question "How was your day?" *is* telling a story. Many conversations between two people contain a story. Whether it's just a simple illustration or an epic tale, children love stories. As the narrative is constructed, attunement to the child's inner thoughts, feelings, and motivations guides the process. The child's day-to-day caregivers are most attuned to him; therefore, the best narratives will come from parents. The following pages describe how to create a warm setting, the elements of a good story, and how to make a narrative come to life for the child.

The setting for Family Attachment Narrative Therapy

How can parents of older adopted or foster children create moments that bond, heal, and teach? These moments of quiet and openness can be few and far between in the normal everyday life of work, carpools, and household chores. In addition, children with attachment disturbances and behavior disorders behave in ways designed to anger and push away adults, especially parents. After months, even years of rejection, parents may be reluctant to engage in activities that may leave them vulnerable. Parenting children with extreme behaviors leaves parents and children upset, and both may just want to be left alone. A better understanding of the child's internal working model and the meaning of difficult behaviors enables the parents to take the risk.

Both the parent and child must feel safe in order to enter into a state in which they are open to one another. For some families, narrative work must be done in a neutral place such as a professional's office. The support of an understanding, nonjudgmental therapist may give the parents the encouragement they need and help them to uncover long buried feelings of empathy towards the child. At home, parents can put aside a special time each day and create settings in which the parent and child will be most receptive to attuned interactions.

A room free of distractions and with comfortable seating, soft lighting, familiar comfort items such as blankets and stuffed animals may help the child to be quiet and relaxed, enabling him to accept the parents' emotional and physical nurturing. The child is invited to sit close to the parents or on one of their laps. This type of setting, though preferred, may not always be possible. Parents tell stories in the car, at the dinner table, during bath time, on the sidelines of a soccer game, and while doing dishes side by side. If waiting for the perfect time and place means that narratives are told infrequently, start talking anywhere and everywhere! In some cases, children refuse to sit near their parents. Safety and comfort are necessary for the success of the narratives. Holding the child is not. Many parents have successfully used narratives with resistant or very active children.

> A five-year-old boy moved continually during the narrative—from lap to lap, between his parents, on the arms of the couch, behind the couch, and he even lay across the back of the couch, smiling at them like a Cheshire cat. Discouraged, the parents attempted the narrative later in the day, adding new material hoping to interest their son. They were surprised when he exclaimed, "You didn't say that part before." Despite his activity, he had not missed a word they said.

Parents may also encourage their child to look them in the eye and may gently remind him throughout the narrative to maintain eye contact. Mutual eye gaze creates pleasurable states in both mother and child (Schore 1998). Eye contact seems to facilitate deep emotional connections. The parent and child "see" and know the mind of the other. If the child has difficulty making eye contact, power struggles should be avoided. As both the child and parent become comfortable with the process of Family Attachment Narrative Therapy, the amount of eye contact usually increases.

Appropriate touch is important too. Shared physical gestures of affection provide a multi-sensory experience of each other. Of course, parents must take into account any factors that might contra-indicate touch, such as sensory integration issues or unresolved sexual abuse. Parents may stroke their child's face, run their fingers through the child's hair, or massage lotion on his hands or feet. Children may respond to this nurturing by reaching out to play with their parent's hair or explore their faces. In this setting, parents may also find themselves relaxing and enjoying the closeness with their child. The synchronized dance that takes place between them as each alters their attention, stimulation, and emotional level in response to cues from the other, results in a resonance (Schore 2001a) or a state of "feeling felt" (Stern 1985).

The perspective

Choosing the perspective from which the story is told is an important component of narrative construction. In a story told from the first person the protagonist is the teller of the story. The events happen to him. The thoughts, feelings, and conclusions drawn are his own. "I looked around for my mother but she was gone" is an example of a first person statement. The first person perspective is often used in claiming or developmental narratives. For example, in relaying family history to a child as part of the claiming process, a father talked about the adventures of his own childhood. He humorously conveyed the message that a child deserves love even when his brother leaves him stranded on the top of a barn and his dad has to rescue him. In developmental narratives, parents may use the first person to describe how they struggled to learn a new skill as a child. As a result, children know that their parents understand something of the difficulties they face.

In a story using a third person perspective the teller describes events, feelings, and characteristics of others. The protagonist is not the storyteller or the audience. Pronouns such as "she," "he," or "it" are commonly used. Third person narratives are useful in developmental, trauma, and successful child narratives. A story told from the third person permits descriptions of the events in the life of a child when not all the facts are known. It is impossible to know the child's experience on a day-to-day, moment-to-moment level. Third person narratives allow parents to recount what is known along with what is supposed. For example, if medical records indicate that the child was diagnosed as failing to thrive, parents could conclude that the child might not have been fed every time he was hungry, or that at times there was no food in the cupboards or refrigerator. Although that might not be totally accurate, the story allows the child to process related memories, thoughts, and feelings.

Third person trauma narratives are also useful in discussing difficult material and protecting the child's fragile feelings for his birth family. Adopted or foster children are bonded to their birth parents. Despite what happened, this was their mom or dad. They are loyal to them. Even children who did not know their birth parents and siblings often cultivate a fantasy of what that family is like and develop feelings for them. It is important to respect that bond. It is not necessary for those bonds to dissolve, or for the child to be angry about the past in order to establish a connection to new parents. Saying, "Your birth mom left you alone in the crib" often results in an immediate denial: "No she didn't!" A third person narrative permits the child to maintain his relationship with his birth parent. At the same time, parents can present the facts so that the child can begin to process those events and make sense of his life story. Third person narratives also give the child a zone of safety. He is free to keep the story in the realm of "just pretend" when the content is difficult. This ensures that the child is not being re-traumatized by the telling of the story. This is discussed in further detail in Chapter 6.

Talking to a child about his behavior may be like talking to a brick wall—it certainly won't create warm fuzzy feelings between parent and child. Telling a child a story about an interesting character with similar problems builds the relationship while teaching new behaviors. The use of the third person perspective in developmental and successful child narratives allows the child to listen to instruction and behavioral alternatives without becoming embarrassed or defensive.

Sarah was severely neglected as an infant and appeared to have some sensory integration problems. She seemed unaware of where her body was in space. As a result she intruded on the personal space of her peers and family. Circle time at school invariably ended up with Sarah in tears because someone had pushed or hit her after she practically sat in their laps. Mom and Dad told a creative narrative about "bubble aliens." Touch one and everyone ends up covered in green, yucky slime. Sarah laughed about the aliens' antics, but got the message too.

The hero

Finding a hero to whom the child can relate is one of the most critical parts of story construction. If parents are successful in doing this, they communicate to the child that he is understood, and the child is more open to receiving the story's message. The stronger the identification between the child and a story's hero or protagonist, the better the child will be able to internalize the message of the story. As the child internalizes the message, adopting the perspective of the protagonist, his own internal working model is challenged. The new perspective must either be integrated into the old, shifting the faulty meanings the child has previously fabricated, or discarded and the old model retained.

The hero can be anyone or anything with which the child will identify. Television, movie, sports, and cartoon characters from the popular media may be used. Sometimes a make believe child with similar problems will work. In addition, some children have a particular animal with which they are fascinated. Dinosaurs, dolphins, stray puppies, and tigers can be used as the main character.

> Andy was a *Harry Potter* fan. He devoured each and every book in the series and bugged his mom and dad endlessly when a new movie was released. Harry seemed like the ideal protagonist for their son, the parents thought. Much to their surprise the story time that night was disastrous. Andy interrupted and argued every point. Ron didn't have the invisibility cloak, Harry did. And it was Hermione that concocted the potion transforming Harry and Ron into Crabbe and Goyle, not Neville. Lesson learned, they sighed: "Do not pick a character that Andy knows more about than we do."

If the character and the situation hit too close to home the child may react defensively. On the other hand, if the situation is too dissimilar and identification doesn't take place, the message may be missed. Attuned parents are usually able to make this determination. If the child doesn't connect with the hero (or argues about the protagonist), a simple change of characters in the next telling usually does the trick.

The message

The content of the story is specific to the task at hand and determined by the child's unique internal working model. Narratives can be used to challenge the child's negative belief system. Stories that introduce an alternative meaning have the capacity to change the internal working model and, consequently, the life of the listener. Answering the question

"What message do I want to convey through this story?" provides the blueprint from which the narrative is constructed.

Every good story has a beginning, middle, and end. The beginning introduces the main hero and the setting in which the action or plot takes place. Details about the protagonist's appearance, personality traits, and the setting help the child visualize the story during the telling. What color are the hero's hair and eyes? Does the action take place in a city, a forest, or on a mountaintop? After framing the backdrop in which the story takes place, the plot is the heart of the narrative and relays the message of the story. In claiming narratives, the plot elaborates on the care the child or character deserved to have as an infant and young child. Trauma narratives relate life events in a coherent fashion and may describe how the negative internal working model developed. The plot of developmental and successful child narratives teaches skills or new behaviors. The actions, thoughts, and emotions of the hero as he faces a crisis or dilemma hook the listener, building interest and suspense. Lastly, there is a resolution to the crisis, which brings the emotional energy of the listener to a calmer state and usually holds the message of the story.

Children traumatized early in life typically have difficulty constructing a narrative in this form. They have trouble considering alternatives, making cause and effect connections, and resolving conflicts. By constructing a story with a sequence of events, a captivating plot, crisis and resolution, parents are able to teach their children about planning and form, not just content.

Bill and Karen decided to start with claiming narratives. They did not believe that Robert saw them as special to him in any way. They were just adults who might give him something he wanted. They also felt that if they started talking about what they would have done if he had been their baby, he would panic and have to either fight or run. For Robert this meant a tantrum or behaviors that would distract him from what they were saying.

Bill and Karen decided to use a third person perspective in the claiming narrative. They would tell a story about another mom and dad who loved and cherished their brand-new baby girl. Karen described how the mother took care of herself during her pregnancy so her baby would have a healthy start. Bill made screeching car noises when he talked about the dad speeding to the hospital. They showed Robert the blanket and toys the baby would have received from happy relatives and friends. He came close enough to touch the blanket. They told Robert how the mommy and daddy took care of the baby all day long and in the middle of the night too. They gave voice to the baby's thoughts and feelings as her parents nurtured her. They told how the baby stared at her mommy's face and grabbed her daddy's pinkie finger. They ended the story by describing the family's bedtime ritual. Karen even sang a lullaby. Robert wandered around the room and lay on the floor kicking the wall but he did not get angry and he did not leave the room. They kept it simple and short and felt pretty sure he had heard at least part of the story.

Incorporating props in the telling

Some children need concrete objects in the telling of the narratives; other children may be distracted by them. Parents can usually predict whether or not props will enhance their child's experience with narratives. Children who have been institutionalized, neglected, or abused often have difficulty understanding what they see and hear. A child with auditory processing problems or poor short-term memory for verbal information may benefit from incorporating visual props. Enlisting a family of dolls, stuffed animals, or toy cars as the main characters in the story may keep the child interested and attentive. The parent or child can draw pictures to illustrate important parts of the story. Keep in mind that if it appears that the child is operating at an earlier emotional or cognitive stage of development he may enjoy props or toys that are appropriate for a much younger child.

Even adolescents may need to see and touch the baby layette that parents would have bought for them. Parents of a teenager, adopted as a preschooler, picked out a beautiful infant dress, pink (her favorite color), with lace and ruffles and black patent leather shoes. She was tickled with the purchase and kept it with other mementos from her childhood. For children who are in the developmental stage of concrete operations props may transform the abstract thoughts and feelings of the narrative into a concrete, realistic representation. A handmade blanket, special stuffed animal, baby rattles, bottles, pacifiers, a toddler's blocks, and trucks can make the narrative come to life.

One mother brought her child to the baby department of a local store, showing her all the things she deserved to have as a baby. Her foster daughter had never seen a bassinet, walker, baby swing, and the other baby gear available to parents today. She was amazed as she walked down the aisle gently touching the articles. She continued to ask, "Would I have had that?" questions for weeks.

In designing the setting for Family Attachment Narrative Therapy, Bill and Karen purchased a double rocker so that all three of them could comfortably participate. They chose a room in their home that could easily be de-cluttered in order to decrease the distractions and sensory stimuli. Recognizing Robert's anxiety and hypervigilance they carefully placed the lights to dispel shadows. Karen provided pillows and blankets around the room in anticipation that Robert would not sit on their laps for long. Although he had difficulty tolerating close physical proximity, they felt certain he would continue to listen to the story even from behind the rocker. Because he often rubbed his cheeks on the bed and floor, they bought a soft, velour baby blanket for him. A bottle with his favorite juice, baby lotion, and a few baby toys completed their purchases. They were ready.

Additional thoughts

Parents are very aware of their child's learning style and language skills. Vocabulary and sentence structure vary in relationship to the child's age, developmental level, and expressive or receptive language skills. Parents can adjust stories for a perfect fit. In the case of international adoption, English may be the child's second language. Translators may be used in the telling of narratives. Parents may also incorporate vocabulary from the child's first language into the narratives. Many narratives are told in the child's native language if the parent is fluent in that language. We have heard stories told in Russian, German, Bulgarian, and Spanish. Although the therapist learned some words and short phrases by observing each day, for the most part she was unable to understand the narratives told by the parents. These narratives were highly successful, reinforcing our belief that parents are indeed capable of helping their children with Family Attachment Narrative Therapy. *They* are the agent of healing, not the therapist.

We have listened to thousands of narratives over the years. There seem to be three common themes which run through each narrative:

- From the first, the child deserved to be loved and cared for by parents he could trust.

- Even though the child experienced abuse, abandonment, or neglect he deserved to be loved and cared for by responsible parents.

- The child's behavior does not define his value and the parent's will be there to love and support him as he makes changes.

These themes appear over and over again regardless of the child, the child's internal working model, or who is telling the story. Because they occur repeatedly, we believe they are an important factor in shifting the child's negative beliefs.

Summary

Stories have the potential to change lives. Constructing a narrative that will shift the child's negative internal working model is a challenge. In telling stories that bond, heal, and teach, it is important to create an environment as well as a story that promotes attuned physical and emotional nurturing. Parents and children who have been hurt and rejected have difficulty approaching any situation that exposes them to further pain. The storytelling setting must provide physical and emotional safety as well as invite openness and vulnerability. Props may be used to make the narratives concrete and believable. Emotional safety is generated through parental attunement. The child who feels understood is open to begin the attachment process with a new family.

For some parents making up a healing, bonding, or teaching story for their child seems like an impossible task. "I'm not very creative," "I won't know what to say," "I'm not very good at telling stories," and " I don't think I can do this," are thoughts and feelings shared by many parents endeavoring to learn something new. We believe that storytelling is a natural way to communicate. In most cases, with a little instruction, support, and encouragement, parents have the ability to tell a story that touches the child's heart and mind. Appendix B contains a story construction guide or worksheet that parents may find helpful as they consider and choose the elements of the unique story they are designing for the child.

Constructing specific types of narratives that make up Family Attachment Narrative Therapy is described in the next chapters. The examples given are designed to illustrate features of each narrative type. The best narratives are individualized to the child and told by the parent. Parental attunement, intuition, and hunches based on day-to-day interactions with the child are the key to constructing effective narratives.

Chapter 4

Parental Attunement and Regulation

One gave you emotions, the other calmed your fears.

Emotional attunement to the child and the parent's ability to provide regulation are the foundation for a secure attachment relationship. When parents are attuned they seem to have an inner eye and ear for the child's thoughts, feelings, needs, and desires. For example, a mother correctly interprets her inconsolable baby's cries as stress and overstimulation and removes her from a lively family gathering to calm her. A father, hearing the familiar five o'clock whine of his toddler, puts aside the day's mail, and snuggles with him, touching, talking softly until his son hops up to fetch a toy. Each of these parents is demonstrating attunement to their child's cues. Each of them provides soothing when the child is overstimulated, tired, and unable to manage stress.

As new parents become acquainted with their child, whether a newborn or an older adopted child, the meaning of nonverbal behaviors such as facial expression, posture, and movement becomes clearer. Eventually they are able to read her signals and anticipate her needs. As the child acquires language, words and gestures combine to signal her needs. Many parents excitedly anticipate holding, rocking, singing, and playing with their newly adopted child. In these quiet moments the bonds of love begin to grow. But what if the child spent the first months of her life alone in a crib?

Infants naturally demonstrate attachment behaviors such as smiling, babbling, crying, and reaching out. When parents respond to those behaviors by smiling back, cooing, soothing, and touching, the child's social–emotional development is enhanced. The first year is a critical time in which infants are discovering who they are and organizing strategies to relate to others. When attachment behaviors work, the child tries them again and again, not only on her parents but also on others she encounters. The expression on her parents' faces tells her she is special, important, and loved.

When Tyler arrived at the airport with his escort from the orphanage overseas, he did not look at his parents, smile, or respond to their attention. He lay limp and lifeless in their arms. This special moment for which they had waited two years was silent and eerie, nothing like they had expected. His mother knew she had to bring this child back to life. She bounced and danced and twirled, and sang loud, silly songs to him. She stroked and tickled him, and gently coaxed her son back into the world. Soon Tyler was laughing and mimicking his mother's facial expressions, holding his head up, and sitting alone.

Intuitively, his mother had provided the essential sensory stimuli needed to heal his past neglect. Quiet rocking and cuddling became a regular nightly ritual, promoting a strong emotional connection. The road to healing and attachment was begun by the intuitive actions of his mother, not the result of professional education and training.

When parents are consistently attuned and available to the child, her relationship model and self-image is positive, and will evolve into a cooperative exchange. During the first months of a child's life the responsibility for initiating and realigning attunement lies with the parent. If the parent misses the cue the first time, it is important to try again. As the child develops language and cognitive skills, however, there is a move toward a more reciprocal relationship. Older children are able to consider the needs and wishes of a parent. They begin to give back. A securely attached child notices the parent, initiates interactions, and becomes an active partner in the relationship.

After doing narratives intensively with her adopted daughter one parent reported that her daughter offered her baby blanket to her when she was lying on the couch recuperating from the flu. She was shocked, as her daughter is usually very needy and demanding when mom is sick. For the first time she had noticed her mother's needs.

Without the experience of attunement in infancy the child struggles to reach a goal-directed partnership (Bowlby 1969/1982, 1980). For adoptive parents, it may feel as if they give and give, yet cannot fill the child's insatiable needs. They get little from the child in return for their generosity, except more demands and arguments. Securely attached children have a history marked by sensitive, attuned responses. Those caring interactions create a template or model for the child about the role of parents in providing consistent love and protection. In the process, parental attunement assists in regulating the child's internal state as she navigates the challenges of her environment.

How attunement and regulation enhance or alter development

The early relationship between a mother and her child is characterized as symbiotic. This physiological dependence suggests that the wellbeing of the primary caregiver influences the welfare of the baby, and vice versa. Beginning at conception, this relationship affects the course of development for a child. What a mother ingests (nutrients or toxins) during her pregnancy, combined with her stress level, has an impact on the fetus. The mother's ability to shape the child after birth is of equal importance. If she suffers from depression, is drug or alcohol dependent, or excessively anxious, her baby does not have enough life experience to think, "What is wrong with that woman?" Instead, the actions of the caregiver are seen as a reflection of the child. They are taken personally. This feeling of being "at one" with another person is called attunement, and affects the child's beliefs and expectations, forming a model for her self-concept and future relationships (Bowlby 1988; Bretherton et al. 1990).

The quality of attachment experiences and the nature of early environment not only affect a baby's expectations but also brain development. An infant is born dependent upon the nurturing, consistent care of a caregiver to help her organize and develop. As Schore (2005) notes, "attachment relationships are essential because they facilitate the development of the brain's self-regulatory mechanism" (p.206). Regulation refers to the ability of an individual to regulate body, emotions, and states of mind (Siegel 2001). Attachment relationships help regulate the amount of stress hormones in the developing baby's brain. In small doses, stress hormones help a person to assess an unsafe situation and act in a way that ensures survival. In higher doses over long periods of time, these same stress hormones can impair brain function (Robbins 2000; Siegel 1999; Sunderland 2006). Early life stress can impact a child's physical, emotional, cognitive, social, and spiritual development (Engert *et al.* 2010; Finzi *et al.* 2001; Granqvist and Dickie 2006). It influences the capacity of a person to communicate with others, regulate strong emotions, develop a strong sense of self, and adapt to and cope with an ever changing stressful environment (Schore 2005).

Section 1: How to Attune to your Child

How can parents have an emotional connection with a child who seems unable to accept love and care because she experienced neglect, abuse, and abandonment by another parent? How can parents be expected to understand and empathize with violent behavior that seems hatefully directed towards them? We believe parents can successfully care for and nurture such children. The key is looking beneath their behavior and understanding the internal beliefs that drive the behavior.

The experiences of some adopted and foster children include adequate attunement in their first years of life. Consequently, they may be better able to verbalize and organize their behavior so that adoptive parents can attune to them and meet their needs. However, children who did not experience adequate attunement as infants may not have developed such an organized or effective strategy. They have an expectation that the adult will ignore them, deny them, or even mistreat them. Underlying that expectation may be a belief about their value. They may believe they are unworthy of help because they are defective, bad, or not loveable. Consequently, children with negative working models often ask for help in a manner that sets them up for failure, further reinforcing their faulty beliefs.

The child who yells at her mother, "I want it NOW!" is stating a perceived need in an inappropriate manner. It is unlikely that the parent will say, "Of course, this is what you deserve." Instead, the parent is likely to withhold the item because of the child's demanding approach. This dynamic between parent and child occurs frequently with children who suffer from attachment difficulties. It is important for parents to look at what drives a child's behavior so that their response challenges the underlying, mistaken belief.

One mother told a story about how she had to be hospitalized, leaving her seven children at home with her husband. When she returned home she found that every item in the freezer had portions eaten out of it. There was cookie dough missing from its container, chunks of pie torn from the tin, and opened packages of frozen vegetables. She gathered her children around her and said, "I can think of two children who may have done this. My guess is the person who ate this food was Tanya. I know that when Tanya is scared she chooses to misbehave. I think she was afraid I might die, so she ate all food that she knew she shouldn't eat." The mother reported that Tanya began to cry and confessed that what she said was true. The mother hugged her and told her that she was going to be fine—she was not going to die. Recognizing her child's fear, she elected not to give her a consequence.

The mother in this story understood the thoughts and feelings fueling the misbehavior of her child. She acknowledged it and named the emotion when she confronted her. Tanya's mother adeptly tuned in to the emotions and beliefs of the child, and calmed her daughter by providing an appropriate response with her words and actions. In attachment language, this mother was attuned to her child.

To determine the meaning of a child's behavior it is important to ask why the child is behaving in this way. There are many possible questions to ask, but just start with one and build on that. Returning to the example of the demanding child, parents might ask: Why is she asking for the item in that way? Does she know how to ask appropriately? Is there something else going on? Is she being triggered by a memory in the past—is she replaying a pattern of interaction she had with a former caregiver? What is the emotion driving her demands? Why does she have that emotion? Does she need to be in control of the situation? Why does she need to be in control? Is her demand a distraction? Is she upset over an unrelated event? Is she covering up a disability? Can she do what the parent asked her to do? Does she know how to do it? Asking these kinds of questions will help a parent figure out the beliefs of the child. Taking into account the child's developmental level, learning style, possible deficits, response to stress, and her history will provide a caregiver with clues to her belief system and why she is behaving in a certain way. Although a parent may not be able to clearly understand her motivations in the moment, it is important to make a guess. If the parent is wrong, the child will tell her about it—through words or behavior. If the parent is right, then she can respond appropriately and the attachment with the child will be strengthened.

> Renee needed special shoes to help her ankles develop appropriately. But the shoes were ugly and different from the shoes her friends wore. She deliberately dragged her toe on the sidewalk, wearing a hole in her new shoes, hoping she would not have to wear them ever again. Renee's mother could have speculated that the deliberate destruction of property was due to an underlying anger and rage. That hypothesis might have led to a logical consequence such as earning enough money to replace them. Was Renee angry about having to wear the special shoes? Yes, but that misses the underlying thoughts and feelings and leaves Renee feeling misunderstood and still angry. Instead, Renee's mother understood and clued into her underlying emotion of embarrassment at having to wear ugly shoes. In fact, years later when Renee was older she revealed that she had cut a hole in her own hated black Oxfords as a child. She truly understood Renee's feelings. Renee received another set of therapeutic shoes—which she had to wear. But in addition, she received a coveted pair of black patent leather shoes to wear to church and other special occasions. Renee learned about respecting property and the relationship was enhanced by the exchange.

When a child has an attunement deficit she is not capable of a goal-directed partnership. She cannot see or understand her parents' needs. Instead, she is focused on getting her own needs met. When an attuned parent disciplines a securely attached child, the child may protest and argue. Ultimately, she trusts and understands that limits and consequences represent her parent's love and desire to protect her. She might think, "I'm not going to do that again!" Without this partnership and an attachment to the parent, requests and appropriate parental interventions appear punitive and unfair to the child. This child may think, "You're mean!" and her behaviors are unlikely to change in spite of the consequences.

Components of attunement

Daniel Siegel (2001) proposes five basic requirements for fostering secure attachments: collaboration, reflective dialogue, repair, coherent narratives, and emotional communication. *Collaboration* is the experience of sharing nonverbal signals such as eye contact, gestures, facial expressions, tone of voice, and body language. As the parent and child exchange nonverbal cues and adjust their responses according to the other person there is a profound feeling of connection between the pair. This is clearly demonstrated when a mother mirrors her infant's sounds, facial expressions, and movements. She allows her to lead the dance, increasing the intensity of her reactions in response to her child's excitement and soothing the child when excitement and glee evolve into agitation. Siegel suggests that such collaboration is essential in developing a sense of self. The parents must also verbally communicate to the child their sense of the child's internal experience in a *reflective dialogue*. This allows the child to attribute meaning to the experience.

Verbal narrative accompanies the nonverbal communication that takes place within the mother–child dyad. Interpreting the infant's movements, sounds, and cues, the parent narrates the infant's inner state: "What a happy baby you are! You like kicking your strong legs. Mama's watching you. What a big smile! Oh, it's OK, Mama's right here, you're OK. You just scared yourself, didn't you? Mama's here, Mama's here." This conversation allows the infant to "know" what she is feeling (Fonagy and Target 1997).

Sometimes signals go unnoticed or misread, and the internal state of the child is not responded to or incorrectly communicated to the child. The parent must then re-attune or *repair* the connection to the child. While running errands, a mother misses her toddler's signs that she is tired and a tantrum over something minor occurs. Rather than giving her overwhelmed daughter a time out, she instead cuddles her close, softly reassuring her, "You are so tired, aren't you sweetie? It's OK, we're going home soon. We'll find your blanket and rest." When adults join the child in constructing stories about past, present, and future, the child is able to integrate her experiences and to form a *coherent narrative*. Day-to-day chatter remembering the morning's trip to the library, talking about lunch as the peanut butter is spread, and planning what to do after naptime are examples of how a parent might narrate a day in the life of a child. Reminiscing about past events, telling the story with a beginning, middle, and end, also helps the child make sense of her world. Parents who reflect their child's emotions facilitate the child's ability to identify and express feelings appropriately. "Your face looks mad right now. What do you need? Can Mama help?" These are examples of *emotional communication* that is attuned to the inner state of the child and helps her understand that emotions are acceptable.

All five of these elements are present in Family Attachment Narrative Therapy. During the storytelling parents pay attention to the child's nonverbal signals. They may mirror or reflect those signals and feelings in their voice or facial expressions and incorporate them into the story. One child immediately made the connection between himself and the character that was telling the "big fat lies." He looked away and squirmed. In response his mother lowered her eyes and head, illustrating how the character in the story looked away from his parents and fidgeted in embarrassment. Then the fictional parents encouraged their son that he could and would make the right decision next time.

Parents may also adjust the content, pacing, and length of the story based on the child's reactions during the telling. For example, shallow breathing and increased muscle tension may indicate that the topic is painful or scary. Parents may respond by revealing less detail about the event in the narrative or touching and cuddling the child closer to them. Parents also help the child make meaning of her experiences by attributing to the protagonist the thoughts, feelings, and perceptions they believe are similar to the child's internal experience. If they believe the child thinks that her birth mom "gave her away" because something was wrong with her, then the character in the story has the same belief and same feelings.

Parent repair any misunderstanding or miscommunications based on the child's reactions to the narrative. After an emotional narrative about a child's grief when she was placed in foster care, a 12-year-old told her adopted mom that she could not remember her birth mother doing anything with her. She said she missed her mom a little but not her old life because there was nothing to miss. Another child disagreed with her parent's statement that the hero was scared when she was locked in the closet and said, "No, she liked it in there. Nobody could see her." If the narrative has "missed the mark," adjustments can be made in the story or in the next telling. Many children will correct any misperceptions during the story, allowing parents to immediately integrate new information into the narrative. Finally, the telling of what happened to the child in the past, and what may happen in the future, facilitates a coherent narrative. Throughout the process parents include both factual information and emotional communication. Through voice, facial expressions, and nonverbal signals parents communicate that they share the child's hurts and joys. The parents name emotions for the child and reassure her that all feelings are valid.

Goal-corrected partnerships are difficult to achieve until the deprivation of attunement has been rectified. Family Attachment Narrative Therapy provides a way for the parents to convey that they know and understand their child's experience of neglect and abuse. They understand the mixture of confusion, terror, sadness, and rage their child may have felt. The parent accomplishes this by using narratives that bond and heal, and that help the child make sense of the past and reduce the anxiety about an uncertain present and future. The parent also needs to explicitly name and challenge the child's faulty, destructive conclusions about self, others, and her environment. The focus is on renewing the child's mind so that the emotional connections necessary for growth can occur.

Factors affecting attunement

There are many factors that affect attunement in a relationship between a parent and child. Attunement involves a regulatory response in both parties (George and Solomon 1999). If an individual in the dyad is emotionally distant, dysregulated, or unable to appreciate the perspective of the other, attunement falters. Just as in a telephone call, if there are problems with reception, communication is impaired, resulting in a one-sided conversation. Making a connection and attunement are difficult if a parent has an insecure attachment pattern, unresolved trauma or grief, mental illness, an overload of responsibilities, or limited family and community support.

Parents' own attachment style, reflective capacity, and relationships with their parents

Collaborative communication between parent and child increases attunement and security. Parent and child co-construct a coherent narrative about thoughts, feelings, and events. In order to accomplish this task, it is important for the parent to be able to talk about the mental states and emotions of others. It appears that parents' ability to reflect on and talk about their relationships with their parents, their beliefs, and expectations about themselves and their children significantly affects their capacity for attunement (Fonagy 1999; Fonagy et al. 1991; Fonagy and Target 1997).

What kind of relationship did parents have with their mother and father? What are the parents' expectations and hopes about parenting? What are their expectations and hopes for their child? What kind of relationship do they want with their infant, toddler, child, and adolescent? These kinds of questions can help parents sort out their model for parenting and determine their attachment style.

For example, one father complained that his teenage son was overly dependent. He hung around when he was working in the garage, asking questions and getting in the way. When he was asked about his expectations for the relationship with his son, he answered the question by describing his background. He stated that his father was very distant, giving him the message that he was not to be bothered. As a result, he avoided his father and found things to do that did not involve interacting with him. As this father began to discuss his beliefs about father–son relationships via his own story, he became aware that he wanted something different with his own son. His son's actions were in stark contrast to his pattern of avoidance while growing up with a distant father. His expectations had to be altered to form a healthy attachment with his teenager.

Knowing what model of parenting a caregiver desires to use is critical. Does the parent want the child to come to her with problems? Does the parent expect his teen to talk with him about her day or does he assume that she will be distant towards caregivers through her adolescent years? Does the parent want something different with the child than what she experienced? The answers to these questions affect how parents interact with and attune to their children.

Parents who can "read the mind" of the child, or look beneath the behavior to the underlying emotional state, will react to the emotional state rather than the behavior. Such a skill facilitates understanding and modifying the behavior. This is particularly important with children who have histories of attachment difficulties and have formed negative working models. A negative working model can result in the child miscuing or incorrectly signaling the parent regarding her needs. Common examples of miscuing include: the child kicking the parent when, really, she just wants to be held, ignoring the caregiver when she needs attention, and arguing when she wants to spend time with her parent. In such situations, parents who are able to "read the mind" of the child will react differently than parents who only see the behavior.

> It would be easy to misinterpret David's behavior. He wanted his dad to spend more time with him instead of watching television after work. When Dad's new leather recliner arrived from the store, he stabbed it repeatedly with a pocket knife. A weird way to say, "Play with me, Dad!" His father was understandably furious and did not understand the message David was trying to send.

In the moment while being kicked and pummeled or watching furniture being destroyed a child's signals are difficult to interpret. Upon reflection on the child's mental state parents may begin to see the frustrating and annoying behaviors of their child as covering a deficit, reenactment, avoidance, or attempts to satisfy a need. With children who have attachment difficulties, it is important to look underneath the behavior and meet the unspoken need.

The mental state of the parent

If a parent cannot focus on her child and be present in the moment it will be difficult to attune to her. Parents with their own unresolved trauma may have difficulty dealing with a child's attachment-seeking behavior or strong emotions and may respond inappropriately as a result (National Child Traumatic Stress Network 2003). Judy, a recovering drug addict, had a tough childhood strewn with chaos and violent, abusive relationships. Her mother, trapped in her own addictions, did not provide a healthy model for parenting.

> When Judy's son was born, she was elated. However, due to her past experiences she could not consistently be emotionally present in her care of him. His attachment behaviors elicited annoyance instead of nurturing in her. As a result, he was highly anxious and poorly behaved. He was often provocative and learned that negative behavior got him a lot of attention that he normally did not get otherwise.

By becoming aware of one's automatic responses a parent can choose to respond differently (Dozier, Manni, and Lindheim 2006). Intentional parenting involves conscious, consistent attention, praise, teaching, and correcting. It requires that the parent envisions and works towards goals for the relationship with their child. If attuning is difficult due to difficulties such as anxiety, depression, grief, or chemical dependence it may be necessary to seek professional help.

Quantity versus quality of time

Secure attachments take time. Researchers have found that most mothers would prefer to stay home with their infants and young children if financially able to do so (Leach 1994). Parents are irreplaceable in a child's life no matter the skills of the substitute caregiver. Often parents who work outside the home are expected to have the same level of commitment to their job—putting in extra hours, bringing work home, taking negligible leave and vacation—as their childless coworkers. Much has been made of the concept of quality time, or intensely focused, positive interactions between parent and child. However, if a child is in daycare for ten or twelve hours a day parents may have problems attuning to the intricate nuances of their child. There is no substitute for quantity. The mental states of both parent and child are affected by the stress of repeated separations and reunions adding to the difficulty with attunement. Center-based childcare causes stress in the child as evidenced by higher cortisol levels throughout the day (Vermeer and van IJzendoorn 2006). If the child is tired and hungry after school or daycare and the parent is distracted, rushed, and irritable it may be hard to reconnect after a long day. Scheduled play times or cuddle times do not work; just try to convince a baby to stay awake for quality time when she is tired and sleepy.

Janice adopted her daughter when she was in her late thirties. She planned on continuing her successful career as a salesperson. As a consequence of her status in the company, she routinely traveled abroad and worked long hours at the office and at home. She was highly compensated and had a very comfortable lifestyle which included a large home, lavish trips, and nice cars. However, the time away from her new daughter proved to be excruciatingly difficult for this woman who had waited years to be a mother. Although the daughter did well in the care of a nanny and daycare, Janice found that their relationship was compromised due to their inability to spend sufficient time with each other. After careful consideration, she and her husband chose to sell their large home and purchase a small one-story house. She stayed at home to care for her child and experienced a closer relationship with her daughter.

Support from family and friends

Parenting is hard work! It is particularly tough when the child has developmental, learning, or behavioral issues. The phrase, "It takes a village to raise a child" may be worn out and overused, but it is true. Researcher Susan Crockenberg (1981) studied mothers with colicky infants. She found that if the mother had a good support system she could attach to the most difficult baby. However, if she was not supported by her spouse, family, or friends, forming a secure attachment with her child was significantly more problematic. It is important that the primary caregiver feels supported in his or her role as parent. If not, it is more difficult to meet the needs of the child and form a healthy, secure attachment. Social and community support are related to both quality of parenting and child outcomes (Sroufe *et al.* 2009). Likewise, increasing parental support improves the quality of the relationship between the parent and her child.

Section 2: Regulation—Helping your Child to Calm

When professionals mention regulation, they refer to a person's ability to calm or self soothe. A child who has endured a stressful early life may have a hard time regulating. She may be moody, have frequent temper tantrums, be defiant, or aggressive. An adult may recognize when he or she becomes dysregulated and take action, such as eating if hungry, taking a short nap, going for a walk, or indulging in a hot bath. Infants cannot self-regulate. They are dependent on parents to figure out what they need to calm them. Older children who have received sensitive care in the past may attempt a variety of means to regulate themselves. Some crawl up in their parent's lap and fall asleep on the spot. Others find a place to hide away, read a book, or listen to music. Teens might shoot a few hoops, play a video game, skateboard, or contact a friend. Children without a history of loving parents providing attuned care do not have the skills to self-regulate. Their misguided attempts at self-regulation may include binge eating, hitting someone or something, rocking back and forth, isolating themselves or zoning out, chewing holes in clothing, or moving and talking constantly. Many parents assume that what works for them or what worked for their other children will work for a child with attachment difficulties. They are surprised when what calms them causes the child to lose control. In these cases it is important to think outside the box and be creative. Food, drink, music, television, video games, exercise, and sensory input like baths, water, or sand play may regulate some children and dysregulate others.

Factors affecting regulation

Sensory integration

Regulation is the founding principle of sensory integration. Sensory processing is a term that refers to the manner in which the nervous system takes in sensory data and responds to the messages of sight, sound, smell, taste, touch, perceptions of speed and movement, position of one's body in space, and pressure on joints and muscles. A good processing system enables a child to function in, and interact with, her environment. It can assist her in coping with difficult emotions, calming down after a stressful moment, navigating social situations, and succeeding academically (Delaney 2008). Children who experience orphanage or domestic care where they were not regularly held or permitted to move at will are most susceptible to processing difficulties (Miller 2007).

Difficulty with sensory processing may be compared to having a migrainous headache. Typical features of a migraine include sensitivity to light and sound coupled with pain. Imagine that while enduring the pain of a migraine a woman's spouse decides to mow their lawn. Just as she is about to lie down, her teenager rushes through the front door with two of her loudest friends and promptly turns on the radio to its highest volume to listen to their new favorite song. Meanwhile, her youngest child, who she told repeatedly throughout the morning to go outside, decides to wrestle with the family dog in the living room. The dog is big with a long, menacing tail that can send books, magazines, and small figurines flying with one swipe. Fido is excited and runs circles around the coffee table barking. To top it off her middle child, who loves orderliness, has decided to clean the kitchen. She has loaded the dishwasher full of unclean dishes, starts it, and the motor roars. In this moment, the woman might feel overwhelmed and her response may be one of the following: to tell her loved ones to pipe down, to lock herself in a darkened room and put in some earplugs, or to burst into tears.

The anguish of a migraine helps us understand the child who suffers from an over-responsive sensory system. Many children who have experienced neglectful care have trouble appropriately processing sensory data. It is difficult for a child to achieve balance between her emotions, body, and internal state if she does not appropriately process what she sees, hears, feels, smells, and tastes.

When thinking about what is driving a child's behavior, it may be helpful to assess whether or not she has sensory integration issues that impair her ability to regulate. The following questions may assist parents in evaluating whether sensory processing problems may be contributing to their child's current difficulties.

- Is your child clumsy?

- Does your child have difficulty with clothing or food textures?

- Does she wrap herself in clothing or bedding, or layer clothing?

- Does he strip off clothing and insist on being barefoot?

- Or, on the contrary, does she refuse to undress and prefer long sleeves and long pants or even layer her clothing?

- Does he resist grooming tasks such as: hair washing, bathing, tooth brushing, hair combing, etc.?

- Does your child insist on large personal space or is she unaware of others' personal space?

- Does your child avoid being touched?

- Does your child put things in her mouth that are inappropriate?

- Does your child push or rub his body against objects, walls, or people?

- Does your child avoid crossing his midline (an imaginary line down the centre of the body) when reaching for objects?

- Does your child bump into objects, or have difficulty walking around furniture or people, and going through doorways?

- Does your child exhibit hesitancy at stairs or ramps?

- Does your child pace, rock her body, or walk in a bouncing gait?

- Does your child tire easily, is he passive unless encouraged in movement, or does he demonstrate a weak grip?

- Does she have slurred or mumbled speech?

These symptoms may be severe or so mild that in some cases it may take years to recognize. Parents generally know that their child's functioning is not quite right, but the task is figuring out what is wrong. Many times the children exhibit Sensory Processing Disorder in addition to another disorder such as Attention Deficit Hyperactivity Disorder, Posttraumatic Stress Disorder, Autistic Spectrum Disorders (Autism, Asperger's, and PDD-NOS), Anxiety Disorder, Tourette's, and Obsessive Compulsive Disorder (Miller 2007). If you suspect that a child may not process sensory data appropriately, an assessment by an occupational therapist who specializes in sensory processing disorders is recommended. Through sensory processing exercises a child can help her brain learn how to process sensory input more effectively, making regulation easier.

Other factors to consider

Other factors that influence attunement and regulation may include sleep, allergies to foods or additives, nutrition, chemical imbalances, medication and lack of connection with others.

Mental health depends upon adequate sleep. Jason was adopted from Russia as a toddler and from the beginning he never slept well. At the age of ten he often roamed the house hours after everyone else was in bed. He rummaged through cupboards for sweets and broke passwords to illicitly surf the internet. He was tired and cranky in the morning. Without sufficient sleep he could not control his violent impulses when he got upset. Jason's parents were at their wits' end. Finally, they sought a sleep aid for him. In his ten years, he had never slept through the night. With his nightly medication, he was able to stop many of his problematic behaviors, cope more effectively with his siblings, and perform better in school. More importantly, he seemed to enjoy life more. Likewise, his interaction with his parents proved more pleasant.

Certain inputs into a child's system may produce negative behaviors. One child may have intolerance to gluten, feeling sick to her stomach and light-headed after eating a sandwich, while another may become aggressive if she consumes certain dyes in foods. The parent needs to play detective and determine what behavior changes occur when specific foods, food additives or medicines are introduced. One way to help facilitate this process is periodically to make a log of the child's negative and positive behaviors, triggers, foods, and medications to determine a possible cause.

After painstakingly discussing the tantrums of her 12-year-old son, one mother came to the realization that his outbursts occurred when his ADHD medication was wearing off. With this knowledge, she was able to explain his behavior to him in a way that helped him realize that these overwhelming feelings were not necessarily connected to anything but the medication. Thereafter, she assisted him in participating in set activities to keep him calm and occupied during these times. Another parent was puzzled week after week when her daughter raged violently for hours after every appointment for sensory treatment. At first she thought it was an expected side effect of the treatments and exercises but something did not feel right. She discovered that her daughter was playing in shaving cream at the therapy clinic. The chemicals in that foam caused a reaction in her daughter, triggering the tantrums. She asked the therapist to cease that particular activity and the rages stopped occurring.

A sense of connection and belonging can be a tremendous regulating factor for an individual. Many adults find connecting with a close friend in times of stress invaluable. Unfortunately, these connections are difficult to form for children who suffer early childhood maltreatment. Excessive stress affects a child's ability to develop emotionally and socially. It is hard for a child to pick up the nuances of a social relationship when her brain is in survival mode. The early relationship with a caregiver affects the activation of the child's capacity for reflective functioning or mentalizing. She is able to consider the implicit meaning of others' words and behaviors (Fonagy and Target 1997), or consider the implicit meaning of others' words and behaviors. Implicit in this function is a fundamental component in any relationship—empathy. Empathy requires that a person not only perceive the thoughts, feelings, and attitudes of another, but also identify with them based on her own experiences. It is hard to share, say nice things, or be helpful if one cannot take the perspective of another.

Many times children may have empathy but are unable to consistently read social cues and interpret them appropriately. This impairment, coupled with possible negative beliefs about others, has a detrimental impact on relationships. Furthermore, the quality of early life experiences may affect not only a person's ability to access relationships with others but also with the Divine. The concept of God may be likened to a parent or attachment model. When early experiences of love are mingled with neglect or abuse the working model for relationship with parents and God is one of mistrust and fear. Interestingly, the views of God may also become compensatory—i.e., "The great attachment figure" (Granqvist and Dickie 2006).

Of course, sometimes children cannot control their behavior regardless of the parent's good intentions to control their diet, sleep, amount of exercise, and overall environment. At these times, a child's mood changes may be linked to chemical imbalances that can only be controlled by medication. Tracking behavior and moods can assist a parent in determining whether psychiatric care is necessary.

Techniques to enhance attachment and increase regulation

A primary purpose of parenting is to assist a child in physiologically regulating her system. When a baby cries, a responsible parent will soothe and calm her. This pattern of stress and calming assists the child's brain to wire in a way that helps her cope with future circumstances. However, if a child does not have a caregiver who consistently soothes her when overwhelmed, a pathway of dysregulation is formed. As a consequence, in everyday experiences such as transitions or learning new skills the child cannot regulate herself enough to act appropriately. Many children "short circuit" when they encounter something stressful; they defy requests, throw temper tantrums, or make up some outlandish lie, buying time so that they can process information and calm down. One 16-year-old boy described his tactic to understand his piano lesson. He said that when the instructor asked a question about the lesson, he often refused to answer. Exasperated, his piano teacher would explain over and over again to convince him to try. While she talked, he had time to process what was said and calm down so he could proceed successfully.

The question arises, "How can parents help their children reduce stress so that they can explore, play, and learn?" The primary principle in parenting a dysregulated child is attuning to her and creating an environment that will help her self-regulate. Depending on the child's needs, this environment may be calm or stimulating. Either way, the key to success is in the concept of consistency.

Consistency

The most important thing one can do to help a child regulate is to be consistent. Consistency for a child is a building block of trust. If a child can count on certain actions and events her anxiety will decrease and she will be better able to use the skills parents teach her. For some children, reliable care from their parent, habitual routines and daily rituals, and consistent consequences for misbehavior may be extremely important. This structure can act as a security blanket, assuring the child that she is cared for and protected. Some ideas and tools to help in consistency may include keeping the daily routine simple and regular and writing down expectations, rules, chores, and family agreements. Maintaining attunement and consistency can be exhausting.

Being structured and consistent is easy for some parents but harder for others who have a temperament that prefers to go with the flow. It is paramount for parents to get help and feel supported as they endeavor to create consistency. Parents are their child's lifeline—if they are having trouble, the child will struggle. Remember that if Mama (or Papa) is not happy, no one is happy!

Being in control reduces a child's anxiety. One mother related that her seven-year-old daughter's constant questions about "What's next?" were driving her crazy. Every morning the mother reviewed the plan for the day. If there was a time with nothing scheduled she knew her daughter would pester her all day about it. She tried writing the day's activities on a white board in the kitchen. Next to it she placed a list of optional activities for her daughter to choose from when there was a gap in the schedule. This allowed her daughter some control over her free time. More importantly, every time her daughter asked the question "What's next?" she could simply respond, "Check the board."

Parenting for connection

Many parents state that there is no one parenting methodology that works all the time with all their children. With children who had tough beginnings this is pretty typical. Despite decades of new parenting techniques the hearts of parents have always known what is best for their children.

> A method of child-rearing is not—or should not be—a whim, a fashion or a shibboleth. It should derive from an understanding of the developing child, of his physical and mental equipment at any given stage, and, therefore, his readiness at any given stage to adapt, to learn, to regulate his behavior according to parental expectations (Fraiberg 1996).

When choosing a form of discipline for the child, it is important that it both regulates and improves the attachment between the parent and child. We believe that Family Attachment Narrative Therapy is a way of parenting and connecting with the child that meets both these criteria. However, telling stories while the child is pounding her little brother's head into the wall does not seem practical or wise. At that moment, parents must act swiftly to protect their child. Later, after tempers have cooled, a story about jealousy and rivalry may help resolve the underlying feelings of insecurity.

Choosing a method of discipline that assists the child in regulating and does not reinforce her negative working model can be difficult. One clue to choosing a disciplinary technique is the parents' feelings during this process. If parents dislike the child or themselves more after using a discipline technique, then it is not the right one. In the end, parenting techniques should create a more connected relationship between the parent and child, aid in regulating the child's emotions and behavior, and give the child a sense of mastery. Some parenting techniques that we have found to be regulating, nurturing, and connecting are listed in the recommended reading section at the end of the book.

Structuring the environment

Choosing an environment where the child can be successful is extremely important. If the environment outside the home is too stressful, it can affect how a child views herself, and ultimately her attachment with the parent. Managing the outside environment may include advocating for her within the school system. In the US, a 504 Plan or an Individual Education Plan are helpful to create a supportive environment for the child. Good communication with teachers and care providers about the child's unique needs is invaluable. If a child struggles in school, involving her in nonacademic success-producing activities may also improve her confidence and self-worth.

One mother decided that in order for her adopted daughter to be successful in school she needed to connect with her throughout the day. The mother became a helper at the school's office so that her daughter could check in with her regularly. During lunch, the mother often sat with her daughter and other children from her class, modeling appropriate conversation. After months of frequent contact, her daughter did not seem to need those moments of reconnection as much. Many times, a phone call was enough to calm her and give her the encouragement to cope with the next challenge of the day.

Movement and touch to calm

The mind-body connection is extraordinary. There is a plethora of written material today about this connection suggesting that specific movement can lower stress in an individual, improve processing of sensory data, and even help form brain connections. Figuring out how to incorporate needed activity in the child's day to help her regulate is essential to her success. Some parents have found that certain movements assist their child in remaining calm and focused. Activities such as running, jumping, swimming, swinging, spinning, and heavy lifting may calm a child. Fine motor work such as playing with Play Doh, stringing beads, or coloring can also be helpful. Additionally, food or oral input can be overstimulating or calming— chewing gum or crunchy foods, drinking with a straw or sucking on hard candy may improve attention and focus. Certain types of touch may be more calming for a child who has sensory issues than other types. For example, heavy pressure may be calming whereas light touch painful for one child while another prefers a light tickling touch. Keep in mind every child is unique; for some children these same activities may overstimulate them and cause a meltdown. Attunement and sometimes just experimentation helps parents find what is most helpful.

Years ago, a four-year-old girl with sensory issues was brought to our clinic by her adoptive mother because of emotional and behavioral problems. During the intensive therapy she constantly squirmed while cuddling with her mother. Seeing her distress, her mother said, "I know this is hard for you. I can see that. However, if we are to be a closer family, we need to do this." The girl turned to her mother and said, "If you're going to hold me, hold me like this!" She firmly grasped her mother's arm and applied all her strength. The mother complied with her daughter's request. Amazingly, her progress was astounding after she verbalized her need. Her mother massaged her arms and leg as she told the stories. Her daughter was calm and focused during the sessions. Their attachment was strengthened.

When evaluating the needs of a child it is important to realize that sensory input may calm and improve focus. The sensation of touch, in the form of massages, back rubs, weighted blankets, bins of beans to run fingers through, or being held in a nurturing manner, may assist a child to regulate. There are many other sensory activities that may meet the needs of a child. Consulting an occupational therapist may be helpful in assessing and designing an individualized sensory program.

Alternate therapies

It is daunting for a parent to experience the three-hour tantrum of her five-year-old and not know how to calm the rage or prevent the next one. Understandably, many parents want to try different approaches before considering medication. Often the children we see in our clinic are on multiple medications for attention, sleep, emotional control, anger, and aggression. Many alternatives to traditional medicine may be extremely successful in helping a child regulate. Some of these alternatives are listed below. Parents will also find additional information about these resources in the recommended reading section at the end of the book.

Digital Audio Visual Entrainment (DAVE) is a passive form of biofeedback designed to temporarily alter brain waves for a specific desired effect. Problems that may be alleviated by regular use include insomnia, attention difficulties, memory and learning, anxiety, irritability, and pain. An individual can listen to desired music while participating in DAVE. The programs typically last from 20–30 minutes.

Nutrition and Homeopathic Medicine are common strategies for parents seeking answers for their child. Stress coupled with genetic sensitivities may account for intolerance to certain foods and chemicals. Many parents report decreased behavior problems when they have addressed nutritional aspects of their child's health. One mother sought psychological services for her preschool daughter for sleep difficulties. Together, the mother and the therapist uncovered that her daughter was able to sleep through the night after she removed cow milk products from her diet. Another mother found that her daughter's disobedient behavior was much improved when she was on a gluten-free diet. Additionally, parents have reported that certain supplements such as omega 3, vitamin D, zinc, and magnesium have greatly improved their child's mood and mental abilities. Consulting with a nutritionist or homeopathic doctor may helpful.

Animal-Assisted Therapy may be a powerful tool for regulation and self-awareness. Research suggests that being near animals may decrease hyper-arousal (Parish-Plass 2008). Some animals appear to be highly sensitive to the internal state of those around them and can assist a child in regulating her mood. Horses used in equine assisted therapy seem to mirror and respond to the thoughts, feelings, and body language of a child. Numerous clinical examples seem to suggest that the child spontaneously "mentalizes" about past interactions, experiences, behaviors, and the conclusions drawn about those experiences. Animal-assisted therapy may challenge previous negative internal working models.

Summary

Emotional attunement is the foundation for secure attachment relationships. When parents are attuned they are able look beyond behavior and determine the thoughts and feelings of the child. Attunement helps parents select the most effective parenting strategies for their child. There are many factors that affect attunement in a relationship between a parent and child. Attunement requires that parents first regulate themselves and then the child. A child who has endured a stressful early life may have a hard time regulating. Even the most minor stress causes a major meltdown. Parents must creatively experiment to find out what regulates their child. Sensory processing issues may contribute to problems with regulation. Other factors that influence attunement and regulation besides faulty or conflicting beliefs may include allergies to foods or additives, nutrition, chemical imbalances, and medication.

Chapter 5

Claiming Narratives

The first gave you a need for love, the second was there to give it.

Imagine answering a knock at the door and being told by the adult waiting there that she has come to take you to a new home. The friendly woman states that it will be a "forever" home. Not only is there a new home and family but there is a new school too. It may take a while to meet new friends and learn the routine, she counsels, but it's for the best.

This scenario is not far from the experience of adopted and foster children. In the case of international adoptions, some of this information may have been given by people speaking in a different language. The new home may be in a different climate and culture, and with people of a different race. The child may never see the same trees and flowers, smell the same smells or taste the same foods again. Is this traumatic for children? Absolutely! However, the child's need for safety and a permanent family often outweighs the pain and confusion of change.

Being claimed by a family is extremely important to children who have been abandoned, abused or neglected, and moved from home to home. A claiming narrative establishes the rights of the parents of an adoptive child to provide physical and emotional nurturing. A claiming narrative establishes the rights of the child to belong, to be accepted, and to be cared for by loving, responsible parents. The word "claim" is defined by Webster's Dictionary (Collin 1999) as "to say you own (something) which was left or lost" (p.77). The experience of being accepted and belonging to a family is a basic psychological need. This feeling of belonging provides a secure base for children to learn, grow, and venture out in the world.

After adopting a seven-year-old from Ukraine, parents were dismayed to see her willingly hug strangers, ask them for food, and even ask if they were her next mama and papa! Having gone through their adoption agency's pre-adoption training classes they had heard about behavior like this but were unprepared for how much it hurt. They were in love with this little girl from the first time they saw her referral picture and video. She belonged to them. But after two years she still did not know it and was shopping around for alternate caretakers "just in case."

Section 1: The purpose of Claiming Narratives

Claiming narratives can strengthen existing emotional connections or bonds between the child and family members, such as parents, siblings, and extended family. The narratives can also be used to pass on important family-specific information to the child, such as family traditions and history. Finally, in the telling of claiming narratives, parents may come to terms with issues such as infertility and relationship problems within their family of origin.

When parents find it difficult to bond

Adoptive or foster parents were not there when the child entered the world wet, slippery, and squalling. Connecting with older children is difficult. Connecting with older children who have been abused and neglected is even more difficult. The new parents were not the cause of the damage yet must deal with the behavioral and emotional fallout of the child's traumatic history. Parents are understandably angry about the child's difficult behavior and struggle to develop an emotional bond toward a child who makes himself very unlikable. Narratives allow the parents to experience the possibilities of what this child could have been like if he had received optimal, responsive care as an infant. Stories about "what it would have been like if..." allow parents to see their "challenging child" in a new way, as an innocent baby who from the first deserved to be cherished. Claiming narratives help parents see the child with fresh eyes. The child's loveable potential is revealed and behavior becomes just that, behavior. Separating the child from the behavior allows parents to empathize and provide unconditional love and acceptance.

Many parents enter our center's door at the end of their ropes. This is their last hope. If this does not work they are out of ideas and options. This was the case for Mark and Sherry. They were not even sure they could go through one more therapy with their son. "Honestly, we have nothing left to give. We don't even like him anymore." They went on to describe years of verbal and physical abuse at the hands of their adopted son. He had destroyed his room and just about every possession they cared about. He injured them and his siblings and no one in the family felt safe anymore. These parents got it—they knew why he did what he did but they did not know how to help him move forward. "I don't think I can stand to even be in the same room with him anymore," Sherry admitted guiltily. Mark and Sherry felt like failures and horrible parents.

With support, understanding, and nonjudgmental encouragement they agreed to try. Beginning with claiming narratives they described what their son's life would have been like had he been with them from the beginning. He interrupted, made sarcastic remarks, and looked bored. But to Sherry's surprise her eyes filled with tears. The realization of what he could have been like if he had the love and care they would have given him hit her like a ton of bricks. Her heart softened.

When the child finds it difficult to trust

In claiming narratives, children experience the joy of being warmly accepted into existence. The love an infant deserves is not based on merit, but on the mere fact that he exists. Many traumatized children missed this unique experience, and claiming narratives provide an important opportunity to re-experience those moments as they should have been.

Children who have their physical and emotional needs met by caring adults feel important and trust that adults will continue to be available, accepting, and responsive in the future. Children who have been abandoned and maltreated often assume they deserve it. Instead of trust, they feel anxiety, shame, and anger. All children deserve a safe, loving upbringing. When the child hears that he deserved attentive, loving, responsive parents, it may be a revelation. Hearing what the parents would have done if they had been there when he was an infant encourages trust on the part of the child. Parents who use Family Attachment Narrative Therapy report that their children ask "Would you really have…" questions for days and weeks after beginning claiming narratives. "Would you really have rocked me every day? Would you really have bought me these booties?"

Many families find creative ways to extend the claiming process beyond story time. Carrie and Tom had three biological children before they adopted Rachael. Their biological children each had a baby book, scrapbook, and a box of keepsakes and favorite treasures. Realizing the discrepancy, Carrie and Rachael started a baby book for her based on the claiming narratives they were doing. They started by borrowing a few pregnancy pictures from the older kids. Together they imagined how big Carrie was at each prenatal visit. They added an ultrasound picture that they found online. They pasted catalog pictures of a crib, changing table, and rocker on the page for baby's first room. They pored through baby name books before deciding on Rachael. Carrie found and printed a picture of the local hospital in which Rachael would have been born. Because they did not know exactly when Rachel was born and how big she was at birth they made up the time of birth, her weight, and length. Over the next few days they added information about her Well Baby visits, developmental milestones, first words, and favorite foods. They even cut a lock of hair to put in the envelope labeled "Baby's First Haircut."

Shifting the child's internal working model

For many children this is the fun part of Family Attachment Narrative Therapy. Hearing what it would have been like if they had been with this family from the beginning answers many questions and affirms their value to the new parents. Many relish the one-to-one time with parents and being the center of attention. They may even ask for the story over and over again. However in some cases, hearing what it *should* have been like leads children to remember what it *was* like. Those children experience sadness and grief. One four-year-old slid off his adoptive parent's lap after the story and exclaimed, "What a rip-off!" He immediately recognized that he had missed out in his first family. And for others, being loved and cherished may be incongruent with the child's existing model of who he is and what he expects from the adults around him.

Stories about what the child deserved in his early years may be met with resistance if the child believes that he is inherently bad and undeserving of love and responsive care from adults. It is not uncommon for us to see children covering their ears and refusing to listen to that "stupid baby stuff." Some try their best to destroy the mood and the moment. Each time one mother emphasized how she would have fed and cared for her preteen son if he had been with her from the start, he interjected statements like

"Yeah, I would have peed in your face!" and "I would have barfed all over you." It was discouraging. She eventually discovered that he would tolerate stories about some other mom and baby and switched to the third person perspective. Over time, repetitive and consistent physical and emotional nurturing with claiming narratives can shift a child's negative conclusions about himself and the adults responsible for him.

Establishing birth order

Claiming narratives can be used to establish a child's place in the family. When a child enters the family, whether through birth, foster, or adoptive placement, a new hierarchy must be established among the siblings and roles adjusted accordingly. Conflicts may occur as the children work out this pecking order. Age is not the only criterion for arriving at a new order. Because children who are in out-of-home placements have often experienced multiple caregivers, trauma, and neglect, there may be delayed development in one or more areas. The new child may be chronologically older but physically smaller and emotionally like a much younger child.

Scott and Mary adopted two teenagers from Russia. Tanya, age 14, and Nick, 12, joined Jill and Ben, their biological children. Jill was two months younger than Tanya. Ben, was 13. Tanya and Nick had spent six years in an orphanage and experienced abuse and neglect in their birth home before that. Two years later Tanya has accepted her role, not as the oldest but as the third child. Both Jill and Ben will be going through driver's education before she does. She recognizes that she has a lot of ground to make up.

An older sibling sometimes shares in welcoming and caring for a new baby or child. In other cases, the new addition is not appreciated. Parents may choose to have siblings participate in the narratives. One family involved older sisters in claiming the adopted brother as their own by having them pick out baby things for him and presenting their new sibling with these keepsakes. Another older sibling told a newly adopted sister of her joy when she arrived, her love of the big sister role, and how she worked through occasional feelings of jealousy and competition. It came as a quite a surprise to the adopted child that a birth child could be jealous of her. Sibling conflicts, hierarchy, and roles can be worked out in the telling of a narrative.

Claiming the extended family

The extended family is also involved in the claiming process when a child is born or adopted. There may be an endless stream of visitors after the arrival, all wanting to see and touch the newest member. Grandparents, aunts, and uncles often note that the baby has Uncle George's ears and Grandpa Joe's eyes. These family characteristics, both physical and personality traits, are also important in the claiming of an adopted child. Many times there are remarkable physical similarities, but in the case of international or transracial adoption the focus may need to be on how the child's sense of humor is like Aunt Martha's or how his mother loved to dance as a child too. Grandparents and other members of the extended family may take part in the claiming narratives as well. There is so much adopted and foster children don't know. Children of all ages enjoy stories about Mom and Dad when they were young. They are fascinated to hear that a great-great grandparent fought in the civil war. And of course there is the all time favorite of how far kids used to have to walk to get to school. Adopted children have years of experiences and history to catch up on. Claiming narratives answer the endless questions children have but may not ask.

Michael was adopted as a preschooler. By the time he entered school, his adoptive sisters were already in high school. They were busy with homework, sports, friends, and jobs and never had time for him. It seemed to him that they got whatever they wanted. They got treated better—it was not fair.

Recognizing that many of Michael's behaviors were attention seeking behaviors fueled by jealousy and insecurity, his parents arranged (actually pleaded) for his sisters to attend a family session. Embarrassed at first, once they started, the story just seemed to create itself. His sisters described how at age ten and eleven they would have been excited that their mom was having a baby and they have been the envy of all their friends. They told Michael how much fun it was to play with him and teach him things. Then the sisters presented Michael with a stuffed animal and toy truck, relating that Mom would have taken them shopping so they could each bring a gift to the hospital when he was born. All this time Michael had thought his sisters did not like him or want him in the family. It was a surprise to hear how much they wanted a baby brother.

Passing on the family traditions, history, and rituals

Inside jokes, pet names, rituals, and holiday traditions may seem strange to newly adopted children, and may be hard for him to accept. Claiming narratives teach family history, traditions, and rituals. Providing shared memories helps the child to feel as though he belongs to the family. Everyday dinner table conversation can be a mystery to the adopted or foster child. He does not have a shared history with his new family. Sharing the stories behind the family jokes helps the child identify with the family. A story about the time Uncle John and Dad almost drowned catching frogs explains the mystery of why everyone calls Dad "Kermit" at family gatherings. Parents may share their own life story, struggles, and joys in these narratives. Claiming narratives about the child's special role in holiday celebrations relay family traditions to the new child. How does the family celebrate birthdays? What will happen on the summer camping trip? Are gifts opened on Christmas Eve or Christmas Day? Will there be fireworks on the 4th of July? These questions and more can be answered in a claiming narrative.

Faith and values can be transmitted in family narratives. Descriptions of religious rituals such as baptism or first communion can be included in the claiming narrative. Meaningful narratives have been constructed around how the family would have prayed for the child—prayers for normal development, safe arrival, protection, happiness, and prosperity. Parents who are committed to values such as giving to others, honesty, and integrity incorporate these principles into whatever narrative they may be constructing and telling (see Chapter 8 on Successful Child Narratives).

Other issues

For parents who have struggled with the pain of infertility or family of origin issues, Family Attachment Narrative Therapy can help heal those wounds. Claiming narratives that begin before conception may assist parents in processing the loss and grief of infertility. Couples have dreams about their future family. They envision themselves as a mother or father nurturing, teaching, and playing with the child. They dream of picture-perfect family holidays. They anticipate the loving feelings they will have for that infant. The loss of that dream is as real as a death. As parents tell the older adopted child a story about their eager anticipation, the care taken during the prenatal period, and the joy of the first glimpse of that new person-to-be in the claiming narrative, both the child and parent share a healing experience.

There are no "perfect" parents. Most adults enter into parenthood with unresolved needs, losses, and even traumas. These issues may interfere with the process of attachment with a child. Claiming narratives describing children's early interactions with parents provide a model for parenting. The ideal parenting described in the claiming narratives help parents realize that if this child had been theirs from the very beginning they would have given him everything he deserved. Immersed in loving care and attention, they would have witnessed the child's full potential emerge.

In the midst of a claiming narrative one parent realized that she would have wanted to be loved and cared for like this by her own parents. Claiming narratives allowed her to re-parent herself. As she told her child about the love and nurturing he had deserved as a baby, the child within her was listening. In the telling, his possibilities became her possibilities.

The child's behavior also affects marriages, sibling relationships, and relationships with extended family, friends, and neighbors. When dealing with a challenging child, parents often feel isolated and unsupported by others close to them. Drawn together as a team through the narratives, partners begin to see and appreciate each other's strengths and characteristics. Siblings and other family members may choose to participate in the narratives. Understanding how the child's problems developed and the potential of the child (had he received the care he deserved) reawakens empathy for the child. Empathy for the child reduces feelings of anger and frustration. Siblings, family, and friends again have the energy to support and help the parents.

Summary

When a child experiences abuse or neglect in his early years he is at risk of forming a negative view of the world and the adults in it. Adults are perceived as unreliable, unavailable, and even dangerous. This world view or internal working model is applied to all adults in his life. Claiming narratives allow new parents to experience the child as their own precious baby. Narratives allow the child to experience the possibility that he deserved to be loved and cherished. The sense of belonging to the family is established by involving siblings and extended family and sharing the family history. Attachment is strengthened.

Section 2: Telling Claiming Narratives

Claiming narratives begin the process of healing, attaching, and adjusting to traumatic life changes. Through narratives the child begins to learn about the new parents, what he deserved as a baby, and what place he has in the family. Many children with attachment disturbances assume that the care they received from their birth family is "normal" and something all children experience. Some believe that rejection is deserved, because there is something wrong with them or because they did something wrong. In the claiming narrative the child's original life story is not being denied; instead, alternate possibilities are being presented. This begins the process of shifting those negative beliefs to a healthy model that will help the child begin to trust and feel secure in his new family.

If you had been...

Good stories have an inviting setting, a protagonist or central character with which the reader or listener will identify, a plot or dilemma, and a resolution. Start the claiming narrative by constructing the setting. Rich detail will add to the believability of the story and aid the child in visualizing the surroundings. Possible backdrops for claiming stories might be the birthing room at the local hospital or the baby's nursery at home. It may even be a room in the house on Maple Street where the parents lived at the time the child would have been born. Bonding may begin during pregnancy. If parents choose to start the narrative with the experience of being pregnant, the setting may be the doctor's office where they would have learned that they were pregnant or perhaps the romantic restaurant where Mom shared the news with Dad.

"Joshua, you know that you were in another lady's tummy and that we had to wait a long time to come and get you?"

"Yeah," he said.

"Well, we want to tell you a story about what we think it might have been like if we had been together from the beginning. You know we wished we could have come to get you sooner."

"Why didn't you?" Joshua asked. They have talked about this before but they answer each of his questions patiently.

"We had to fill out lots of paperwork and answer lots of questions. They wanted to make sure we would be the best parents for you. When they finally said, "OK" we were on the very next plane to get you. But if we had been there from the first I would have cried when I saw you. Not because I was sad, but they would have been tears of happiness. You know I cry all the time, don't you? Then I would have counted your fingers and toes and kissed your nose. You were a beautiful, perfect baby who deserved to be loved from the start. Daddy and I would have held you close, looking into your beautiful blue eyes as we rocked you to sleep. You know the bassinet your sister used?"

"Uh huh," he mumbled.

"We would have wanted you right next to us so we could hear if you needed something. And the minute we heard you making a noise our eyes would have popped open and we would have been right there to see what you needed."

"Really? In the middle of the night?"

"Yep," said Dad, "and there would have been a fight to see who got to feed you every time." Joshua's eyes sparkled with laughter at the thought.

"In the morning," Mom continued, "you would have had another bottle. Then it would have been bath time. I would put just a little water in that small yellow bathtub, you know, the one in the attic. I would check how warm the water was with my elbow like my mother used to do. It would be nice and warm, not too hot, not too cold."

"Not cold, right?" said Joshua.

"Nope, my baby deserves clean, warm water for his bath. I bet you would have splashed water all over the floor and me!"

"Yep!" Joshua exclaimed gleefully.

"After your bath," Dad added, "it would have been play time. We would have put a clean, soft blanket on the floor and surrounded you with toys to look at and touch. We would have stayed right next to you, helping you grab them, teaching you how to hold on and shake your baby rattle. Then it would be time for another bottle and naptime. We would always rock you to sleep and be there when you woke up. You might be hungry again or you might want to play. Life is pretty routine and boring for little babies. Tomorrow we'll tell about what it would have been like if you had had your first birthday with us."

The protagonist of a claiming narrative is "the baby." The child immediately understands that this baby represents him. He identifies with the baby. He experiences what the baby experiences with a new "baby like" wide-eyed openness. Children may intently watch their parent's face and gaze into their eyes. Often children ask questions and add to the story. It is not unusual for a child to ask questions directly related to his past history. For example, a child who had frequently been locked in a room for hours asked her new parents if they would have ever left her alone. Others ask if they would have had a certain toy or article of clothing. The child's identification with the protagonist helps him consider new possibilities. His view of himself, the world, and the people in it begins to parallel that of the baby/child of the story.

In claiming narratives the plot is the story of how the child would have been physically and emotionally nurtured in this family. The child would have been loved, cared for, and protected. Many parents begin with pregnancy, birth, and infancy, followed by toddler and preschool years. The narratives may continue until the parents grow the child up to the age at which he did join the family. The narrative may focus on a holiday or special event such as baptism or a birthday. The story may underscore the child's known background and history. For example, if the child was often hungry and ate food out of the garbage it might be helpful to emphasize how he would have always been fed when he was hungry and given healthy food to eat. Children who have lived in a chaotic environment need, yet resist, structure. They often create familiar chaos in their new family. Hearing that they would have had bath time, mealtime, naptime, and playtime day after day provides the consistency that was missed and teaches the new family's routine and expectations.

"Remember yesterday when we talked about what it would have been like if you had been with us from the start? If you had been my baby back then, I would have baked you a cake shaped like a race car for your first birthday. We know how much you like race cars. Your room still has race cars on the wall doesn't it?"

"Yeah, and I have more race cars than anyone at school," Joshua piped in.

"Your sister would have wanted to blow your candle out for you. I would have let you try first but one-year-olds aren't very good at blowing yet. I would have funny pictures of you with blue frosting all over your face and in your hair. Grandpa and Grandma would have been at your party too, and they would have given you a little race car that you could sit on and push with your feet. You would have made funny race car noises as you sped around the dining room table."

"And you know," said Dad, "I would have had the video camera going the whole time. I probably would have given you a model race car but…since you were so little, I would have just *had* to put it together for you." Dad laughs; Mom groans.

"Joshua, half the toys you would have had would be ones that Dad bought so he could play with them!"

"What kind of toys?" Joshua asks.

"Well," said Dad, "first there would be the baseball and bat. That you would have had before you even left the hospital after you were born. Then there was the football, the basketball hoop, the fishing pole, and the hockey stick. Boy, come to think of it, I would have had a lot of fun while you were a baby!"

"Tell me more, what presents would I get for my second birthday?"

"Remember Josh, you were with us when you were two," replied Mom.

"Oh yeah, so what did I get?"

"How 'bout we talk about when you came to our family in tomorrow's story?" asked Mom.

"OK," said Joshua.

Emotional attunement will help parents determine when the child is ready to leave story time. Sometimes it is as obvious as the child hopping off the parent's lap with "That's enough baby stories for today." At other times the child's emotional state and degree of relaxation will signal he is ready to stop. The ending may also leave the child wondering what happens to the protagonist next. What will he experience on his second birthday? Children typically look forward to story time. An adopted or foster child has faced many, many challenges; he may not have experienced many resolutions in his life. There is a satisfying ending to this story.

Be prepared for continued "Would you really have…" questions following the narrative. The babyfood aisle at the grocery store, driving by the hospital, bath times, and mealtimes bring questions to the child's mind. These questions, as well as the child's behavior between story times, give clues as to what the next narrative may need to cover. Nighttime insecurity may suggest a focus on bedtime rituals and Mom's and Dad's role in protecting children, while hoarding food may indicate the need for stories about the parent's role in satisfying the infant's needs.

Props and reenactments are commonly used in the claiming narratives. Baby blankets, a baby bottle with the child's favorite beverage, baby toys, and a massage with baby lotion will make the story come alive to the child. If the child resists any of the props or acting out the story, simply show the bottle and other items that would have been used if he had been born into the family to assist him in visualizing the experience.

Because of Robert's traumatic history and difficult behaviors Bill and Karen sought the help of a therapist trained in Family Attachment Narrative Therapy to facilitate the attachment process. Robert had resisted most of their stories and nurturing efforts at home. In the therapy session, however, he smiled charmingly at the therapist and chatted happily.

"I got new shoes on, see," he said as he turned the lights in the room off and on again. "Do you work here? Do you have kids? My mom yelled at me yesterday. Can I have this [pointing to his mom's water bottle]?" He did not hesitate to climb into his parents' laps to listen to a story. As they started to tell him what babies deserve from loving parents, he glanced and smiled frequently at the therapist looking on.

"Robert," Karen began, "If you had been our baby, right from the start we would have picked you up every time you cried. We would have never left you alone. When you were hungry we would have warmed a bottle of formula for you. Formula is like milk, only for babies. I would have boiled the bottles and the tops in hot water to make sure they were clean for you so you wouldn't get sick. Daddy would be the champion diaper changer in the family. Babies get a sore bottom if they are wet or poopy for a long time and we would have kept you clean and dry."

After a few minutes of the story Robert became restless, moving and bumping awkwardly into them. Robert asked them to stop and said it was time to go home. He asked them questions about lunch and where his brothers and sisters were. He eventually got up and hid behind the couch. Initially exasperated and feeling rejected, Bill and Karen considered stopping. Underneath this resistance, however, they thought maybe he was nervous and uncomfortable. He wasn't in control. Instead of stopping they continued the story holding a doll and switched to a third person perspective.

"All babies are precious," Bill continued. "Babies need parents who are responsible. Moms and dads need to pay attention to what their babies need. Babies can't talk, you know, so parents have to watch the funny faces they make and listen for their cries."

Robert began chanting "I can't hear you!" and covered his ears. They finished the narrative despite the distractions. Throughout the remainder of the day, Bill and Karen made simple statements about other things that parents do to take care of babies. As Bill prepared dinner, he talked about how moms and dads put food into the blender to make food the baby can eat. As Karen helped Robert with a bath she talked about special yellow bathtubs that babies need to be safe. Finally at bedtime, when Robert refused to sit with them for story time, they sat on the edge of his bed and talked about how babies need to be rocked to sleep each night and how music played softly keeps babies from feeling alone at night.

In order to be in control, Robert needs to know everything. Bill and Karen were banking on that fact and hoping that he was indeed listening. As Bill and Karen continued to tell claiming narratives in session and at home, Robert appeared to be distracted. However, they overheard him talking about the story with a boy down the street, confirming that he was indeed paying close attention. Karen gave him a hand-knitted baby blanket during one story. He immediately stated, "This is a stupid baby blanket! I'm not a baby!" and threw it behind the couch. Bill later found it under Robert's pillow. Bill and Karen felt a glimmer of hope that their love for him was finally getting through.

Problem-solving tips

Not all story times together will be precious moments. At times the child will resist or behave in ways that make it difficult for the parent even to be in the same room with him. And life happens: older siblings need to be at soccer practice, there are bills to pay, appliances that flood basements, phones that ring; the list of demands that parents face each day is endless. Don't despair if problems occur, if the story seems lacking, and the child (or parent) seems bored: try again and again. Some commonly asked questions about telling claiming narratives are addressed below.

I'm not very creative; what if I can't think of what to say?

Creativity is not a requirement for successful Family Attachment Narrative Therapy! Use past life experiences to build plots. If the parents have any past experience with infants and young children, they may draw upon that. Maybe they babysat as a teenager, worked in the church nursery, or spent lots of time with a nephew. All these experiences can provide ideas about how the parent might have cared for a younger child. Words spoken from the heart are more believable and effective than scripts or reading books. Remember that it is the attunement and connection between the parent and child that is most important, not the words that are said.

What if my child refuses to make eye contact with me?

Most children with attachment difficulties resist eye contact. Eye contact is an intimate connection between two people and this can produce anxiety in children who have come to expect only pain and hurt from caregivers. Eye contact will be even more difficult if a story has emotional content. Take care to not over-emphasize eye contact. It will naturally occur as attachment security and level of comfort increases.

If your child resists eye contact determine the meaning of this resistance. What feeling is behind the child's difficulty looking into the parents' eyes? The response to the refusal to make eye contact depends on what is driving the behavior. If it is fear, eye contact may improve over time as the child becomes more comfortable with story time. If it is a need to be in control, to not let the parent have power over him in any way, this may be addressed in future narratives. Story time should be pleasant and enjoyable for both the parent and child, not just another area for the child to engage the parent in a power struggle. Keep in mind too that some cultures avoid eye contact. So, your child's avoidance may have nothing to do with attachment whatsoever!

What if my child refuses even to sit on my lap?

Again, ask the question "What is the meaning of this behavior?" The answer to that question will help decide what plan of action to take. Avoid power struggles. Perhaps the child will make some physical contact, rest his head on a shoulder, or hold hands. Dramatic facial expressions, a soft voice, and props may interest the child and draw him closer. We have had parents successfully tell stories to children on the couch, behind the couch, under a blanket, and on the floor. One child was not even in the same room and watched his mother tell a story to a doll on a television monitor.

My child tries to control the story; should I let him?

Some children will ask questions and guide the telling as they attempt to answer questions about what their life would have been like with the family. In this case, including the information they seek in the narrative will satisfy their need to know. If the child controls the story to the point that the time together becomes adversarial it may be appropriate to ask the child to wait until the end to ask questions or end the story time altogether for the day. Try to understand why he needs to be in control of the narrative. This awareness may provide direction for another story. For example, if he is trying to control the story time due to anxiety about doing something new and different, a future story plot may be about a character that is afraid of anything new.

One parent avoided arguments, interruptions, and attempts by the child to control the story by doing "one-liners" throughout the day. At every opportunity she interjected a line about what it would have been like before her son could make a face, cover his ears, or rudely butt in. For example, at breakfast she casually stated that if he had been her baby he would have been gleefully throwing handfuls of cereal on the floor. On the way to school, spotting a parent pushing a stroller she exclaimed, "That's the kind of stroller we would have had for you!" And at suppertime she reminded him that as a baby she would have put all the vegetables in the blender for him because he did not have any teeth yet.

My child always asks for story time when I'm busy and then refuses when I try to do it later; do I have to drop everything?

The internal working model for many children impairs their ability to trust adults. Being in control decreases anxious feelings. They seek to control the adults and environment around them at any cost. A set time for stories each day may give the child the structure he needs to feel more secure.

When he asks, a simple reminder that story time will be at 7:15 as usual may be enough reassurance for the child. For others, a parent's willingness to be flexible and meet the child's need sends the message that he is loved and special. Some children reinforce negative internal working models by setting themselves up to be rejected and then becoming angry when their requests for nurturing are not met. This is the child who has to talk about his abusive past the minute the phone rings, or the child who demands a hug when a parent's arms are full of grocery bags. The response depends on assessing the meaning of the behavior. Putting down the grocery bags in the middle of the driveway to give him a hug may surprise him and lets the child know that he is more important than daily chores. If it becomes a pattern, the focus of future narratives may be to reassure the child that parents love him even when they are busy.

Summary

Claiming narratives begin to shift the child's dysfunctional internal working model developed as a result of his early attachment experiences. The parent conveys to the child that he is someone who from the first deserved to be cherished. Claiming narratives also help the child adjust to his new family. The child identifies with the main character in the story. The possibility that the child deserved responsible, loving parents becomes imaginable. Parents often report that their child appears happier, smiles more, and seeks out physical affection frequently during the period that they are telling claiming narratives. The parents' emotional attunement to the child helps them to find creative ways to deal with any resistance.

Chapter 6

Trauma Narratives

One sought for you a home that she could not provide.
The other prayed for a child and her hope was not denied.

A common childhood fear is the loss of a parent through death or separation. This theme permeates children's fairy tales and movies. Whether the movie is based on a classic tale such as *Peter Pan* or *The Jungle Book* or more recent family films, the story often involves characters who have lost one or both parents. The plot unfolds, revealing their triumph over danger and search for love and family. This underlying and pervasive fear can sometimes be seen in children's play. Games such as hide-and-seek, peek-a-boo, and imaginative games where the children are lost and surviving on their own help children master their fears of abandonment and loss. This fear can also be seen in children's dreams and nightmares of their parent's death in natural disasters, being kidnapped, or left behind. For many children the trauma of danger and loss is part of their everyday experience, not just a fairy tale. Every year millions of children experience some form of trauma.

Section 1: The purpose of Trauma Narratives

Every life is a story unfolding day by day, sometimes dramatic and sometimes ordinary. Many people wonder what their life would have been like if they had been born into another family, grew up in another city, married someone else, studied a different major, or had one more child. Every event in life changes the story. Sometimes the story is changed intentionally by a decision; at other times, a chance accident changes the course of life. Looking back one can see how events, actions, and choices brought them to this point. But no one can go back and redo life. Or can they?

Children who have been abused or neglected often develop negative beliefs about life events and themselves. Looking back on their story they see only a myriad of mistakes, misfortunes, predicaments, losses, and emergencies. They judge their life and themselves as "bad." Any "good" is forgotten or dismissed as chance. Van der Kolk (1996) has postulated that a person's fear response can be allayed by an attachment figure and by internal schemes of security. Trauma narratives can not only heal the child's old wounds; moreover, they can shift the child's negative internal working model. As the internal working model is changed, new behavioral and emotional responses are available to the child.

Healing the pain of trauma

Language utilizes and links many areas of the brain (Cozolino 2002). Because new experiences can change the brain early negative experiences can be repaired. Growth and healing are possible. Narratives or stories may be used to reorganize the brain. Trauma narratives can be used to help a child recover from past abuse, neglect, and loss. The telling of the child's life story facilitates a reprocessing of the events and decreases distressing emotions connected to the events. If the child's life story is told in third person narrative format she can do the work of reprocessing without triggering fear or defensiveness. Many children can not or will not tell the story, but in the telling of the trauma narrative parents can open the door for discussion. Through the story they can convey their acceptance of the child no matter what, as well as their belief that what happened to the child was not her fault. All of these components can help the child to heal. Children may express anger at the person who perpetrated the abuse one day and staunchly defend that person the next. Or they may not talk about it at all. There is no single, right way for them to go through this process.

Shifting the child's internal working model

Trauma narratives can create new working models and shift the child's negative conclusions about her life story. In the telling of the story the child's perspective becomes more realistic and judgments of the events more accurate. The child sometimes experiences genuine sadness about past losses. In the trauma narrative the child's love and loyalty to birth parents is recognized and the child is then free to separate the feelings about the birth parent from the feelings about the abuse and neglect she suffered. A child may love her birth parent but hate what happened. The child's feelings of shame and responsibility for the traumatic event often diminish as a result of the trauma narrative. Effective trauma narratives can shift negative conclusions children have made about the event, themselves, and the adults around them. In our experience this seems to happen spontaneously. Sometimes, a child will make a matter-of-fact observation like, "My birth mom wasn't very responsible but my new mom keeps me safe."

Creating understanding and empathy

In the telling of the child's trauma narrative adoptive or foster parents often regain empathy for their child. The past is not used to excuse current behavior problems. However, hearing the child's life story again assists parents to put behaviors into perspective (Hodges *et al.* 2003). A child who steals food, leaving the remains and wrappers stuffed everywhere, may be driven to hoard because of her background of malnutrition and neglect. This behavior is less irritating when the parents understand the meaning of the behavior. Telling and hearing their child's story also increases their understanding of the child's difficulty in trusting and attaching to them. Empathy for the child fosters bonding feelings. This empathy also helps parents become more attuned to their child and brings up feelings of anger toward the person who caused their child such deep pain. Children may be surprised and even pleased when parents thoughtfully express their outrage. Although criticizing the birth parent can be counterproductive, championing the cause of the child and what she deserved may give the child permission to feel her own anger, if only vicariously through the adoptive parent.

After telling a detailed trauma narrative Marty felt angry. As a dad he could not comprehend how any father could hurt his child the way his adopted son had been abused. His father had taught him that dads are supposed to protect their families. Because of his past, his son did not trust him and over-reacted whenever Marty lost his temper. Sometime he even flinched as if he expected Marty to hit him. After careful consideration, Marty decided to share his angry feelings with his son. He started by telling his son stories about his childhood and the trouble he was always giving his father. Marty also related the consequences of his boyhood antics, explaining that in the family he grew up in the punishment fit the crime. He had to help replace the garage door after using it for throwing practice and he got grounded for a week for missing curfews.

"No matter how mad my dad got I always knew he loved me and wouldn't hurt me." Carefully and with a wry smile, Marty added, "When I think about what happened to you, I wish I could meet that guy someday, because I'd like to tell him what I think about men who hurt kids."

"Really?" his son responded incredulously. "You'd fight him for me?"

"You bet I would! Nobody hurts my son!" That simple statement made a huge impact on the child's existing model for parents.

Empathy and understanding may also develop in children through the use of narratives. When the abuse was severe, children may numb themselves to both the physical and emotional pain. They may talk about intense, horrific trauma with very little emotion. Many traumatized children seem baffled when they observe others displaying strong emotions. This confusion may be interpreted as lack of concern and caring. One child laughed when she saw her mother and sister crying during a tragic scene in a movie. She did not realize that her numbness toward the scene was strange, not the crying. As trauma is processed, however, some children regain their ability to experience emotions more fully. They may be able to experience a range of emotions such as sadness, loneliness, anxiety, anger, and fear. As these emotions become integrated, children may begin to show signs of developing empathy and understanding for others. Because they have felt sad, children can recognize that feeling in another.

Because her daughter, Hannah, loved dogs one mother decided to use a puppy as the protagonist in her story. She began by describing the hard life the mother dog led, living in alleys and eating and drinking whatever she could find for herself. Her daughter typically talked constantly but she did not speak a word during the story. Hannah kept her face turned away so the mother was unsure if she was even listening or if she was off in her own world. At the end, Hannah declared, "That puppy had a very sad life." Her mother was shocked. Hannah seldom used feeling words other than "mad" and she had never expressed sadness about anything before. Reluctant to say anything that would disrupt Hannah's mood, her mom just nodded agreement. Hannah casually added, "That puppy needs a new family," as she left the room.

Summary

Traumatic events initiate a stress reaction in the body as the child attempts to organize a protective response to the danger. When the trauma is the absence of a caring, nurturing relationship with the parent or another caregiver the child may develop a negative internal working model of herself and adults. The child may see herself as bad, adults as untrustworthy, and the world as an unsafe and dangerous place. Trauma narratives heal the wound. Hearing the story helps the child make sense of what happened. In telling the story the parent can reassure the child of her innate value and that it was not her fault. Presenting the facts challenges the internal working model and leads to new conclusions. As parents develop and tell the story behavior is put into perspective. The child develops genuine emotions and empathy.

Section 2: Telling Trauma Narratives

The telling of trauma narratives honors the life experience of the child. It is her history, how she came to be the person she is. In the arms of her parent the child experiences herself as loveable despite her past. Although some children are able to listen to their trauma story and reprocess those events with apparent ease, other children are resistant. Not thinking about the events and not feeling the fear, sadness, and anger are effective defense mechanisms children often develop to protect against painful memories. Use of third person narratives may decrease the possibility of resistance or dissociation to the reality of the child's experience. When the storyteller utilizes the child's favorite animal or character as the story's protagonist the child's attention is captivated and the child is less defended against processing her own traumatic life events. Third person narratives also provide safety. The child can identify with the experience and emotions of the character yet maintain enough distance so that she does not become overwhelmed. Some children immediately recognize that this is their story and may say, "That's my story so why don't you just use my name?" Others keep it in the "it's just a made up story" category until they are ready to handle the content and feelings. Some children do not consciously recognize the story's similarity to their life at first. As the story is repeated the traumatic material becomes less sensitive and children may begin to see the parallels to their own life.

Throughout the narrative the message that the protagonist did not deserve what happened and that it was not her fault is essential. After selecting a character with which the child will identify parents may begin by describing the setting and events leading to the trauma. Some trauma is prenatal and the narrative depicts what the life of the birth parent(s), may have been like before the character appeared. Once the stage is set the story is told. The amount and extent of detail revealed about the trauma depends on what the parents believe the child can handle in this first narrative. If parents are unsure how their child will respond it may be wise to keep it simple and keep it short. Additional facts and details may be added in a subsequent telling of the story. Parental attunement to the child will help them know when the child has heard enough or whether she is ready to assimilate more information.

The story content is often difficult to hear. Lack of eye contact, restlessness, and fidgeting may indicate some normal anxiety and discomfort. This is to be expected. The past is painful; but remember, she has already survived it. Recalling it with a safe and nurturing caregiver will not re-traumatize her. Taking the child one step beyond her comfort zone helps her to begin to reprocess and reevaluate her past. Avoiding it may send the message that it is too scary, too shameful, and too bad to be brought out into the open. And again, the third person narrative allows her to examine the events and feelings from a safe distance.

Children may anticipate rejection when their new parents know everything about them. Weaving in the message that the child was not at fault and deserved something very different assuages these fears. Out in the open there are no more shameful secrets. Experiencing unconditional acceptance from parents helps the child to accept the experiences and herself. New beliefs about herself take hold and strengthen as the negative internal working model becomes obsolete and inaccurate.

"Instead of reading you a story I want to tell you a story tonight, OK?" Mom asked. "It's kind of a sad story but it has a happy ending. Ready?"

Angie said, "Okaaaay..." somewhat suspiciously.

"Once upon a time," Mom began, "there was a family of cats who lived on a farm in the beautiful countryside. The kittens lived in an old shed with holes in the walls and roof and when it rained they would get wet and cold. But they loved to play in the meadow on sunny days and chase butterflies. The mother cat was a very young cat and did not know how to take care of her kittens. The father cat was a big old alley cat from the city. Sometimes he brought the family big fat mice from the barn for dinner. But sometimes he drank bad water and he would get angry and even mean. He would snarl at the mama cat and swipe her nose with his claws. Sometimes the mama cat would run away and leave the kittens behind. They cried and mewed for her until the father cat hissed and swatted them with his claws. The little kittens were afraid and lonely but they learned not to cry. Sometimes the father cat would go away somewhere for days and then there would be no food for the cat family."

"Weren't there any people around to take care of them?" Angie asked.

"No, I'm afraid not," said Mom. "This family lived out in the country on an old farm and there weren't any people living in the old farmhouse."

"But why didn't the mama cat do something?" Angie interrupted again.

"Well, remember, she was a very young cat, almost a kitten herself. She didn't know how to take care of her kittens. Sometimes when she was running away from the mean old tomcat she would find some other cats and stay with them. Because she was such a young cat she would play like a kitten and forget to go home to her babies. But the little kittens were smart little kittens. Pretty soon they figured out how to find food on their own. They found bugs and worms, even grass to eat. It wasn't the good kind of food kittens deserve, but they survived. One day they left the shed to find food and wandered all the way to a town. Towns have lots of garbage cans, you know. They thought they had found a feast. But it still wasn't the kind of good food they needed."

"Did the mama cat miss them? Did she look for them?" Angie asked earnestly. There was a tension in her voice. Not sure what Angie needed to hear at that moment, Mom asked, "What do you think the mama cat did?"

In a very matter-of-fact voice Angie said, "I think she looked but she gave up to soon. Can we stop now?"

"Don't you want to find out what happened to the kittens?"

"Not right now, maybe later," Angie replied. The tension was gone from her voice, so Mom let her go.

As the story is told and retold the child's anxiety and discomfort usually subside. She will become more comfortable with the narrative. Sensing the parents' love and acceptance, the child may begin to reveal new details about the past, which are then incorporated into the story. The goal is not investigation, it is helping the child integrate these memories into her life story and shifting the faulty, negative conclusions she drew based on those memories. Some children believe that they are protecting the new parent by not revealing their trauma history. Or they may be protecting their perpetrator. Accepting new information from the child in an empathetic yet matter-of-fact way signals to the child that adults can be trusted with her memories.

"Are you ready for another story, Angie?" asked Mom.

"Not the cat story again, Mom. I know that's just my story," said Angie in the "do it my way or else" voice Mom knew so well.

"It might be like your story, but it's about a bunch of cats, not a beautiful little girl. Who should the story be about tonight then?"

"How about a Barbie and Ken story?" Angie asked, feeling pretty sure this would start an argument.

"Are Barbie and Ken the mom and dad or the kids in the story?" said Mom, calling her bluff.

"The mom and dad, I guess," said Angie, knowing she wasn't going to get out of it but thinking maybe she could make it short like last time.

"Barbie and Ken lived in Malibu, in a pink house by the beach."

"Wait!" said Angie. "My mom and dad didn't live together ever!"

"This is about Barbie and Ken though, not about your mom and dad. The stories aren't exactly the same. I don't think they ever lived in Malibu either. Anyway, Barbie and Ken lived by the beach. It was a lot of fun for them. They could lie in the sun, play volleyball, go swimming, and have parties with their friends."

"See, this is going to be about me!" Angie tried again. Not deterred, Mom kept going.

"Now this Barbie and Ken aren't like the ones in your coloring books. When they had a party it got pretty wild. Sometimes the police would show up to tell them to quiet down so the neighbors could sleep. Sometimes they missed work because they were so tired from last night's party. If they missed work, there wasn't enough money to pay for stuff and then Barbie and Ken would get into big fights. Life went on like this for quite awhile until Skipper came to live with them. By this time the house was getting pretty run down. Nobody cleaned; they just wanted to have fun. There wasn't always food in the house. There were lots of loud, noisy fights, and lots of parties. Skipper was pretty little so she couldn't take care of herself, or talk or walk. She could only cry and then Barbie and Ken would get mad and fight."

"I'm tired now, I'm going to sleep," announced Angie. She did not appear anxious or upset, and Mom's intuition was telling her that this was more of a control issue.

"That's fine," said Mom, "Close your eyes and sleep while I finish the story. It's OK if you fall asleep. Anyway, as Skipper got older she learned to find her own food. She liked to make Barbie and Ken and their friends laugh so she sang songs and danced dances, wiggling her hips like she saw the grown up ladies do. Everybody smiled and laughed and called her their little princess when she did that."

"Stop talking, I can't sleep if you're talking!" Angie exclaimed.

"I'm almost to the end, honey," said Mom as she began rubbing Angie's back. She could tell Angie wanted to start an argument but she knew she loved back rubs too, and hoped that would settle her down. "Some days Skipper would wake up and Barbie and Ken would still be sleeping. They slept most of the day after a party. Skipper would find something to eat and watch TV. It was boring.

"One morning she found the door open. Usually it was locked and she was too little to reach the door knob. She went outside and wandered down the beach. It didn't take long for her to realize that she was lost. She couldn't see the pink house anymore. Skipper started crying. A nice lady stopped and talked to her and called someone on her cell phone. Pretty soon a police officer came. Skipper knew all about the police. They came to the pink house a lot. People ran out the back door or hid. She was scared of them. She told the lady that she lived in a pink house. The policeman put her in his car and drove just a little while until she saw the house. He took her in. It was a mess from the party. He looked around at the bottles and needles all over. He seemed very interested in the white powder all over the coffee table. He took her back to the car and used his radio to call someone. Then he went back to the house. Another police car came. This time a lady police officer took Skipper and put her in the other car. She was talking to Skipper as she drove away but Skipper wasn't listening. She was looking out the back window watching Barbie and Ken get in the other police car. She was really scared. She didn't know where they were taking her or what was happening to Barbie and Ken. 'How would they find each other again?' she wondered. That's enough for tonight I think,' said Mom. Angie was pretending to sleep and just made some noise. Mom was pretty sure she had heard the whole story.

"I'll tell you what happened to Skipper tomorrow. Goodnight, sweetie."

As discussed previously, children commonly dissociate from the strong emotions that may have accompanied their trauma experience. Intense fear, sadness, and hurt are too painful to feel for any extended period of time. When abuse or neglect is repetitive some children endure the incident disconnected from the emotion. Trauma narratives begin to connect the thoughts and feelings to the memories to facilitate integration. The parent, as the narrator of the child's life, gives voice to the internal dialogue going on within the protagonist. If the child blames herself for what happened then the character also blames herself. If the child might have been afraid, heart racing, body trembling, then the character experiences terror. Even though it may not be 100 percent accurate, the child is reassured by the fact that another child had the same thoughts and feelings when bad things happened to her. Sometimes the child will correct you: "Nah, she didn't feel scared anymore, it happened all the time."

Utilizing the inner dialogue, the protagonist models the healing process for the child. In the story the character begins to consider that she might be loveable and valuable. Self-blame changes to understanding that the protagonist deserved something different. Anger changes to sadness, and then acceptance and moving on. The child identifies with the loveable character and may consider the possibility that her birth parent loved her despite the abusive behavior and irresponsible choices. Accepting that she is loveable, she also realizes that her new parents can love her. And if those parents can love her no matter what, maybe they are worth her trust.

Skipper's story might continue with Mom talking about the fear and confusion she felt as she was taken to a shelter home. The story might describe how she constantly thought about Barbie and Ken. Where are they? Are they in trouble? Why don't they come get her? Have they forgotten about her? Don't they want her back? The story might follow her journey to a foster home, on reunification visits, through the process of termination of parental rights, to an adoptive home, and finally to the courtroom where she becomes part of a new family. If Angie refused to listen to another Skipper story, which seems likely, the narrative would be just as effective if Mom picked up the story with a different cast of characters.

In a variation on trauma narratives, parents have used life books to help children develop a coherent life narrative. The life book is an ongoing autobiography of a child's life (Keck and Kupecky 2009). Pictures, videos, drawings, and mementos may all be included to tell the child's life story. The chronological discussion of the child's memories and of the book becomes a story with a beginning, middle, and end. The child may reveal more information about the past, but that is not the purpose of reviewing a life book. The goal is to help the child make sense of the past, understand how she got to the place she is now, and recognize future possibilities.

John and Marsha put their narratives in writing for their daughter Samantha to read over and over again. In pencil, marker, or crayon the words were carefully transcribed on the pages. Together they added illustrations—clip art, pictures cut from magazines, and crude crayon stick figures. With the many word processing and publishing programs on the market today, binding the story into a real book was an affordable possibility. Samantha was proud of her accomplishment and asked to put other narratives in books too.

As a general rule of thumb, parents tell trauma narratives over and over again. Sometimes it is the same story, sometimes the setting and characters change and additional details are added. When a child has worked through and developed some mastery over the story material she may want to move on. If the child is no longer interested in any version of it, displays no emotion during the story, and there are no behavioral difficulties after the story she may be done with it for now. Parents may revisit trauma narratives with their child again if she brings up new information, asks questions about her past, or displays behavior that parents believe is related to her traumatic experiences. As children enter a new developmental stage, for example moving from concrete operations to formal operations where they are able to think in abstract terms and consider hypothetical situations (Piaget and Inhelder 1969), trauma narratives may be used again. Hearing the story this time in a different developmental stage, the child is able to consider possibilities that may not have occurred to her before. Adolescents may ask difficult questions as they realize past events are not as black and white as they used to seem. The fact that her birth mom did not know how to take care of babies was an adequate answer at six. At 12 she may want to know why she did not take classes to learn how to take care of her baby. At each stage of development, trauma narratives may help the child reprocess her earliest life experiences.

Rich and Sarah went through therapy with their son when he was in elementary school. It did not solve all their problems but little by little things got better. However, when Trevor hit adolescence they felt like they were back at square one. They were not sure they had the time or energy to go through that turmoil again.

Before going back to a therapist they decided to do stories with him again. Enduring constant eye rolls and sarcasm, they persevered through the claiming narratives. They knew that the old trauma narrative about a mother dinosaur leaving her egg unprotected against predators would not go over well with a 15-year-old. The story was basically the same but they believed that Trevor needed more information at this stage if it was going to work. Using a recent movie they told the story of a professional football player's beginnings—growing up with a crack addicted mother, sometimes homeless, and moving in and out of the foster care system. It was similar to Trevor's story but not close enough that it would trigger his defenses. It turned out that he had watched the movie a couple of weeks ago at a friend's house.

Unbelievably, he hung around after the official "story time" and asked questions about his birth mother. Some they could answer, some they could not. Over a late night snack they showed him the social history and court reports they had received from the social worker before he was adopted. For the first time in a long time, they had a conversation without arguing.

When to seek professional help

There are times when parents should seek a professional to help their child work through past trauma. Some indicators that narratives alone may not be sufficient to shift the internal working model and change behaviors related to trauma include the following:

- Some children dissociate when memories of the trauma are triggered. A young child, unable to escape the abuse physically, may have discovered that she could escape psychologically and emotionally. Dissociation became her defense of choice. Now the child seems to "space out" in the middle of everyday activities. When something reminds her of what happened early in her life, the child automatically dissociates to defend against possible fear and pain. Seeking help from a professional who has experience with dissociative episodes may be wise.

- Many professionals assert that parents should not bring up the past with a child who has been traumatized, but rather allow the child to bring it up when she feels safe. This is good advice in some cases, but every child is different. Some children will bury the memories, thoughts, and feelings. They are unable to understand the connection between their current anxiety, anger, and behavior and the trauma. Trapped in the past, they do not develop an emotional connection with their current caregivers or the skills to deal with the stress. When defenses impair children's ability to function in the family, school or community, professionals and parents can develop a plan to help them face the past and thus move forward in life.

- The process of resolving past trauma is difficult for both parent and child. At times problem behaviors intensify as the child is working through her past. While most parents will not experience behavior any more difficult than they have previously, some prefer to have the support of professionals during the work. If behavior progressively deteriorates, professional help should be sought. If the child threatens to harm herself or others, seek help immediately.

- When narratives alone do not resolve the past, other techniques, such as Eye Movement Desensitization and Reprocessing (EMDR), may be added by a professional to work through trauma issues (see Appendix A).

Bill and Karen sought the assistance of a therapist to help Robert process through his past losses and traumatic life events. Bill and Karen chose a baby brontosaurus as the protagonist of their trauma narrative. Robert has been fascinated with dinosaurs and repeatedly asks to watch an animated dinosaur video. They recently took him to a science museum to view a dinosaur exhibit and he talked about it for days. Robert was relieved to hear that the story was going to be different today and that he wouldn't have to listen to that "baby stuff." He sat between his parents as they began the story.

"Once upon a time there was a little tiny dinosaur inside his egg waiting to be born. But this little egg had a mother who was just a teenage brontosaurus. She didn't know anything about taking care of eggs. She just wanted to hang out down at the big water with her friends. Sometimes she left the egg alone, cold, and unprotected. The baby brontosaurus wasn't growing as fast and as big as he should have.

"The big day came and with a loud crack he came into the world; he was alone. His mother came along later and showed him where the big water was. He drank thirstily but his stomach hurt and he didn't know what dinosaurs should eat. He followed his mother and her friends but they didn't even look at him and he had to move fast to avoid being trampled on. Sometimes they shoved him with their great feet if he was in the way.

"One day he fell and got a big cut on the back of his head. He found things to eat but sometimes it hurt his stomach bad. Nobody paid him much attention or told him what was good to eat and what would make him sick."

Robert moved, talked, and seemed distracted as usual. Bill and Karen were by now sure he was hearing every word and continued the story until the baby found a safe herd who would teach him and care for him.

In the second session with the therapist Robert wouldn't sit still. He wandered around the room touching things as Bill and Karen told another dinosaur story. They added more detail and began to describe the inner thoughts and feelings of the baby dinosaur. Although he looked disinterested, he made comments that the baby was sad or mad or that the mother wasn't "nice." Bill and Karen told versions of this story at home between sessions with the therapist. When Robert began to seem bored with the narrative they told a new trauma narrative, this time with a human protagonist. Robert was getting used to story time and didn't argue about sitting between them and even sat on Karen's lap sometimes.

"Once upon a time," Karen began, "there was a girl named Tiffany. Tiffany lived with her mom. Her mom said her dad had left before she was born. Tiffany was 15. Her mom sometimes had boyfriends stay overnight and they would do mean things to Tiffany. So one day Tiffany ran away. She drank alcohol and used drugs with her friends. She didn't care about going to school. She just liked to have fun with her friends.

"One day she found out she was pregnant. That means there was a baby growing inside her. Tiffany was only 15, just a teenager. She wasn't ready to be a mother. She still drank and used drugs and had fun with her friends. That wasn't good for the baby inside her. She didn't go to the doctor either to make sure her baby was healthy.

"When the baby was born she knew she would have to go home. The street isn't a place for babies. She named her baby boy Rory. Tiffany didn't know much about babies. She tried to take care of him when he cried, she really did. But no one taught her how to make bottles or give her baby a bath. And when Rory cried and cried, her mother and the boyfriend would yell at her. Sometimes she just left and went to find her friends. Rory would cry and rub his cheek on the bed until he fell asleep. He was hungry and mad and scared.

"It wasn't Rory's fault his mom left. Babies don't know how to talk. They only know how to cry. Rory deserved to be picked up and loved and fed and rocked and played with. But Tiffany just didn't know how to be a mommy."

In Karen's lap, Robert sat very still. He seemed to be listening intently with a very serious look on his face. Karen and Bill kept going until Rory was safe in a new home with new parents. They tried to give voice to what they thought was going on inside Robert; for example, how Rory didn't like being told "no" because he had always been the boss in his first family. And how Rory got into lots of trouble, not because he was a bad kid but because he didn't yet know how to be part of a family. They emphasized how much Rory was learning as he grew up into a big boy.

Problem-solving tips

Trauma narratives are difficult for both parents and children. Hearing the child's past history may be painful and sad; however, empathy for the child may increase. Telling the story replaces chaotic memories and feelings with a coherent life narrative, helping the child make sense of the past. Children often form new conclusions about the events. Some children may resist. "Not that story again!" It is important to consider the meaning of the resistance. Commonly asked questions are answered below.

My child refuses to listen to the stories anymore. I still think there is more of his history to process. What can I do to engage him?

Finding out why the child is refusing to listen can help determine how to approach this problem. Refusal or apparent boredom may indicate that the child is done with this story, at least for the time being. In other children this behavior may indicate that they are having difficulty coping with the material. They may need a break or perhaps additional coping skills to continue. The story's character can model for the child how to deal with difficult emotions, thoughts, and even dreams that may arise during and after the narratives.

Some children are fearful that they might get into trouble for what happened. They might fear that their birth parent or someone else they care about would be in trouble. Many abused children have been threatened. They are fearful that they will be found and punished for telling. If the child is anxious, returning to claiming narratives may reassure him that he deserved responsive care and love. The character in the narrative can also experience the same fear but courageously learn to face the fear. She may come to realize it wasn't her fault and that her new parents will keep her safe.

If you assess that the child is resisting for some other reason, construct a narrative that addresses the underlying cause of the refusal. One mother noted that her daughter was complaining about hearing the "boring billy goat story" all the time so she changed the cast of characters and began revealing more details of the trauma history. During the new narrative the girl called out to her brother, "Joey, now we're bears!"

Now that her story is out in the open my daughter brings it up at inappropriate times. Should I let her talk about it? I'm afraid if I set a limit she'll stop talking.

In many cases, children are reluctant to share information about the past. However, others have poor boundaries. They reveal disturbing details about their trauma histories to teachers, friends, or even strangers. Again, determining the underlying reason for the behavior is the first step in addressing this issue. Children with poor boundaries usually need simple rules and lessons communicated through narratives about what is OK to talk about in public. Children who use stories about the past to shock and control adults or be the center of attention may respond to narratives addressing the feeling underlying those needs.

We have told the story many times now but she doesn't seem to feel anything. Shouldn't she be mad or sad?

Dissociation allows the child to physically remain with an abusive parent upon whom she depends for survival. In essence, the child sets aside feelings of hurt, sadness, shame, and anger in order to maintain her relationship with the caregiver. When dissociation is successful the child is able to endure repeated abuse and function in the family, school, and community. During Family Attachment Narrative Therapy children frequently recall past memories of abuse; however, they may not experience the expected emotions during the narrative. Attributing the pain and emotions to the main character may help the child claim, experience, and express feelings. Other children appear not to have any feelings about past events or, for that matter, present events that the parent would expect them to be upset about. However, after processing the trauma they are able to feel and express a wider variety of genuine emotions.

My child wiggles and squirms and it's very uncomfortable for me. How do I make her sit still?

It is important to determine the reason that the child is wiggling so the underlying feelings and meaning of the behavior can be addressed in narratives. Increased anxiety expressed through restlessness and fidgeting is normal during trauma narratives and may be calmed when the parent reassures the child of his or her constant and unconditional care and acceptance. Retelling the trauma narrative may desensitize fears brought up by the subject matter. If the child is attempting to push the parent away with the behavior it may be appropriate to let her know that it is not all right to hurt anyone. Emphasize that story times are important. Vary the story somewhat if the child is bored—change the character or setting. Sometimes telling an adventurous, fun tale that does not have any underlying message keeps the child engaged in the daily storytelling routine.

Some children with attachment issues or past trauma may have a concurrent diagnosis of attention deficit hyperactivity disorder (ADHD) or Sensory Processing Disorder. Sitting still for an extended period is difficult for such children. Allowing them to shift and move during the narratives is fine and does not decrease the effectiveness of the story. For a child with ADHD moving can be a way of maintaining an attentive state. Provide an acceptable means for the child to stay alert. For example, let the child manipulate a soft, squishy ball or cuddle with a favorite toy. A short break with a drink or snack may help the child continue to pay attention. Some children will move about the room during the story, yet are listening closely. Parents have successfully used a weighted blanket or heavy pillow to supply the sought-for sensory input so that their child can sit for a longer period of time.

Summary

Trauma narratives provide a means for the child to process the events, thoughts, and feelings of her early life experiences. The love and comfort the child receives in the safety of her parent's arms communicates that she did not deserve what happened and that it is not her fault. As in claiming narratives, parental attunement to the child guides the selection of characters, the content, the intensity of emotions, and length of the story. Discovering the unique meaning of resistance and difficult behaviors during and following the narratives leads to adjustments in the narrative process. The experience of parental attunement and unconditional acceptance makes the old internal working model obsolete. Trauma narratives decrease the anger, hurt, shame, and sadness associated with the traumatic memory and allows the child to form a new meaning for her experiences.

Chapter 7

Developmental Narratives

One saw your first sweet smile, the other dried your tears.

The joy of watching an infant master developmental tasks and pass through stages such as playing peek-a-boo, speaking his first word, taking his first drink from a cup, learning to walk, or doing something all by himself contributes to the development of a reciprocal relationship between parent and child. Milestones and other firsts that parents excitedly videotape or record in baby books may be unknown by adoptive parents. Developmental narratives provide parents with an emotional experience of these events. Stories about babies, one-year-olds, two-year-olds, and so on allow parents to experience their older child as an infant or toddler and encourage him to achieve normal milestones. These narratives provide children with the experience of a caregiver celebrating their accomplishments and reveling in their uniqueness. These shared experiences and the positive feelings aroused by them build the bonds between the parent and child.

Section 1: The Purpose of Developmental Narratives

Trauma or other developmental injuries may impair how a child thinks, interacts with others, and solves problems (Cozolino 2002; Sroufe *et al.* 2009). He may appear "stuck" emotionally and/or behaviorally at an earlier stage of development. Parents can often accurately assess at what level their child is functioning. For example, they may report that with peers their ten-year-old acts more like a preschooler, dictating what his friends do rather than negotiating with them. Children deprived of parental encouragement and support may have delays in physical growth, gross and fine motor skills, speech, and cognitive, social, and emotional development. A complete discussion of child development is beyond the scope of this book, but parents may need to consult other resources in order to construct appropriate developmental narratives. For our purposes we will focus on areas in which we commonly see altered development in children with an insecure attachment.

Facilitating cognitive development

Lack of attention and care may impede cognitive development. These changes may not be evident until the child grows older and the discrepancy between adaptive age and chronological age increases. Maladaptive changes in the process of development constrain the child's ability to think, solve problems, and play.

Sensitive, attuned care conveys to the child that his actions and cues are effective and valued. Deficits in cause and effect thinking may arise when cues are repeatedly ignored or misread by parents. A child whose cries were not answered may not grasp that actions have reactions. Later, he may display the same behavior day after day despite receiving consistent consequences from parents, never seeming to learn from his mistakes. A child who lacks cause and effect thinking may also be a risk taker—constantly putting himself in dangerous situations without the normal fear inhibitions.

Alison's birth mother used alcohol and drugs during her pregnancy. After her birth, she was often left unsupervised, strapped in her car seat in front of the television or dropped off with a sitter. Although there was little documentation of abuse, her behavior led her adoptive parents to believe that she had been physically and sexually abused. But what they struggled with most on a day-to-day basis was Alison's constant lying and stealing. They joked that if it was not nailed down it would end up in her pockets. If she did not have pockets she stuffed her socks full. Money, candy, jewelry, trinkets, and just plain junk ended up hidden all over the house. Even when her socks jingled she innocently responded "What money?" when confronted by parents or teachers. Time outs did not work. Extra chores, loss of privileges, making restitution, apology letters, and even rewards and positive reinforcement for empty pockets and socks did not change her behavior. She just did not get it. Alison did not understand the concept of "mine" and "yours," and warnings of "If you do that, this will happen" did not seem to matter. They had tried everything and nothing worked. Her parents understood that exposure to alcohol most likely was the underlying cause but it did not make returning a box of stolen goods to school at the end of every week any easier.

Older children who have been deprived of optimal care may remain in the cognitive stage of preoperational thinking or concrete operations. Children view themselves as the center of the world and are very egocentric in the preoperational stage (Piaget and Inhelder 1969). They frequently have difficulty with attribution. For example, if Mom and Dad announce that they are getting a divorce shortly after the child has thrown a tantrum he may believe that it is his fault. Children in the stage of concrete operations are black and white thinkers, unable to imagine possibilities or see options. Jokes, sarcasm, and witticisms are simply not understood. One 12-year-old who had a background of serious neglect was told by a peer to stop "pulling my leg." She replied in all seriousness, "Mom, I didn't touch her leg."

Solving problems is also very difficult for such children. They get stuck repeating the same strategy over and over again even when it seems clear that it will not work. Whining for help and eventually breaking down into tears, a ten-year-old collapsed in frustration after trying over and over to pull a large object through a much smaller opening. She was unable to step back and consider the options of going around the obstacle or removing it.

Delays may also be seen in the play of children who experienced neglect and inadequate stimulation as an infant and toddler. For example, symbolic functioning is normally evidenced between the ages of three to five. In symbolic play children are able to use objects and language to represent something else. The child pretends that a box is a crib or says, "Let's pretend we're at McDonald's" as he sets out play dishes. Older children who have a history of trauma and attachment disruption may not demonstrate developmentally appropriate imaginative play with a coherent narrative, but simply manipulate or stack toys like a much younger child. Another example of delayed play is a ten-year-old child who opened and closed the blinds of the therapist's office, playing peek-a-boo with his mother's car.

Before children can use symbols they must master object permanence, or the understanding that objects or people still exist when out of sight. Children normally master this task between the ages of 4 and 18 months. This ability may be impaired in children who experienced deprivation in their early years.

Eric, a six-year-old who had been institutionalized for the first three years of life, worried when he lost sight of his parents, his toys, and possessions. Every night he placed his treasured belongings in the doorway to his bedroom and then insisted on sitting at the end of the dinner table so he could see them while eating supper with his family. Although his mother consistently told him when she was going to the bathroom, to her room to change clothes, or downstairs to do laundry he followed her everywhere, shouting through the closed doors to make sure she was still there. In his distress he even called down the laundry chute to the basement, "Mom, Mom, Are you there? Mom? Mom? Mom!"

When told to put a piece of candy in his pocket for later, Eric lost it and burst into tears, crying, "But I can't see it!" For him, the candy placed out of sight meant that it had disappeared. Because of his early history, he could not form a mental representation of his parents, possession, or even candy and know that it was safe in the pocket of his jeans.

Developmental narratives can be used to assist children in moving forward, learning and becoming proficient in areas where they may be lagging behind their peers. Embarrassed and fearing failure, many children may be reluctant to back up and try something they may feel is "babyish." Through imagination and stories children are able to practice these new skills.

Facilitating emotional development

Emotional growth may also be arrested and the child may lack the ability to modulate strong emotions. An infant's ability to accept comfort and eventually develop self-soothing strategies begins to form when a mother, attuned to his cues, relieves the stress and calms the child. A neglected or abused child who has not mastered the ability to accept external comfort or internally soothe himself may be overwhelmed by strong feelings and regress to more primitive coping strategies.

Imagine a boy waiting in line, anticipating recess. It's noisy and he's being bumped. This anxiety and stimulation initiates his stress response.

Without a pattern to soothe and calm himself he becomes more agitated and finally strikes out at another child who inadvertently bumped him. Sitting in the principal's office during recess is unlikely to change this child's internal reaction to stress or his behavior next time he is bumped while waiting in line.

Developmental narratives promote the growth and maturation of patterns that can help the child deal with strong emotions. Physiologically, many emotions may feel similar and may trigger the child's stress response. Learning to tell the difference between excitement and anxiety, or embarrassment and anger, and then expressing those feelings appropriately, can be taught and modeled through narratives.

Building relationships

Socially, children who have been deprived of physical and emotional nurturing lag years behind their peers. They have difficulty recognizing nonverbal cues and misinterpret facial expressions and verbal information. Their attempts to interact are immature and even bizarre. Institutionalized children often display the most severe deficits in peer relationships. Behavior that may have been prevalent and even tolerated in an orphanage may ostracize children in current social situations.

Sasha spent three years in an Eastern European institution before she was adopted. Her sometimes bizarre and intrusive behavior emerged when she entered kindergarten. In a large room filled with lots of children and one adult she began running around, making odd noises, grabbing others' belongings, and bumping into and hitting other children. Although unusual, her behavior made sense in the context of her institutional background. Part of the daily regimen included "play time" when the children were put in a small room with few toys and no supervision.

A Romanian adoptee recalled being in a room full of cribs and silent infants. When asked where she was in that room she replied, "Oh, I'm crying and they're rocking me." She survived by acting in a way that caused the adults around her to pay attention to her. She also learned to be rude to her peers, whom she perceived as competition. This attention-getting behavior did not go over well with her new family or with peers in the school setting.

New behaviors can be shaped through developmental narratives. Children also learn how to read nonverbal signals as the parent tells stories with emotion and animation.

Disinhibited behavior with adults is common among children who have been neglected. Without a selective attachment to a primary caregiver the normal inhibitions about strangers may not develop. Any adult becomes a possible source of attention, food, or gifts. Parents commonly report that their child will approach strangers, hug, sit on their laps, or request help in the bathroom from them. One parent related the chaos her two newly adopted boys caused in a European airport by taking food and belongings from everyone.

After using a claiming narrative to establish parents' claim to children, developmental narratives may be used to present information about how children behave when they are attached. Through the protagonist they learn secure base behaviors. Securely attached children prefer the primary attachment figure, check in with him or her, and exhibit anxiety when separated or when they see a stranger. Narratives can be used to teach caution with strangers and to reinforce that parents are capable of meeting children's needs.

Kevin was four. Placed in a pre-adoptive home less than a year ago, it seemed he had no fear. His foster parents reported he ran off in stores, played with other families at the park, and talked to anyone and everyone. He had already asked at least three teachers if they were going to be his next mom.

During the first developmental narrative on attachment, his parents described how as an infant he would have stared into their eyes and memorized their faces. He would have turned towards the sound of their voice, protested when they left the room, and checked in when he began crawling and toddling around the house to show them every wonderful new discovery. They also described how as a toddler, if the teller at the bank tried to give him a piece of candy he would have buried his face in their shoulder, refusing even to look at her. He immediately piped up to interject "Not me, I would have taken it!" Funny and, unfortunately, true.

Remedial skill building

Children's maladaptive behavior in a family makes bonding with them more difficult. Lying is frequently a problem in children with attachment disturbances. A tall tale may be cute when coming from the mouth of a three-year-old, when developmentally the line between reality and fantasy is blurred. But the same imaginative tale from a ten-year-old is frustrating to parents. Tantrums with flailing arms and legs accompanied by tears and wailing may be tolerated in preschool. However, teachers in middle school cannot stop everything to soothe and calm an out of control preadolescent who has been denied extra time on the computer. Daily phone calls from frustrated teachers are often followed by angry confrontations that evening between parents and children. When behavior is viewed as a component of the child's past and a result of disturbed development, the focus is not on a consequence but on "How can we help this 12-year-old learn what he needs to know to survive middle school?" Narratives can teach children the difference between truth and a lie, how to delay gratification, and handle frustration.

Children tend to have periods of regression when mastering a new skill. Learning new behavior is stressful for them. When teaching new skills through narratives, parents can provide permission to regress. One parent allowed her nine-year-old daughter to play with baby toys during their nightly bath ritual. But when she asked to take them to school her mother replied "No" while gently reminding her that the toys would be available again at bedtime. Another intuitively knew that on some days her adolescent son was not going to be able to make it through the day without a toddler meltdown. It is hard to be 14 all the time. She allowed him to stay home and just "play," avoiding the explosion that might further ostracize him from his same age peers. When staying home or changing the routine to allow for regression isn't feasible, the parents could tell a story about a child's frustration while learning to do something new. This narrative demonstrates to the child that the parent understands just how difficult it is to grow up.

Vika had a history of early deprivation and delayed development. Her parents discovered that she needed periods when she was allowed to regress. When she just cannot hold it together anymore, she tells her mom that she needs to be two, and that being five is too hard. Her mother gives her permission to regress. She stays home from school, skips soccer, and experiences all the structure and nurturing necessary for a two-year-old. With her needs met, she can often return to age appropriate behavior within hours.

Enhancing development

Narratives are an effective tool to encourage growth in children whose behavior is reminiscent of that of a younger child. What appears to be maladaptive behavior in a ten-year-old may be normal (maybe even cute) in a four-year-old. Seeing his problem behavior as typical for a four-year-old also provides clues about the child's internal working model and brings up the question of what was happening in his life at the time that may have changed his developmental pathway. Parents can then empathize with their child's developmental challenges rather than being angry at the behavior.

When observing difficult behavior, parents can ask themselves at what developmental stage or age this behavior would be appropriate and then modify their response to the behavior accordingly. Recognizing the child's need to regress may mean changing parenting techniques. For example, parents respond to stealing in a three-year-old differently than in a 13-year-old. Developmental narratives put behaviors in the context of developmental needs and stages.

When behavior is seen as consistent with the child's internal working model and as normal for his stage of development, it no longer appears pathological. When the behavior is identified in this way parents enjoy watching and being the child's cheerleader as he moves ahead. Putting difficult behaviors in the context of altered developmental pathways not only changes the way parents discipline their children but also decreases the shame children may experience about their behavior.

Anna's parents successfully drew a distinction between orphanage behavior and family behavior using stories about an adopted animal. Wanting to be like the story's character, she eagerly practiced her new family behaviors both at school and home. Sasha was able to label her own behavior, proudly calling herself a family girl.

Summary

Children who have been traumatized in the early years of life may behave like a much younger child. There are physical, cognitive, emotional, and social delays. Cognitive concepts such as object permanence, causality, and symbolic function may not appear until much later than expected. Emotionally, the child may have difficulty modulating feelings and become overwhelmed. Children who are raised in chaotic environments may not recognize social cues and may respond inappropriately to their peers.

These delays are not permanent. In a safe, consistent, supportive environment, the child is free to move ahead. In fact, studies have shown that children adopted both domestically and internationally make gains in physical growth, attachment security, emotional and cognitive development, and school achievement once they are in a nurturing environment (IJzendoorn and Juffer 2006). Attuned parents can create new patterns for responses to stress. Developmental narratives teach children how to grow up. Cognitive, emotional, and social skills improve when parents lovingly encourage and support children as they struggle to master new tasks.

Section 2: Telling Developmental Narratives

Developmental narratives encourage children to move through developmental stages they missed when they were simply surviving in an abusive, neglectful environment. We have found that many traumatized or deprived children want to behave better at home. They want to have friends, but just don't know how. They don't have the necessary skills to succeed in family and social situations. Hearing stories about what they would have been like at an earlier developmental stage teaches children what is "normal." Developmental narratives educate both parents and children about a range of behaviors that children typically present at various stages of growth. Both may recognize stages and behaviors that were missed. Parents can then encourage children as they struggle to move forward. Older children are able to evaluate and label their own behavior. Following narratives it is common to hear a child state, "I'm really being eight, aren't I, Mom?" Children and their parents engage in stories, play, or reenactments, which allow them both to experience the pride of mastering developmental tasks.

After telling developmental narratives to her daughter one very surprised parent related the following story. Expecting an immediate meltdown when she said "No" to a cookie, she waited and it did not happen. Her daughter paused as if thinking.

"But I really want a cookie," she said.

Mom empathetically and firmly said no again. Once more she waited, expecting the scream. Nothing happened. Her daughter paused again and then just groaned with a disappointed, frustrated tone in her voice. No meltdown. The parent could not believe it. Later, her daughter talked about the incident and said that she had been thinking hard about whether she should get mad like a two-year-old or act like a six-year-old. She wasn't exactly sure what a six-year-old would do so she groaned.

"Was that OK, Mom?"

After daily tantrums for the past four years, it was definitely okay with Mom.

When you were a two-year-old you would have...

Developmental narratives begin at an age where the child missed some critical emotional or physical nurturing or experienced a traumatic life event. For some, this may have occurred in the prenatal stage and the developmental narrative should begin at the point of conception.

Once upon a time there was a mommy and daddy whale who lived in a deep blue ocean called the Pacific. This mommy and daddy decided that they wanted to have a baby whale to swim and play with them. They traveled south to the warm waters, where they spent the winter waiting for the baby to be born. The mommy and daddy whale loved the baby whale before he was even born. The mommy ate lots of plankton to make sure her baby would grow big and strong inside her. She stayed away from the poisons they sometimes found in the water because she knew that the poison would hurt her baby. The daddy swam close to protect the mother from hunters...

Even if the child's complete history is not known, her current behavior may give clues to what emotional and physical care that may have been lacking. A child who refuses to dress herself may be perceived as oppositional or as expressing a desire to be nurtured. A child who hugs strangers and will sit on anyone's lap may not have mastered the primary developmental task of attachment because of experiencing a multitude of caregivers in her life. When analyzing behavior it is important for parents to continually ask what the child might be thinking or feeling. In an institutional setting for care, like an orphanage, disinhibition is very adaptive. It allows the child to connect with and receive attention from many different caretakers each day. It is important for parents to consider the meaning of the behavior. Is this behavior related to the child's early attachment experience or past trauma that may have caused her to miss a key developmental task or stage, to take a maladaptive pathway?

Jenny's foster parents knew that she had been passed around between relatives and friends and neighbors. Her birth parents were addicted to crack cocaine and had been in and out of jail. Jenny had been born while her birth mother was incarcerated. She spent her first month of life with her grandmother. When her mother got out she found her dealer before she found her daughter. She would leave Jenny with a babysitter and not come back for days.

At four Jenny treated all adults the same. She hugged everyone. She ran off in the department store and her foster mom would find her chatting happily to another customer. It got so bad that as soon as she heard the loudspeaker, she knew it would be an announcement for "Jenny's mom to meet her at the Customer Service desk." Her parents were scared for her. Her disinhibition made her vulnerable. They had talked until they were blue in the face about "stranger danger" but she didn't heed their warnings.

Mom and Dad decided to try a story about how babies learn who their parents are and don't like strangers. One Sunday morning as they were all snuggled together on their big king size bed, Mom said "Jenny, we have a story we would like to tell instead of reading the comics today OK?"

"OK," Jenny chirped happily.

"Once upon a time there was a new mommy and daddy. Their baby had just been born. When babies are born they are wide awake for awhile so the mom and dad held him close. The new baby looked around until he came to his mother's face. He stopped. His eye stared into her eyes, almost like he was trying to memorize her face. He looked at her for a long time then he looked away. Pretty soon his eyes found their way back to hers and they gazed at each other for a good long time. Eventually he fell asleep. But he never forgot those eyes. They were the first things he looked for when he woke up."

"What was the baby's name?" Jenny asked.

"The mommy and daddy named him Charlie because that was his grandpa's name. Charlie spent most days sleeping, eating, and growing. But each time his mommy or daddy fed him they held him close and they stared into each other's eyes. As he got old enough to play he would reach up his chubby little fist and touch his daddy's beard or grab his mommy's glasses. As they played "Pat-a-cake" and "This Little Piggy," he would watch them with big eyes, smiling, drooling, and blowing spit bubbles."

"Spit bubbles! That's funny!" exclaimed Jenny.

"That's just what babies do," Dad said.

"Pretty soon little Charlie was sitting up. He watched his mommy vacuum or wash the dishes. Sometimes he would shake his rattle and then look to see if his mommy was watching. She was always there smiling, clapping her hands and saying, "What a big boy, Charlie." After a couple more months Charlie started crawling around. He could chase after the cat or explore the den. But he never went very far from his mommy. Charlie followed her from room to room and if he couldn't find her he'd start to cry."

"Why did he cry?" Jenny asked.

"If Charlie could not see his mommy, he got scared," Mom replied.

"I don't get scared when you get lost," Jenny proudly asserted.

"I know," said Dad with a wry grin. "But maybe if you had been with us from the very beginning you would have learned that it was safer to stick close to Mom and Dad."

Mom continued, "Remember how Charlie memorized his mommy and daddy's face? Well, at about the same time that he started crawling, he started to be afraid of faces he didn't know. If someone walked up to the stroller and said, "Oh what a cute baby!" he'd cry and look for his mommy and daddy. He cried because he didn't know who that person was. Babies go through a stage when they are afraid of strangers. They only want their mommies and daddies to take care of them. Charlie would sometimes cry if Grandma and Grandpa held him."

"That's silly, he should know his Grandma and Grandpa," said Jenny.

"Charlie did know his Grandma and Grandpa," Mom explained, "But if he could see his mommy, that's who he wanted.

"Charlie kept getting bigger and soon he was walking. He could toddle off toward the swings at the park all by himself now. He kept looking back at his daddy, just to make sure he was watching. He was big enough to stay in the nursery at Church now. He cried when mommy and daddy left and watched them go all the way down the hall. Eventually he stopped crying and would play a little. When they came back, he smiled a great big smile. He put his arms up high so they would pick him up.

"At home he could play by himself for a little while. He didn't follow mommy around anymore but she talked to him as she moved around the house cleaning, so he always knew where she was. Sometimes he would go find her and show her a toy.

"One day they went to the department store. He didn't want to ride in the cart, he wanted to walk. So mommy showed him how to hang on to the side of the cart so he wouldn't get lost. At the checkout lane, the nice lady asked him if he wanted a piece of candy. He hid behind his mommy's leg and wouldn't even look at her. Mommy had to take the candy for him. Charlie knew his mommy and daddy were safe; he didn't trust strangers," said Mom. "It's a mom and dad's job to teach their children not to trust strangers. Maybe if you had been with us from the first, you would have learned that moms and dads are safe and that strangers could be dangerous."

"Oh," said Jenny thoughtfully.

"What do you say we go make some French toast?" asked Dad.

"OK!" said Mom and Jenny in unison.

The hero of the story can be the child, a favorite animal, or a cartoon character. When the protagonist of the story is a character with which the child identifies, the hero's challenge becomes the child's challenge. The child can then take on the attitude and perspective of the character. In the telling, the main character experiences the love and care necessary to support mastery of developmental tasks appropriate to the stage that is the focus of the story. The length of the story depends on the age and attention span of the child. A young child listening to the normal development and behavior of a one-, two-, and three-year old may feel overwhelmed with expectations and information. Stories are more effective if they focus on one developmental task, stage, or age rather than multiple stages.

For example, one parent constructed a story focused on the concept of object permanence. The story was about a little girl who lived in an orphanage and was adopted by a family in the US. In the orphanage caregivers, toys, and other belongings were not constant. They changed continuously and disappeared. In her new family the little girl learned that mommies always come back and that toys do not disappear at night.

The plot of developmental narratives typically focuses on a particular task or stage the child has not yet mastered. Emphasize the protagonist's desire to grow and accomplish the task. The hero does not have to succeed immediately: she can struggle and experience regressions just as the child hearing the narrative does. Describe the character's efforts, persistence, and attitude while accomplishing the task.

Not all experiences in life have happy endings, and neither should every story. Although narratives encourage new behaviors and mastery of tasks, failures and setbacks are a real part of a child's experience of growing up, so include them as well.

As mentioned previously, props and reenactments may help the child understand and assimilate the information. Filming a ten-year-old taking tentative steps between her mom and dad may initially seem silly, but it may fill a longing for a child who has no pictures from her early childhood. We have watched a seven-year-old struggle like a two-year-old to fit shapes into the right hole and a five-year-old lie on a baby quilt contentedly playing with baby rattles. Children seem to understand that they missed something back then, something that they need to go back to and experience. There are no limits, so be creative and have fun with the narratives.

"If you had been our one-year-old back then we would have been there to cheer and clap when you took your very first step. Daddy would have had the video camera out ready to go all the time so we would not have missed that exciting moment. You had already started pulling yourself up on furniture. You would have walked from one end of the couch to the other. But one special day you would have turned, let go, and taken your first step. We would have been right there with our arms reaching out to encourage you and catch you if you wobbled."

Five-year-old Nate fell on his bottom right on cue and laughed with his adoptive parents. Suddenly, a little embarrassed, Nate said, "This is stupid, I'm not a baby,"

"No you're not, but we didn't get to take pictures of your first steps. You were in Romania and we were still in America waiting for you," said Mom. "Let's go get some frozen yogurt, babies and big boys eat that don't they?"

Bill and Karen speculated that Robert was functioning in the range of an 18- to 24-month-old child. He had an intense drive to get what he wanted and do things independently. In their minds they could visualize him as a toddler struggling to reach the cupboard where the crackers are kept. He still tries over and over again to do things by himself and then collapses in frustration when his efforts are thwarted. Robert refuses assistance, attempts to distract him, and any comfort. They admire his persistence.

Bill and Karen also recognize that four-year-old Robert is much smarter than an 18-month-old. He has learned many more strategies to get into that cupboard. Robert's level of functioning was assessed using a Vineland Adaptive Behavior Scale. The detailed parent interview confirmed that Robert was indeed operating much more like a toddler than preschooler in day-to-day activities. They noted that his receptive communication, interpersonal relationship, and coping skills were delayed. Could it be that some of his oppositional behavior was in fact a lack of understanding of what was being asked of him? Could his aggression in preschool be caused by not knowing how to approach peers, share during activities or use words when frustrated?

At home Bill and Karen began to simplify their communication and directions when talking with Robert. They gave one-step instructions, paired directions with visual cues, and demonstrated tasks for him. It didn't solve all their problems but he became a little less defiant. Bill and Karen decided to use developmental narratives to teach Robert how to share. They initially decided to use the same baby brontosaurus as the protagonist in this story.

"This story is about the baby dinosaur again," started Karen.

"Not again," groaned Robert.

"Well, who should the story be about today?" asked Karen, sidestepping a possible argument by recognizing Robert's cue and changing the protagonist.

"I want a story about elephants!"

"OK, George the baby elephant had trouble making friends in the herd. He tried to get the other baby elephants to play with him. He would bump them, tease them, and sometimes he would grab something away from them hoping that they would chase him, but they never did. But when an elephant tried to play with George, George would nudge all his toys into a pile with his long trunk and stand over them. He didn't want anyone to take them away. So the elephant would walk away and go play with someone else who would share toys. George was mad, but he was sad too. George wasn't being bad or mean" (words Robert had probably heard to describe him), "he just didn't know how to play with friends. None of the adults in the herd had taught him.

"One day a wise old elephant stood rubbing her tough skin against a tree. She saw that all the other baby elephants stayed away from George. She saw him guarding his toys but not really having any fun with them. She had been around so long that she knew every elephant in the herd. Her name was Jumbo."

"Oh, just like Dumbo's mom," said Robert.

"Yes, just like Dumbo's mom. Jumbo remembered that this baby elephant's mom was just a young elephant. She had had a baby before she knew how to take care of one. Jumbo decided that she would adopt this baby elephant and teach him everything he needed to know to be in a herd. The next time another elephant came to play with George's toys she was right there and told him to push a toy closer to his new friend. 'Watch what the other elephant does with the toy, George. And then you take a turn and do exactly what he is doing.' George tried it and the elephant didn't leave. They took turns playing for a long time and then the other baby elephant had to go home to sleep. George wasn't sad that night."

Bill and Karen constructed a developmental narrative to teach Robert the basics of "how to be a friend." Unlike other times when they had tried to coach him through social situations he didn't get defensive and respond with, "I know that already!" He seemed amused by the baby elephant's poor attempts at making friends and even told them what the elephant should do next time. Each time Robert faced a new social situation, Bill and Karen were able to use the baby elephant to model behavior for Robert.

Problem-solving tips

Developmental narratives encourage progress toward more age appropriate behavior. Commonly asked questions are answered below.

What if my child wants to stay a baby?

Once a child's emotional and physical needs are met he is able to move forward developmentally. If a child wants to listen to the infant stories over and over again there is most likely a reason, some need that he is attempting to satisfy. New narratives may be introduced, telling the child what he would have been like as a one-, two-, three- or four-year-old while the parent allows periods within each day for the child to hear or reenact the infancy stage. The child may move back and forth between ages and stages until the developmental needs are met or until his needs are satiated at that stage. The feeling of safety and security does not happen overnight. Everyday stresses may cause the child to regress at times, but there is a drive toward growth, so don't give up.

This is my first child and I adopted him when he was seven: I don't know what infants and younger children do.

Before constructing a developmental narrative, new parents or parents of older children may need to review basic child development books such as: *The First Twelve Months of Life* (Caplan 1973), *The First Three Years of Life* (White 1975), and *The Common Sense Book of Baby and Child Care* (Spock 1945). Social workers, therapists, and other professionals may also be able to assist parents. Children may identify with the narrative if they recall how younger siblings or infants and toddlers observed in the extended family or neighborhood behaved at the age the narrative is taking place.

My son is stuck in the "terrible twos." How do I get him to move forward fast?

When a child is behaving like a two-year-old, it may be tempting to start developmental narratives at age three in an attempt to grow him up quickly through the "terrible twos." A focus on the need behind the behavior is critical. A child will only move forward developmentally when his basic psychological and emotional needs are met. Determining what is underneath the difficult behavior may suggest to parents where to begin a developmental narrative.

Summary

Developmental narratives help children master the "how-tos" of childhood while providing parents with the emotional experience of parenting a child through earlier stages of development. Cognitive, emotional, and social deficits may be ameliorated as children progress through ages, stages, and phases by identifying with the narrative's hero. Understanding that children are functioning at a much lower adaptive level than might be expected given their chronological age decreases confrontation and anger in the family. This perspective helps parents view difficult behavior as a need for knowledge and skills. Armed with the knowledge that children need their help, parents teach and cheer them on. Adversaries become teammates working toward the same goals. This shift in how parents view behavior is a critical factor in improving the emotional connection between parents and children.

Chapter 8

Successful Child Narratives

One gave you a talent, the other gave you aim.

A child who has been hurt in the past may behave in ways that drive parents crazy. Many challenging behaviors develop in order to help the child survive physically and emotionally in a neglectful, abusive environment and these can be difficult to change. Some problem behaviors occur simply because the child lacks the basic skills of how to do life. Overwhelming emotions such as fear, anxiety, sadness, or anger instigate other behaviors.

The majority of parents contact our clinic because the child has extremely difficult behaviors. They have read book after book, attended workshops, sought the help of educators and professionals, and still the child has defeated every parenting strategy. They feel angry, frustrated, and defeated. Behaviors exhibited by many children with attachment issues go far beyond the bounds of developmentally normal problem behaviors. The narratives used in Family Attachment Narrative Therapy help children create new stories about who they are, what happened to them, and who they can be. New stories teach and guide new behavior (Cozolino 2002). Successful child narratives address the child's behavior problems, giving the parents the relief they seek without triggering the defenses of the child.

Section 1: The Purpose of Successful Child Narratives

In the telling of successful child narratives the parent's goal is not to confront the child's behavior. Instead, stories support and encourage the child as he learns to control whether or not he behaves in a respectful, responsible way. Many problem behaviors can be addressed through enjoyable narratives while teaching the child values, reinforcing cause and effect thinking, presenting alternative behaviors, and explaining the basics of how to do life. Successful child narratives are extremely useful to teach, guide, and direct all children. Use of claiming, trauma, and developmental narratives usually precedes successful child narratives with a child who has an insecure attachment. Attachment provides the support needed as he tries out new behaviors. The experience of attunement with a trustworthy, responsive caregiver is necessary to shift the child's negative internal working model. It is important for parents to be attuned to their child's feelings. Why is the child behaving in this way? Successful child narratives are most effective when the underlying feelings and purpose of the behavior are understood.

Teaching children values

Values are best conveyed within the safety and security of an attachment relationship. The interactions between a parent and child involve both verbal and nonverbal communications. In this exchange of information the parent communicates values, ideals, and a way of viewing the world. This is the process of moral development. As the child learns to talk, this process becomes an internal dialogue. The parent's voice is present, guiding and helping the child to judge whether or not an action is acceptable. Small children can sometimes be heard repeating parental prohibitions out loud even as they impulsively disobey a rule. Because of the emotional bond between parents and children they usually make the right choice to avoid disappointing the parent and causing a rift in the relationship. Many parents of older adopted children report that their children seem to lack the intrinsic motivation to please others or make the right choice. Successful child narratives can be used to convey values, right choices, and ways of behaving.

Ella loved Disney movies. She watched them over and over. She could sing each and every song and recite most of the dialogue. Disney trivia games were not fun when Ella was playing because she knew every answer.

Fables and fairy tales have been used to communicate morals for hundreds of years. Her parents thought that these stories might be the key to teaching their daughter some valuable life lessons. First they watched Pinocchio together during their Friday movie night. From that story came four more stories about lying, obeying parents, trusting that rules and limits keep children safe, and that true love is transforming.

Reinforcing cause and effect thinking

Cause and effect thinking begins to develop in the first months of life when the child experiences that actions cause reactions. Cries result in nursing and rocking, smiles and coos lead to reciprocal smiles and sounds, throwing a rattle to the floor causes a strange, new sound and then, predictably, Mom or Dad pick it up. When there is a consistent reaction the infant or toddler begins to realize that she has an impact on others and the world. Conversely, when the infant does not experience predictable, congruent responses to her cues she may feel powerless and fail to understand that actions have consequences. Successful child narratives contain dilemmas, choices, and consequences to reinforce cause and effect thinking. As the parents respond to the child's cues during the storytelling the child experiences the power of her actions and feels valued and important.

To help Matthew understand that actions have consequences his parents encouraged him to participate in the creation of the stories. At various points throughout the narrative they paused to ask, "What do you think might happen if he did that?" Sometimes he did not have an answer, shrugging his shoulders in an "I don't know" gesture. But sometimes he got it. When the character did something pretty outrageous (something even Matthew had not done before) he smirked and commented sarcastically on the protagonist's choice. "Bet he got detention for that one! That wasn't too smart."

Presenting alternative behaviors

Children who have been maltreated early in life have difficulty coping with everyday stress and problems. When angry or fearful they cannot see options. Coping strategies that would be appropriate for a toddler or preschooler are used over and over again by much older children unable to conceive of alternatives despite repeated failures. Instead they may choose a response that is familiar. They may emulate adults they observed in a previous home or resort to behaviors that appear to lack insight and organization. Because of existing internal working models they react as if they are in the old unsafe environment, using the same inadequate tactics to handle problems. The same old behaviors elicit the same old responses from new caregivers, thus reinforcing the working model (Sroufe *et al.* 2009). They are unable to evaluate what went wrong or formulate a new plan.

Successful child narratives provide alternatives to habitual negative behaviors and increase coping abilities. A classic example is an 11-year-old throwing herself to the floor of the grocery store wailing for candy. When a two-year-old does not get her way, she may resort to pouting, whining, and tantrums, which sometimes work. When an older child behaves like the two-year-old in public parents may want to pull a hat down over their face and sneak out the back door. Successful child narratives give the child alternatives to her inappropriate behavior. Sometimes a quick story about a greedy, green alien named "I want it" may distract and change the moods of both parent and child. But if the child is lying on the floor screaming at the top of her lungs doing a story at that moment seems ludicrous and other parenting strategies may come in handy (see the Recommended Reading section at the end of the book for more parenting resources).

Jimmy never stopped arguing. From the moment he got up until he fell asleep at night, everything was a fight with him. Even when he got his way he would find a way to argue with that. His mom told the story of "The Arguing Words." Each time the protagonist opened his mouth to argue out poured stinky, smelly nasty words. The words piled up around his feet, his ankles, his calves and his knees until he could not move! Helpless, the boy turned to his mother for aid. "All you have to do to free yourself from that pile of arguing words is listen and obey and, 'poof', just like magic those smelly words will disappear," she said.

The story went on to explain that as the boy listened the pile disappeared and he went out to play. Less than a minute later he was arguing again and stuck again. Without the normal parent lecture, Jimmy did not get defensive and he got the message of the story.

Explaining the basics of how to do life

Problem behaviors may be a way of covering for deficits in social and emotional skills. Children consider their own life experience as "normal" and assume every other family is the same, even if that "normal" included physical, emotional, and sexual abuse. In a new family "normal" might be very different from past experience. New ways of doing things, new routines, new rules, and new expectations can be bewildering. Vacations, daycare, shopping, school buses, and many more situations may be novel to adopted children. In addition, children with cognitive, emotional, and social deficits due to prenatal exposure to alcohol, institutional care, or developmental disorder seem to struggle to make sense of relationships and the world around them. They lack the basic knowledge of everyday life. Successful child narratives can be used to teach countless ways of behaving in every situation.

Diagnosed with high functioning autism, Jake knew that he was different than his classmates. He wanted friends, tried to make friends, but the friendships did not last. He was smarter than a lot of kids his age and at the moment was fascinated with architecture. Using whatever materials were at hand—Lego, playing cards, Popsicle sticks, or books—he built and rebuilt masterpiece structures. His mom signed him up every year for clubs and sports hoping that he would hit it off with someone and make a good friend. This year it was choir. What he liked best was arriving early and setting up the risers and music stands and arranging them; finding the perfect symmetry was fun for Jake. Once the kids arrived, though, he could feel his stress level increase by the minute.

His social skills teacher had taught him loads of ways to put on the brakes when his engine level rose, but in the middle of the choir room he felt lost. He knew the other kids were staring when he sang too loud, but no matter how hard he tried he could not make his voice blend in. He rocked from side to side to calm himself and that earned him some rolled eyes too.

That night his mom told him a story about his dad. His dad could sing but got kicked out of choir! Jake found it hard to imagine his dad getting in trouble. His mom described how his dad had to learn to come into the room quietly, take a seat, listen, and be sure to stand where the director wanted him to. Watching the other kids, his dad followed along as they pulled out the correct sheet music. Most importantly, his dad learned to stick his hands in his pocket and sing, not talk. He got an "A" in choir that year.

Every Wednesday night his mom reminded Jake of the routine for choir until Jake could have told the story in his sleep. He was a full hour into the next practice before he realized that his engine level was cruising along just fine and no one had looked at him funny all night.

Summary

Difficult behavior frequently sends parents looking for help. Trying to change behavior without an emotional bond between the parent and child is frustrating and extremely difficult. The child may respond to behavior management plans if the reward is sweet enough or the consequences severe. However, despite careful implementation and consistent follow through, the child does not seem to integrate the new behaviors and returns to the old behavior as soon as the goal is reached. Parents frequently complain that their child lacks the internal motivation to improve. Discovering the meaning of the behavior, how it is related to the child's early attachment and trauma history, and whether it is related to developmental delays is the key to changing problem behaviors in a child with insecure attachment. Successful child narratives support and encourage the child as she struggles to make changes in behavior. A child may be afraid of making a mistake, afraid of asking for help, afraid of accepting love. These narratives can teach values, new behaviors, and life logistics, and reinforce cause and effect thinking.

Section 2: Telling Successful Child Narratives

Successful child narratives teach new behaviors to a child who may not have the coping skills to deal with everyday stress and disappointments. The underlying message is that the child's behavior is just behavior and does not define the child. Successful child narratives are most effective when one understands the meaning of the child's behavior. Once the underlying feeling and the meaning of the behavior are determined, those thoughts and feelings can be attributed to the character in the story. Some possible meanings of difficult behaviors are discussed below.

The meaning of behavior

There are many possible reasons or meanings for a child's behavior. Although it may appear that the child is committing premeditated acts of destruction and defiance, we have often found that the child is responding to past trauma and life experiences or operating from a deficit. Defiance is safer than admitting that she does not know how to do something or does not understand what was said to her. Defiance is safer than accepting help from an adult, or having to feel sad, lonely, hurt, or vulnerable. From this perspective, difficult behavior is understood as an attempt to cope with everyday stress. Some maladaptive behaviors are a result of missing developmental tasks and stages, or the basics of how to do life while the child concentrates all her energies on surviving. Many behaviors are designed to express anger and reduce the ever-present feelings of anxiety and sadness.

Reducing the effects of stress

In an attempt to reduce fear and anxiety many children want to be in control of everything and everyone. Children who have survived chaotic and dangerous situations did so by learning to take care of themselves. Children attempt to get their needs met by demanding behavior or by manipulating adults. Constant talking and questions keep the parent's attention focused on them. Children identified as having a disorganized/ disoriented pattern of interacting with parents try to control the parent by using aggressive, punitive behavior or manipulative, caregiving strategies (Jacobvitz and Hazen 1999; Main and Cassidy 1988). Stealing, eating disorders, and hoarding food may be related to children's early neglect and deprivation. In a new home with their basic physical and emotional needs taken care of, needs become wants. The perception that the needs will not be met causes anxiety. Children intensify their efforts to get what they want until every interaction seems like a negotiation. In their early experiences, being in control meant the difference between being hurt and making it through another day. Underlying the need to be in control is fear. As such, it is a very difficult behavior to modify. The more parents try to control children, the more threatened they feel and the harder they resist. For the anxious child, control is soothing balm for her fears.

Stealing and lying may also be the child's attempt at reducing stress. The traumatized child may attempt to satisfy her needs by stealing. However, this becomes a more serious problem when a child whose needs are now being met seeks to get everything she wants by taking. In addition, the higher levels of anxiety felt by the child may lead her to conceal mistakes and misbehavior. Lying becomes a way to protect herself. Control may play a role in this behavior; it is as if telling the truth somehow gives an adult power over her.

A child may also attempt to reduce stress by resisting emotional connections with adults. Shallow, phony behavior is designed to keep distance between the child and adults and avoid the discomfort of intimacy and strong emotions. She may approach adults indiscriminately, as if grooming them as future caregivers.

Many children with attachment disturbances and past trauma have well-developed observation skills. They are vigilant and watch everyone and everything. They quickly size up the situation and adults around them. Children may seem to be able to read the mind of others (van der Kolk 1996). They know what to say and what emotions they should be feeling and act the part appropriately. At other times, however, they appear oblivious to those around them and react insensitively to their needs.

Children who have experienced deprivation or abuse may operate in a constant state of alert. They are anxious about everything. Even an event that parents think will make the child happy may cause stress. In the rush to get ready for an out-of-town trip, tempers flare and stress is abundant. Defiance as the family is packing for a vacation may be caused by fear of the unknown. Leaving behind the familiar and experiencing something new is an exciting part of most vacations. However, for children with an insecure attachment it can be terrifying. In addition, packing belongings and loading up the car may remind the child of the many moves she had in the past. Fear of abandonment and loss may result in opposition to the parent's every request. Understandably, such defiance many leave the parent exhausted, exasperated, and ready to haul the bags back into the house.

Developmental needs

Difficult behavior also originates in developmental delays due to the child's history, institutional care, fetal alcohol disorder, or other neurological deficits. Defiance may be due to a lack of basic knowledge about how to do life. Many children who do not understand what is being asked of them simply refuse to cooperate. Opposition often results in behavioral consequences rather than remedial teaching of the necessary skills to do what is required of them. Lying may also be related to arrested development. Remember, chronological age does not equal developmental and emotional ages. If the child is stuck in an egocentric preschool stage she may believe that if she wishes it, it is so and if she says it, it will be believed.

Impaired social skills are also related to the child's past history. Lack of positive, nurturing, attachment relationships impedes the development of social abilities. The child has difficulty interpreting and responding to cues. The child's social behavior may actually be appropriate for her delayed stage of emotional development. Without those predictable interactions, a child may fail to develop the ability to understand cause and effect. Later she acts without considering consequences and has difficulty learning from mistakes. Difficulty with cause and effect also seems to impair conscience development. Without a secure attachment to a primary caregiver the child does not identify with or internalize her parents' values. Because she didn't experience an attuned, responsive caregiver, she in turn has difficulty understanding the thoughts and feelings of others. Children who do not develop empathy do not appear to feel guilt and remorse.

Expressing emotions

The threat of abandonment and loss arouses intense anger. Bowlby (1973, 1988) believed that the goal of this anger is to deter the parent from leaving. When the parent fails to respond appropriately, the child's behavior may become increasingly disorganized and deviant. Children who have a disorganized attachment often exhibit aggressive behaviors (Lyons-Ruth 1996). This anger and aggression may be repressed or directed at other targets (e.g., foster parents, siblings, pets, and property) when the child must maintain the relationship with the parent. An unavailable parent or loss of a caregiver may also be associated with depression (Bowlby 1980).

Depressed feelings may be expressed in feelings of hopelessness and withdrawal from the family, or even self-injurious behaviors and suicidal thoughts and attempts.

Oppositional behavior is also very common and may be a way of expressing anger. On the other hand, the child may be recreating past experiences. Anger and the need for revenge may lead to stealing and destruction of property. Some children with attachment disturbances seem driven to destroy themselves, the family, and belongings. Underneath the anger is sadness, frustration (when she does not get what she wants), or fear—emotions that make the child feel vulnerable.

Changing behaviors with narratives

Successful child narratives may provide a role-model for behavior change. No child likes to be told that she has done something wrong or to be told what to do. Stories about how Joey the Kangaroo sits quietly at his desk and raises his hand to answer questions model respect without causing the child's defense system to go on red alert. The character's behavior is clearly labeled as respectful or not respectful. The behavior is viewed as separate from the character. The character is always valued and loved even though the behavior is not.

As with the other narratives, effective stories involve one or more characters with whom the child might identify. Describe the character and the setting. Where does the action take place? Who else is involved? Explain the dilemma the protagonist encounters, the possible options for solving the problem, the choice the character makes, and the results of the choice. One parent whose son refused to do chores told a story about an irresponsible stable boy and the tragic results of his not caring for the horses he loved. The child later said, "I think I'll go and do my homework." Results may not be that immediate. The child may need to hear the same message several times in order to process the information and gain enough mastery over the skills being presented before she attempts them. A child who has identified with the character often states that she wants to be just like him or her.

Sam didn't like rules. On tough days his mom and dad heard "I wish I lived with another family!" And they did have a lot of rules. Sam's mom and dad recognized that it must be hard for Sam. Sometimes he saw his friends doing things that he wasn't allowed to do yet.

So one night Mom said, "Instead of reading you a story, I want to tell you a story tonight. Once upon a time there was a beaver named Harold. Now everyone knows that beavers are busy. They can't help it; it's just the way they are. Mother beaver was busy in the beaver home adding new sticks and more mud, chewing off any sharp ends that might scratch her children, and smoothing the dirt floor with her large, flat tail. Father beaver was busy in the woods every day, cutting down young sweet trees for his family to eat. He checked his dam across the stream each morning. He carefully examined every branch, making sure it was strong and sturdy. Without that dam his family would be swept away in the fast waters of the stream. But Harold the beaver was different. He didn't like to work. Harold was a dreamer. He liked to lie on top of the dam and look for shapes in the clouds. He was tired of hearing his mother and father say all day, 'Harold, do this, Harold do that. Harold, Harold, Harold' all day long. He wondered what it would be like not to have parents at all."

Mom paused. She did not want the character in the story to say the same thing Sam often did. She figured that if it was too close he would tune her out. But so far so good, so she kept going.

"A world where there was no one telling him what to do. It sounded heavenly. That was his last thought as he drifted off to sleep one warm and sunny afternoon.

"Harold had the strangest dream that day. He dreamed that when he woke up he was in the beaver home all by himself. But it wasn't his home. At least, he didn't think so. This house had a rough floor and the sticks were slapped together every which way. The mud didn't fill in the holes in the walls and the wind whistled through the walls. Harold went looking for his mom and dad but no one was around. He waddled around to the side looking for the tender wood to eat but there was no pile. Well, we all know that Harold didn't like to work so what do you think he did next?" asked Mom.

"Went back to sleep?"

"You got it, Sam; Harold went right back to sleep. But when he woke up later it was still cold and windy and the pile of sweet wood was still missing. So Harold went to play. He went to his favorite meadow and rolled in the soft grass. He climbed the highest hill and watched the clouds and the birds as they flew by. Harold even daydreamed that he was a bird and could fly. It was the best day he could ever remember.

Not once had someone told him what to do. He found some branches on the ground. They were dry and hard but he gnawed on them anyway. He made his way back to the house, took a deep long drink of water from the stream and went to sleep.

"When he woke in the morning he was hungry and cold. This time he decided he better do something. He better find his parents to tell them that the house needed repair and that they were out of food. He went upstream then downstream. Harold couldn't find them anywhere. Worse, when he went by the dam it was leaking. Water was spilling over the top and through a hole in the middle. He had seen his dad fix holes like that but he had no idea how to do it. Harold remembered his dad saying that if too much water got through the house it might wash away. He sat by the dam for a long time watching. He was getting a little nervous. If he went back to the house the dam might break and wash him and the house away. Harold couldn't decide what to do. What do you think he decided, Sam?" Mom asked.

"I don't know, his parents are supposed to take care of him," said Sam.

"Well, Harold was one lucky Beaver," Mom continued. "The sun went behind a cloud and he woke up. It was all a dream. He ran as fast as beavers can run, which isn't too fast, all the way home. There was his mom smoothing the floor. And the house was warm and cozy against the wind. The pile of sweet wood was right where it was supposed to be. Harold gave his surprised mom a hug and ran back out the door. He didn't slow down until he found his dad by the dam, which was not leaking. Dad was checking it over carefully anyway. Harold's dad said he was thinking about adding another branch to the top of the dam. It was still spring, he explained, and you could never tell when it might rain. And when Harold's dad asked him if he wanted to help cut one down, what do you think Harold said this time?" asked Mom.

"He said OK?"

"Yep, he did. But that doesn't mean that Harold started liking to do his chores. Nope, he never liked doing them. Sometimes he still wished he didn't have parents bossing him around. But by helping with the beaver work, he was learning to take care of himself just like a grown-up beaver."

The protagonist is not perfect. He makes mistakes and has grumpy moods. Some mistakes may be comical, others are tragic. Seeing the consequences of the protagonist's choices improves cause and effect thinking. Using narratives, parents can safely allow the child to experience severe consequences that are the likely result of behaviors such as aggression, stealing, or running away. The stories may provide new alternative ways of solving everyday problems. The child internalizes the new behaviors, adding to her own toolbox of coping strategies.

Parents have used classic storytelling techniques such as suspenseful cliffhangers, or letting the child choose the path, to keep children interested and involved in story time. Soap opera lovers have tuned in for years to keep abreast of their favorite characters. Each and every Friday the story typically leaves the watcher in suspense, tuning in next time to find out what happens. This can be a very effective technique with children as well. When parents leave the hero in a precarious situation children look forward to hearing what happens next. When children choose the path, they are given some control over the plot of the story. The protagonist reaches a turning point in the story, a fork in the road—literally and figuratively. For example, if he chooses Road A, he faces a fire-breathing dragon. If Road B is taken, he must cross a raging sea to reach safety. The parallel plots in the story contain valuable lessons both for the hero of the story and for children.

Most children figure out what the story is about and that the character represents them. Children may even resist story time if the intent of every story is to change their behavior. A story with no obvious moral message or teaching, such as the favorite character going on a great adventure, may renew their interest. One adolescent immediately recognized that she was the troubled character of her parents' stories. She did not want to listen to any more "stupid" stories. However, she was surprised when her character in a subsequent story was the hero and was helping others solve their problems.

Teaching behavior with narratives

Successful child narratives can also be used to teach the basic skills necessary to get through each day. Stories about taking the school bus, going to church, getting ready in the morning, or personal hygiene provide instruction in areas where the child may be lacking knowledge. Repetition of the story allows the child to rehearse these new behaviors in the safety of the relationship with the parent.

Timmy had a problem with remembering. He forgot his homework, he forgot to brush his teeth, and he forgot to make his bed. His dad, who had Attention Deficit Disorder too, had tried everything he and the professionals could think of to help Timmy. Nothing had worked so far. After consulting with our clinic and learning how to do Family Attachment Narrative Therapy, Dad told the following story. He deliberately exaggerated the protagonist's forgetfulness. Intuitively he knew that his son felt discouraged that he couldn't remember. Timmy often was heard saying, "I'm stupid." His dad believed that if the story hit too close to home his son would miss the point and hear instead another message that he was "stupid."

He began: "There once was a boy named Webster. Every morning when he got up he forgot to change his underwear, but he remembered to put pants on when it was cold and shorts when it was warm. He forgot to pack a snack for school but he remembered to eat breakfast. He forgot to shampoo his hair but he remembered to wash behind his ears. He forgot to comb his hair but he remembered to floss his teeth. But every day when he went to the door, his shoes were gone. Webster could never find his shoes. Sometimes one was missing, sometimes both. They were his favorite run fast shoes. He would look under the sofa, behind the door, on the porch. He'd eventually find them hiding somewhere, but by that time his mom was yelling at him to hurry up and the school bus was outside honking. All the kids would snicker at him when he finally ran to the bus with his shoes in his hands instead of on his feet. When the pretty redhead girl laughed at him, it was the last straw.

He had to do something about those shoes! But what? It seemed hopeless. It wasn't his fault his shoes disappeared. Someone must be hiding them! Webster decided to find out who was doing it. So that night after his parents put him to bed he lay awake waiting. It was hard to stay awake. He talked and sang to himself. He even got up and did jumping jacks. Finally the house fell silent. Webster quietly crept out of bed and made his way down to the back door. His shoes were already gone! His coat was on the floor. There were his hat and mittens over on the table. His backpack and all his papers were on the floor. But no shoes! He couldn't see them anywhere! He was too late. Mom and Dad heard the noise and found him sitting on the rug looking sad. "What's the matter, Webster? Why are you out of bed?"

"I'm looking for my shoes!" he wailed. "Someone steals them every night. I thought I could catch them. But I'm too late. They're already gone!"

"We locked all the doors and windows tonight, Webster, just like every night. No one came in to take your shoes."

"Then where are they?"

Dad picked up Webster's backpack. No shoes. He picked up his coat and there was one shoe. He looked under the table and there was the other one.

"Well, someone must have moved them," Webster exclaimed.

"I think we have to do something about the remembering problem," Mom said gently.

"I remember taking them off," said Webster.

"Do you remember where you took them off?" asked mom.

"Noooooo," admitted Webster.

"Well, I think the three of us are pretty smart people. We should be able to figure out how to fix the remembering problem. Anybody got any ideas?" Dad asked.

"Well, maybe we could tie Webster's shoes to his feet," Mom teased.

"Or maybe we could glue them to the floor," Dad added.

"Or maybe we should paint them red so we can see them," said Mom. They added silly idea after silly idea until even Webster was smiling again.

"Maybe we should buy ten pairs of the same kind of shoes so we never run out," said Webster.

"That would cost a lot of money, Webster. You would have to help us pay for all those shoes."

"Well, forget that idea then," said Webster.

"We could put a special rug right here by the coat hooks," Mom suggested. "It could even be red so you couldn't miss it when you came home from school. We could paint a picture of shoes on it or write your name on it so you would remember that it was your shoe rug."

"I don't know," said Webster.

"Maybe you should keep your shoes on all the time, even in the shower or in bed. Then they would never get lost," offered Dad.

"I'm out of ideas," said Mom. "Maybe we should think about it and talk again tomorrow. It's getting late and we all have school and work tomorrow."

"OK," said Webster, feeling a little bit better.

"So what did Webster do?" asked Timmy.

"I don't know," said Dad. "We'll have to wait until tomorrow to find out."

Parents and professionals may be tempted to add a few "words of wisdom" after the story or to question the child to make sure she got the message. Resist the temptation. After completing a fun and creative story to help her son with his anxiety, one parent asked about what he had thought about the story. He abruptly cut her off saying, "Mom, I got it." They do get it. If the adult starts talking about how the child can act just like the character, the child may feel shame and then defensiveness. The end result is a lost teaching opportunity.

Robert's behavior was predictable. Every night he pretended to be asleep. After the house was quiet, he would sneak out of his room and get into everything. He ate the cake Karen had baked for another child's birthday the next day. He colored on papers in Bill's desk. He played with toys that did not belong to him and sometimes destroyed them in the process.

Knowing that he was wandering the house while she slept made Karen feel uneasy. Other family members were understandably angry when their stuff was wrecked. Bill and Karen hypothesized that this behavior may have evolved in the birth home. Most likely Robert's early life was chaotic. Parties may have lasted into the early morning hours. There may have been music blaring and bright lights on at all times of the day and night. With no set routine for meals or bedtime, Robert foraged for food when he was hungry and slept wherever and whenever he was tired. This theory helped them to understand the meaning of Robert's nighttime behavior. They now speculated that the behavior might be Robert's way of taking care of his own needs. Bedrooms and bedtimes might be a new experience for him.

Modeling their story on *The Jungle Book* and the *Curious George* stories, Bill and Karen described the life of an orphaned chimp, growing up in the wild jungle. In the jungle, he was free to do whatever he wanted whenever he wanted. Sometimes he loved the freedom of the jungle. But when food was scarce and he could not find a dry place to sleep during the rainy season the chimp longed for a home like the other monkeys had. Bill and Karen continued to tell Robert about the mishaps and fun the chimp had on his own in the jungle. The day's story ended with the chimp staring straight into the eyes of a strange creature that walked on two legs all the time. As usual, Robert feigned disinterest when the story was over but asked when he would get to hear the end.

Later that day, Bill and Karen completed the narrative. The kind man who found the chimp in the jungle took him home to the city and named him Charlie. Charlie didn't know his name and didn't always come when the man called. He didn't misbehave on purpose; he just did not know. Life in the city was very different from life in the jungle. Sometimes the chimp missed his freedom and was angry with the man. He did not like rules. But the man was kind and very patient. He taught Charlie all about hot dogs and other strange and yummy foods, about swinging on the tire swing instead of telephone wires, and about soft beds that were never cold and wet. They emphasized that Charlie was not a bad chimp, he just had a lot to learn.

Problem-solving tips

Understanding the meaning of the child's behavior is the key to successful child narratives. If the meaning is not addressed, the behavior may not change. For example, lying is a common and frustrating problem. There are many possible reasons for a child to lie. A narrative to address the problem of lying might be about a little girl who believes everything she wishes is true, which addresses a developmental need. It may also be about a tiger that changes his stripes and his story to keep anyone from knowing the deep, dark ugliness he hides inside. The second narrative would attempt to shift the child's negative conclusions related to the events of the past. Some commonly asked questions are answered below.

My child seems to enjoy the stories. He even asks for them, but I'm not sure they are changing his behavior.

Be sure the task is developmentally appropriate and within the child's capabilities. If there are developmental prerequisites necessary to achieve the desired behavior change, a series of developmental narratives may be needed to help the child catch up. The problem behaviors exhibited by the child may have developed while he lived in a chaotic, abusive situation. A behavior, like hoarding food, helped him survive. Giving up that behavior is a risk. It may require a level of trust in the adults around him of which the child is not yet capable. Address the underlying anxiety about change in future narratives. Give the child permission to stay stuck as long as he needs to. Reassure him that he is loved and supported as he experiments with new behaviors.

I'm afraid I'm telling too many stories. Will my child get overloaded?

Many children look forward to a daily story time and will even remind parents when the routine is altered. Some parents have developed a cast of characters that they can use to vary the stories and prevent boredom. Telling silly, adventurous stories with the child's favorite character that have no particular moral message or teaching content should prevent boredom and resistance.

I'm not very creative. Where can I get ideas for stories?

The only requirement for Family Attachment Narrative Therapy is love and a firm commitment to the child. A parent's intuition, empathy, and attunement are the keys to discovering the child's underlying feelings and the meaning of her behavior. Once the meaning is unlocked, the exact words of the narrative matter less. The ritual of cuddling together, talking, listening, and demonstrating that the child is understood may facilitate change even if the story is not award-winning material. There are many children's books that teach values and moral behavior. Flipping through a few at the local library may get the creative juices flowing. Family, friends, and other parents may be able to help construct narratives as well.

Summary

Children who did not experience the attuned responses of a loving parent in the early years of life may have difficulty in future relationships. A negative internal working model gives rise to problem behaviors. Children who have been traumatized or who have delays in adaptive functioning present foster and adoptive parents with challenges that beat every parenting technique. Parents use successful child narratives with children to teach and model new behavior. The key to changing a child's behavior is not gaining control over the child. It is not finding a reinforcement or consequence that will work better. The key is discovering the child's internal working model and the meaning of the behavior. Then when she is ready to make a new choice, stories allow the child to see other behavior options.

Chapter 9

Stories, Stories, and More Stories

One gave you a nationality, the other gave you a name.

The best therapeutic stories are unique, created by a parent for a specific child and a specific reason. The stories hold the child's internal working model in mind and are told using the family's vocabulary and speaking style. There are many excellent children's books that tell really good stories. But if reading stories created by someone else worked to heal children from trauma and attachment disruptions there would be no reason for this book. After the first edition many readers requested examples of narratives. We include these with the important caveat that these examples are not intended to be read exactly as written to children. Some of the stories can be used with slight modifications to tailor them to a child—see the notes before and after each story for additional information. We hope readers will use these stories as a guide and a source of inspiration for creating their own unique stories.

This chapter contains full-length examples of claiming, trauma, developmental, and successful child narratives. As often happens in real life, some of the examples combine the narrative types. For example, developmental stages and growth are often part of a claiming narrative as parents describe what a child's life might have been like if he was with them from the first. Additionally, trauma and successful child narratives may be combined when an annoying behavior problem seems to be rooted in an old survival skill. Lying to avoid severe punishment, stealing and hoarding food so that one has enough to eat, and charming the socks off strangers are practical skills for some situations! Finally, stories that address common behavioral, social, and developmental issues are also offered.

We would like to take credit for these stories but we have to give credit where it is due—to the parents. These stories are a compilation of all the stories we have heard over the years.

Claiming narrative example

In a claiming narrative, parents claim the child as their own. Rich detailed descriptions allow the child to imagine receiving the love and care he deserved from the first. Depending on the age and attention span of the child, this story may need to be broken up into even shorter "chapters" describing the prenatal period, early infancy, and the ages and stages of six to twelve months. This story was told by a mother and father to their five-year-old adopted son.

Mom: Even though you were born in Russia, you know how you sometimes wish you had been in my tummy? Well, this is a story about just that. If you had been born here, Dad and I would have been planning for your birth. You were a winter baby so Dad would have been done with the harvest. He would have wanted to be there for everything. The day I found out that I was pregnant with you I would have been so excited that I would have wanted to tell Dad right away. It would have been funny to listen to him whoop and yell to anyone listening that he was going to be a papa.

Dad: Yeah, I would have looked pretty crazy jumping and dancing in the barn. But really we started planning for you way before that. When Mom and I decided we wanted to start a family, Mom would start taking extra-special care of herself right away. She had to start eating healthier—no more coffee or soda pop for her. She would take special vitamins, eat lots of vegetables and drink lots of milk so that the baby would be as healthy as it could be. Mom wouldn't be able to drink any alcohol or take any kind of medicine, even if she had a cold, because that's bad for babies.

Mom: But I would not have given up my chocolate! The doctor said chocolate was fine. Dad would have watched me close all the time; he even would have gone on walks with me to make sure I got my exercise. He'd take off work to go to every doctor's appointment with me. Even at the very first visit we'd be able to listen to your heartbeat. And as you got bigger—so would I. My belly would have kept on stretching until it looked like I had a basketball under my shirt. I would be able to feel you moving and somersaulting around inside. Dad would be able to feel it too.

The doctor would weigh and measure me at every visit to make sure you were growing big and strong. He would even take a very special picture of you, called an ultrasound. It would be our very first picture of you. I would email it to grandmas and grandpas and all our family and friends. We'd even be able to tell if you were a boy or girl in the picture. When we saw that you were a boy we would have started poring over the baby name books looking for just the right name for you. Aunt Diane would have thrown a big baby shower for you and me. You would have received gifts galore. Blankets, towels, cute little clothes and shoes, stuffed animals and loads of books.

Dad: Mom would have had me painting walls and putting furniture together for you. You know how she loves shopping. Your nursery would have been ready weeks ahead of time. The room would have been in blues and greens with cars, boats, trains, and planes decorating everything. Believe it or not, your crib had about a hundred pieces—I even had to read the directions! Mom had a suitcase packed and ready to go right next to the front door so when the big day came, we could be out the door in a flash.

Mom: I packed some pajamas and clothes for me and for you because we would have stayed in the hospital one night together. And of course we had a car seat for you. The hospital doesn't let the baby leave unless the parents have a car seat to keep them safe. All babies seem to want to be born in the middle of the night and you would be no different. At two o'clock in the morning, I would have felt you pushing to get out and I'd wake up Dad to get the car started. I could tell you were in a hurry to get out so I would have made your dad drive faster and faster. We got to the hospital and you were born a short time after that. Dad would have been the very first one to hold you and speak your name. Then I held you and we had your very first breakfast together.

Dad: I'd hate to leave you for a minute but everyone would be waiting for me to call and let them know you had arrived. First I called your grandparents so they could get on the next plane to come and meet you. Then I'd call all the aunts, uncles and cousins, neighbors, and everyone at work. Everyone would be so happy for us and want to meet you, but those first few days after you were born would be a time for just the three of us to get to know each other. Then grandma and grandpa would come, and in the next couple months, you would meet everyone.

Mom: For the first few months you would sleep in a bassinet right next to our bed. If you woke up we would be right there to feed or change you and rock you back to sleep. Babies spend a lot of time sleeping. You would wake up in the morning all smiles; Dad or I would change you, feed you, give you a bath, and play with you for a little while before you fell asleep again. You would sleep for a couple of hours. When you woke up, we would feed you again and change you, maybe play for awhile until you fell asleep again. That's what babies do.

Dad: I loved getting up in the middle of the night to feed you—really! It was the best time of the day. I would take you downstairs so Mom wouldn't wake up and it would just be you and me rocking and rocking until you were full and sound asleep again. Sometimes I would just fall asleep with you sleeping on my chest until Mom came and woke me up in the morning.

Mom: Don't forget all the pictures we would take, Dad. From the moment you were born, Dad would have taken a zillion pictures of you to send to everyone; he would have been so proud of his new son! There would be pictures of you getting your first bath, you being held by everyone in the family, you in your new crib, and you being rocked to sleep. All through that first year, Dad would have taken pictures of everything you did: your first smile, when you rolled over, sat up, crawled, walked, had your first haircut, your first meal in the high chair... Easter would have been our first holiday as a family. We would have dressed you up for church that morning and there would have been an Easter basket of toys and candy. But the chocolate would have been for me.

Dad: Your first summer, we would have one of those baby pools in the back yard. You couldn't sit up yet on your own so I would climb into it too and sit you right on my lap. You love baths so you'd love splashing in the pool too. By the end of the summer you could sit up all by yourself but I'd stay right next to you all the time to keep you from tipping over. Pretty soon you would be crawling everywhere and Mom would make me baby proof the house. We would have latches on all the drawers and cupboards. We'd put away anything that might break or that you might put in your mouth. Babies touch everything and put everything in their mouth, that's how they discover their world.

Mom: About that same time, you would start wanting more than just a bottle. First we would start you on some baby cereal. The first time you tried it more cereal ended up in your hair than your mouth but you'd get used to it. Pretty soon you were eating fruits and vegetables too. As your first teeth started coming in, we would put some Cheerios on you high chair tray and eventually we'd cut up little pieces of fruits and whatever we were eating for you. We'd still have to help you a lot though because you wouldn't know how to use a spoon yet. Sometimes babies are fussy and cry a lot when they start teething, but that's normal for babies, we wouldn't mind. Maybe we'd give you some medicine, but most of the time, we would just hold you, rock you, and try to distract you.

Dad: You would have been just eight months old on your first Christmas. On your first Christmas you would have been old enough to rip open the presents, but you'd probably be more interested in the sound the wrapping paper makes than the present. Your grandparents would have been there too. Everyone would have been taking pictures. Maybe Mom would dress you up in a special Christmas sleeper with the little footies in them. You would still be too little for Christmas fudge or cookies though. More for me!

Mom: Pretty soon you would be babbling and making all kinds of sounds and we would pretend you were saying mama and dada. Before we knew it, you were pulling yourself up on the furniture and taking a few steps. Dad would keep the video camera ready to go so we could catch you taking that first step on your own. I'd sit on the floor a few feet from Dad and he'd be calling you and encouraging you to come to him. You would try and try, until you could let go of my hand, take a few steps, and fall into Dad's arms. We would clap and say hooray! And from that point on, you never stopped moving.

Dad: Mom would be starting to plan your first birthday party; deciding who to invite and what kind of cake to make you. The party would be at our house. Your grandparents would be there and all your aunts, uncles and cousins. Mom would make a cake in the shape of a race car and there would be ice cream too. You would have your own special cake. After we helped you blow out the candle you would have just grabbed that cake and started shoving it in your mouth as fast as you could—remember it would have been the first sweet you had ever tasted, and most babies love it. You would have had a lot of cake and frosting in your hair and I would take pictures of the whole thing.

Mom: Your cousins would probably help you open your presents. You might have got a little school bus that you could ride on and push with your feet. There would have been lots of toys that you could push or pull now that you were walking. Grandma would have given you clothes and more stuffed animals for your bed. Dad and I would give you your very first train set! You have had lots more birthdays since, and we will tell you more about those tomorrow.

Like many claiming narratives, this story describes the normal developmental stages children go through, each of which would have been applauded and cheered if the child had been with this family from the first. With slight modifications it can be used in the cases of domestic adoptions or kin placements.

Trauma narrative example

The purpose of trauma narratives includes desensitizing the child to past trauma and helping him to understand previous life events. However, the value of the story is diminished if the child becomes distressed during the telling. Most parents are able to judge how much detail to include in the first trauma narrative. Additional detail and information that may be more disturbing is included in subsequent versions of the story. This is a sample of a first narrative told when the parent intuitively knew they needed to approach the trauma slowly and gently. This story could be used for children adopted internationally or domestically as the animal shelter may represent an orphanage or foster home.

Once upon a time there was a mama dog. She didn't live in a house with a family or a big back yard to play in. She couldn't count on food or water every day or a dry, warm place to sleep. She roamed the streets, finding food wherever she could and sleeping under the stars.

One day this mama dog found a shed to hide in and she had three beautiful brown puppies. They were so tiny and helpless. They couldn't take care of themselves. At first the mama dog stayed close to her puppies to feed them and keep them safe. But eventually she got so hungry she had to leave them to go look for food. The puppies cried when she was gone; they were cold and hungry too. At first the mama dog came back to feed her puppies every night, but as the puppies got older she was gone longer and longer. And one day she stopped coming back.

The puppies were still too young to take care of themselves but they had to try. They left the safety of the shed to try to find some food and water. It didn't take long before they were hopelessly lost—they couldn't even find their way back to the shed. Strange dogs growled at them, big people shooed them away, and scary machines in the street honked at them.

The puppies were so scared; they ran and ran until they were too tired to take another step. They stopped in the back of a big store and found some food in the dumpster to eat before they fell asleep inside a big box.

They woke up when the box started moving. Someone was carrying them. The man smiled but they just huddled in the corner. He put them in a truck and drove away. They stopped in front of a big stone building. Inside there was lots of noise—growling, barking, hissing, talking, and laughter. The three puppies were put in a cage. They didn't like it but there was a soft rug, food, and water. They ate all the food just as fast as they could and then fell asleep.

The days passed and the puppies got used to the cage and the noise. There was always food and water and the person who brought the food talked softly and petted them gently every day. Some days they got to go outside and play on the grass. Families came to visit the puppies and those were the best days of all. Sometimes there were special treats and toys to play with. The puppies watched some dogs and cats leave with a family. They happily pranced out the front door with a beautiful collar and leash. The puppies wondered if they would ever get adopted by a nice family. The littlest puppy wanted his own boy to play with and he wagged his tail as hard as he could every time there was a visitor. But he watched sadly as his two big sisters received their pretty collars and ran out the door dragging their boy and girl behind them. He curled up in that big cage all by himself and went to sleep. He didn't eat that night.

The days went by and the puppy was getting bigger and bigger, but still no collar. He had almost given up hope of ever getting a new family when there in front of him was a boy. He had brown hair and brown eyes just like the puppy. He looked nice. The littlest brown puppy started wagging his tail, slowly at first then faster and faster. The boy smiled and touched the puppy's nose. Maybe this was "the one," they both thought. The puppy was on his best behavior when the family went outside to play with him. He tried hard not to bark too much or get too excited. He didn't growl or nip like puppies do, but the family put him back in the cage! He had no idea what he had done wrong. He was never going to have a family of his own, he thought, and he hung his head...

But then he saw tennis shoes and looked up. It was the boy, and he had a collar. Hooray, he was getting adopted! The family had a house and a yard with a fence. There were lots of balls to chase and a big soft pillow bed to sleep on when he couldn't run anymore. The puppy liked this new place.

This story might be expanded to cover adjustment issues. Every family has rules, some spoken (don't talk to strangers!) and some unspoken (hidden chocolate in the linen closet belongs to Mom). For an adopted child who grew up in an institution or in a family where there was very little parental supervision and care, these new expectations can be bewildering, even maddening. Imagine the transformation a child must make when he has literally taken care of himself for years and suddenly must ask permission to have a snack, go outside, or watch television. Limits set by parents seem mean. Consequences may reinforce the child's negative beliefs about self and adults.

The next day the brown puppy woke up with lots of energy. To his surprise, the boy went off to school and the mom and dad went to work. At first he felt lonely and even cried a little. But he was a curious puppy and decided to explore. He smelled wonderful aromas, and being not only curious but also clever the puppy figured out a way to climb all the way up to the table and eat the food there. He found shoes to chew on, socks to play tug of war with, beds to nap on, and papers to rip.

[*Aside*] Mom: Can you guess what happened when the family got home?

Child: He was in trouble!

The family came home that night to a big mess and the curious, clever brown puppy got a big scolding. The puppy got scared and worried. He thought that maybe he was a bad puppy and that the family wouldn't want him anymore. Maybe they would even take him back to the shelter. But the family knew he wasn't a bad puppy. He just didn't know how to behave in a family yet. After all, he had grown up in a shed and then in a shelter. He had never lived in a house before. He had a lot to learn. He learned what he could play with and what to stay away from. He learned to eat and drink from his bowls, not from the table. He learned how to tell the boy it was time for a walk so he didn't have an accident. He learned that it was OK to sleep on his pillow but not the furniture. He didn't learn how to be a family puppy overnight. He made a lot of mistakes. The family patiently taught him over and over again. The brown puppy didn't worry anymore. He knew that this was his boy forever.

> Some children ask questions and add their own ideas and opinions to the story. Others remain silent. Some parents prefer a more conversational style of storytelling and ask questions of their child. If a child does not answer a question just continue the story.

Another trauma narrative

> Many parents begin trauma narratives by describing the events of the birth parents, placing the child's experiences into a context that reinforces that what happened was not the child's fault. If parents do not have information about their child's birth parents, the prologue may be omitted. Notice how the storyteller gives voice to the child's innermost thoughts and feelings.

Once upon a time, in a place far away from here, there was a girl. She was just a teenager, really, and she loved a boy very much. One day she found out that she was going to have a baby. She was happy but a little scared too. She had always wanted a baby to love her and she hoped maybe that the boy would be happy too. But he wasn't. He was mad—very mad. He wasn't ready to be a father; he was just a boy. He wanted to play baseball and hang out with his friends.

The boy left and the girl was really scared; she didn't know how to be a mother. She kept going to school and didn't tell anyone she was going to have a baby until she couldn't hide it anymore. She dropped out of school and tried to find a job, but no one would hire a girl who was going to have a baby so soon. She knew she should go to a doctor but she didn't have any money.

The boy came back after the baby was born but he wasn't very nice to the girl or the baby. They fought a lot. They never had enough money for food and diapers. Sometimes they couldn't pay the rent and the landlord kicked them out. They stayed with friends for a while or sometimes just slept in the car. It seemed like they always had enough money for cigarettes and beer though. When they drank, they forgot about their problems for a while and were happy. But if they kept drinking, the fighting got worse—a lot worse.

The baby was a girl. She was beautiful baby with blue eyes and curly dark hair. Like all babies she cried when she was hungry, wet, or tired, or if she was lonely and wanted someone to come and hold her and play with her. Sometimes the fighting got so loud it made the baby cry and then she would get yelled at, which just scared her and made her cry all the more. The baby girl never knew what would happen when she cried. Sometimes someone held and fed her. They even played with her. But sometimes no one came, or she got yelled at or hit. All babies cry to tell their parents they need something. She wasn't doing anything wrong.

When she grew up, she learned how to do a lot of things by herself. She found half-empty bottles to drink or some crackers to eat when she was hungry. But she couldn't do anything about the diapers and her bottom got red and sore. Sometimes her parents would hold her and play with her. Her mom liked to dress her up in pretty clothes and take her to visit friends. If they started drinking, she knew to stay away from them. There were lots of strange people in the apartment, loud music, and lots of fighting. On bad days, her parents wouldn't get out of bed. If she needed something her parents just told her to go away and leave them alone.

One day, the neighbors heard them fighting. They also heard her crying, and called the police. The police warned her parents to be quiet, told them to feed her, and to clean up the apartment or they would call social services. Her parents cleaned the next day and got some groceries, but it wasn't long before they started partying with friends all night and sleeping all day again. And the food ran out.

The next time the police came they brought a social worker with them. The little girl could hear the lady talking to her mom and dad. Her mom and dad sounded mad, and she felt scared. The lady came into her room and looked around for clothes and diapers. She couldn't find anything clean. Then the lady took the baby girl to her car. Her mom and dad followed her all the way down the stairs, yelling. The little girl thought they were mad at her.

The lady drove a long time. She talked in a soft voice the entire ride. Finally the car stopped but the little girl did not know where she was. She was taken into a nice house. It was clean and she could smell food cooking. Now another lady picked her up and took her right to the bathtub. The water was warm and afterwards, she was dressed in clean, warm clothes. Next, the lady strapped her in a funny chair; she couldn't move and she didn't like it very much. She knew not to cry. She ate as fast as the lady could feed her until her tummy hurt. The lady picked her up again, washed her hands and face, wrapped her in a blanket and rocked her until she fell asleep. When she woke up a few hours later it was dark and the house was quiet—too quiet. This house was strange. She climbed out of the crib and wandered around the house silently. She ate some more and then fell back asleep on the couch. She didn't like how quiet it was at night but she liked the food.

One day the social worker lady came back and said she was taking her to a new home. She had no idea what that meant but hoped she would see her mom and dad. Instead she was driven to a new house with a different mom and dad. They seemed nice. There were lots of toys to play with and lots of food in this place. However, her first mom and dad were not there in this new place and it was too quiet at night. She slept, ate, and played with the toys until it didn't feel so strange anymore. When the new mom and dad hugged her, she smiled and hugged them back. They looked happy. Then one day there was a knock at the door and there were her first mommy and daddy. They picked her up and hugged her too tight and kissed her all over. They played with some of the toys with her while the other mom watched. Then they said they had to go. She went to the door but they just waved goodbye to her and left. She heard them yelling at the social worker in the front yard. She didn't see them again.

One morning the little girl saw the new mom packing her clothes and toys in a big black bag. She said she was going to live with a new mommy and daddy, who would take care of her forever. She didn't know what forever meant. She was sad but she didn't cry.

The social worker came back and they rode in the car for a long time. They drove to a big white house. The people there said that they were her new mommy and daddy. They showed her a pretty pink room with a little bed and said it was her room. There were lots of toys and dolls in the room. They showed her the rest of the house too. She didn't say much but gave them a big hug when they asked for one. She knew that hugs make grown-ups happy.

As time passed, the mom and dad thought she was happy, but she was quiet. She didn't talk as much as other two- and three-year-olds, and she didn't sleep. Every time the mom and dad checked on her at night, she would be lying with the covers up to her neck and her eyes wide open. They also noticed that she never asked them for anything. Not for food or a drink, not even for help. She tried to do everything for herself. In the mornings, the mom and dad would find that the big black bag was full of her toys again. They would help her unpack every day, telling her over and over again that she didn't have to move again. The new mom and dad knew it would take a lot of time for her to learn to trust them.

Again, depending on the child's age and attention span, this story may be shortened by omitting some details that could then be included in subsequent trauma narratives.

Trauma narrative example: For older adopted children

This narrative is told from the perspective of the child, which allows the parent to express the character's thoughts and feelings. Telling the story in the third person decreases the possibility that the child will argue with the parent (You weren't there! How do you know what I was thinking or feeling?). The story could also be told from the social worker's or even birth mother's perspective. Remember, there is no right or wrong way. It may take some trial and error to figure out what works best with each child.

As far back as Alex could remember he had been hungry. He and his mom had lived in a hundred different places, sometimes even in the car. Being hungry was the worst. When they had a place, he'd go to school for a while and get the free breakfast and lunch. When they were moving around, he didn't get to go to school. When he attended school, he didn't wear clean clothes and usually didn't have his homework done. He put up with the teasing from the other kids just to get the food. They all thought he was stupid, but he wasn't. He knew plenty.

When they had a place, his mom sometimes had boyfriends over. He knew he had to behave. Some of them were kind of nice and would play video games with him. Some would yell or smack him if he even looked at them wrong. He hated that, but he hated how they treated his mom more. At least there was more food around when there was a boyfriend staying with them.

When the fighting got real bad, the neighbors pounded on the walls and sometimes the cops showed up. Part of him wanted to tell the cops what was happening to his mom, but he knew that if he told he and his mom would be in big trouble. He kept his mouth shut. Sometimes they got off with a warning but sometimes he ended up in a shelter until his mom kicked out the guy and cleaned the place up. Sometimes when he missed a lot of school a social worker would show up with the police. Then he got in big trouble with everyone. He didn't want to tell them that he didn't have clean clothes to wear, or that his books had disappeared in the mess again. He learned to lie. He was pretty good at it too. Sometimes his mom would do the laundry and wake him up on time for a couple of days, but it didn't last long. His mom ended up in treatment promising to never drink again and he'd get sent to another foster home for awhile.

He knew how to take care of himself. He had a system. He knew exactly what time the corner store employees took a break so he could steal something to eat. He knew which restaurants threw out the best food. The old man at the Chinese buffet sometimes set out a bag for him next to the dumpster. On garbage days, when the dumpsters were empty and if the line wasn't too long at the shelter, he would eat there. The old people were usually nice and made sure he got in. If there were a lot of men in line he walked past. If they were in a bad mood, he'd just get pushed around and end up with nothing anyway. By the time he was eight, he was smoking and drinking a little. It helped when he was hungry.

When he was nine, he and his mom were staying in a hotel. She was in the room with a boyfriend so he was wandering the halls. The TV was loud but he heard them fighting anyway. He stayed close because he wanted to protect his mom. When the police came, they caught him with a beer and cigarettes. This time he couldn't lie his way out of trouble. His mom blamed him, saying he must have snuck them out of the room. The police took him to a shelter. He hated foster homes more than he hated life with his mom. They always made him take a shower and put on weird clothes. This place was no different. The lady seemed nice though. She didn't hit him with a bunch of rules right off the bat and the food wasn't bad. There was lots of it and he ate until he was full.

The next day she took him to school. It was a new school and they didn't know him. Maybe that could work to his advantage. He knew better than to pull anything right away though. If he got in trouble while he was living in a shelter they might just stick him in some boys' home.

In a few days a social worker showed up to take him to a foster home. He knew the drill and only asked one question—when would he see his mom? The social worker said his mom was in treatment again and he'd see her when she was done with the program. He knew most programs took a month, unless his mom skipped out again and then it would be a long time before he saw her.

He stayed in the new foster home for a long time. It was OK. He had his own room. They didn't have a lot of rules and he could pretty much do what he wanted as long as he did a few chores when they asked. He helped himself to what he needed and if they noticed they seemed to believe him when he lied. He thought they were kind of stupid. Maybe they were new at this foster care business. They bought him stuff, took him out to eat and to movies, and on vacation with them—like he was supposed to believe that he was part of the family or something.

The social worker visited every month. He smiled and nodded; he said everything was great every time. Just like he figured, she said his mom had left the treatment center without finishing the program. The months passed though and he started to get worried that his mom had really blown it this time and he'd end up in this family forever.

Some stories are more effective when the ending is a cliffhanger, leaving the child wondering what happens next. Some kids who typically resist listening to yet another story eagerly await the next installment.

Trauma narrative example: For an internationally adopted child

Once upon a time in a country far away lived a family. There was a mom and a dad and they had one little girl. Life in this country was very hard. There weren't very many jobs and the family didn't earn much money. They never had enough to eat. Even when they could find work, sometimes they didn't get paid for weeks. They managed but it was hard. It got so hard that the dad left. He said he was going to a big city to find work there and he would write and visit when he could. He packed some clothes and then he was gone.

The mom cried a lot after that. At first, letters with money came but they soon stopped. They were very hungry. After some time, the mom found out she was going to have another baby. She was very worried because she knew she wouldn't be able to take care of this baby. When the baby was born she was happy that her little baby boy seemed healthy. But she was sad too. She wanted the baby to have a good life. A life where he could have enough to eat, toys to play with, and a chance to go to school. She made a very hard decision that day—she left the baby at the hospital because she knew that the doctors and nurses would take him to the children's home. The children's home would have food for the baby, warm clothes, and a crib. The people at the home would try to find a new home for the little boy. It would be a home where there was a mom and dad who would love him and take care of him.

Of course the little boy had no idea what was going on. All he knew was that his mother wasn't there anymore. At first he cried and cried for her. After a while, he stopped crying. But he was still very sad. At the children's home there were lots of babies and children. He got fed and changed, but spent most of the day lying in his crib. It didn't matter if he cried; no one came until it was his turn to get fed and changed. Sometimes he would rock himself to sleep. When he got a little older the nurses would put him on the floor with the other children. Sometimes he held a toy until someone else took it from him. When it was time to eat the nurses scolded him if he didn't eat fast enough. Sometimes they would even give his food to another kid. He learned to eat as fast as he could shovel it in—then he sometimes got seconds. Every morning, after every meal and before bed, the mamas made him sit on a pot. It didn't matter if he had to go or not. He was smart; he learned to go and he learned to never ever have an accident.

What the little boy hated most was naptime and bedtime. After lunch, no matter how old you were, you had to lie down and rest. He couldn't tell the time, but it felt like forever until they said he could get up. If you talked or fooled around, you got spanked or pinched. When the sun went down, everyone had to go to bed. Sometimes he was tired and fell asleep right away. But sometimes the noises kept him awake. He could hear the babies crying, kids talking and moving, and the nurses in the kitchen laughing, talking, and probably eating! Sometimes a kid would get up because they had to use the pot or they were sick or scared. They just got swatted and sent back to bed crying, unless they were a favorite. The little boy wasn't a favorite but he wanted to be. The nurses held their favorites, rocked them, and made sure they had toys to play with. They even got extra food and special treats. They got to stay up late in the kitchen. He was sure they were eating. Some of the favorites got to go home with the nurses on their day off or on the holidays. He didn't know how to be a favorite. He listened and obeyed. He always tried to help but it seemed like they didn't even see him—he was invisible.

Sometimes the Doctor would come to see the children. No one liked him. Some kids started crying as soon as he walked in the door. The little boy didn't like him either. Sometimes he would take a sick child in his car and they never came back. He didn't know what happened to them but he figured it was bad. Sometimes they had visitors. The visitors would bring presents and candy. The nurses would line them up to sing the visitors a song. You had to sing and smile or you would get punished later. The little boy figured out quick that if you smiled at the visitors and hugged them or crawled on their lap sometimes you got extra candy. He tried to hug as many as he could and stuffed the candy in his socks to hide it in his bed later. No matter how hard he looked he could never find any of the presents the next day.

Sometimes the nurses dressed up one of the kids in special clothes and talked about how they were going to meet their new mama and papa today. Later, the Director came to get that child and took them to the special playroom. He could hear them in there talking sometimes. He couldn't understand what the visitors were saying though—it sounded funny. Then the kid would come back and they would take the special clothes off right away. A few weeks later those same people would come back and the Director would come for that child again. The second time the nurses always brought the clothes back to the closet right away. Then all the children had to line up and sing a song to them. A man and woman speaking funny words would be holding the child with big smiles. The nurses told them all to wave goodbye as they got into a car and drove away. Part of him wanted to wear the special clothes and get to play in that locked room, but part of him was scared. He didn't understand what it meant to have a new mama and papa, and he wasn't sure he wanted to go with stranger in a car. The other kids never came back. He didn't know where they went.

But the day came when the nurses told him that he was going to meet his new mama and papa soon. They taught him how to say some funny words (they called it English) and then they dressed him in the special clothes and brought him to the locked playroom. He looked and looked at all the toys in the room. He had never seen so many toys. They made him smile and wave and talk to a movie camera. Then they made him hop, jump, clap, and sing. He couldn't take his eyes off the toys so he got yelled at. He didn't care. When they were done he had to take the special clothes off and put his play clothes back on. He kind of hoped he would be a favorite now, but at bedtime he was sent to bed with all the other boys. After that nothing changed. The days were the same for a long, long time. Once in a while, the Director would walk through and say something about his new mama and papa coming soon.

That day came just like every other day. He woke before daylight, lying quietly until a nurse came in to tell them it was time to get up. He sat on the pot, put on his clothes, made his bed, and then lined up to wait to go to breakfast. After breakfast, they went into the exercise room as usual. There weren't many toys. Most kids ran around and got into fights. He usually stayed away from everyone. In the middle of music class a nurse came to get him. At first he thought he was in trouble; maybe they found the food in his bed. But instead the nurse dressed him in special clothes from the special closet. He tried to ask her what was happening but she wouldn't answer him.

He waited on his bed without moving for what felt like forever before the Director came to get him. She took his hand and they walked quickly down the hall. She told him that his new mama and papa were here to meet him and he must be a good and polite little boy. And then they were in the special playroom with all the toys. There was a tall lady with dark hair and a tall man standing next to each other. They were both smiling and said hello. Then they said a lot of words he didn't understand. They gave him some candy, cookies, a toy truck, and a ball. They sat on the floor near him. He remembered what to do with visitors—he smiled and gave them both hugs. He sat on their laps and held the truck. The Director told him to call them "Mama" and "Papa." They played for a long time. They seemed nice.

The little boy was very worried though. He knew that it was almost lunchtime and he didn't want to miss lunch. He whispered to the Director that it was time to eat, but he just got a mad look and he didn't ask again. After a while, the man and lady gave him a big hug, lots of kisses, and left. They were crying when they left. He wondered if he had done something wrong. A nurse came to get him. He had to change clothes and lay down for rest time. He had missed lunch!

Some of the other kids asked him where he had gone. Some of them seemed jealous that he had a new mama and papa, but some of them whispered that now he was going to be taken away to another country and he would never get to come back. That made him worry. As the days passed and nothing changed, he started to forget about the new mama and papa. He was more worried about moving to the big boys' room. He knew some of the bigger boys. Some of them were mean and took your food, even your clothes if they wanted them. It also meant he would have to go to school. Every morning the big boys and girls put on a uniform and walked to a school somewhere outside. He didn't know where the school was. The little boy worried that he would get lost. He tried not to think about it.

But one day after breakfast, a nurse took him by the hand and walked him down the hall, past the special playroom, past the Director's office, and down the stairs to the older kids' floor. Most of the kids were at school. The nurses made him sweep, mop, and clean until the other kids came home. As soon as the older boys saw him they made a beeline for him. They called him names and pushed him around until a nurse came into the room. At suppertime, he tried to eat fast but they grabbed his food anyway. That night as he was going to bed some of them tripped him and punched his arm. After the lights were out they took his blanket. They said if he told they would *really* beat him up. He lay awake all night listening to the new noises and trying not to cry.

The next morning he had to put on a uniform and walk with the other boys and girls to school. He tried to stay out of reach and avoid the kicking and hitting. The teachers at school wrote down his name and gave him some paper and a pencil. They didn't seem that different than the nurses so he tried to listen and obey. He learned that you had to move quickly when they told you to do something or they'd smack you too. The little boy discovered that he was pretty good at math and he learned his letters quickly. The food was good, too, and he got to eat all of it because the teachers watched and wouldn't let anyone get up out of their seat.

The little boy got used to his new routine pretty fast. He lay in bed until it was time to get up. He used the bathroom and got dressed in the cold as fast as he could. He made his bed. The older children were allowed to go out into the dining room to wait for breakfast. He ate fast, hunched over his food so no one could snatch it away. After breakfast he dressed in his outdoor clothes and lined up to walk to school. Once home all the children sat at the dining room tables doing their schoolwork. Sometimes they had a music class or time to play. There weren't many visitors on the older kids' floor.

By this time, the little boy had almost forgotten about the man and lady that were his new mama and papa. But one day as he lined up for school a nurse told him to sit back down and wait. He figured he had really done something wrong now but he didn't know what. He hoped he didn't get locked in the punishment closet like he had seen happen to other kids.

After a long wait, the Director came downstairs and told him his mama and papa were here to take him to his new home in America. He didn't know what America was. A nurse handed him clothes to put on— new clothes he had never seen before. They weren't from the closet. He had to give his uniform to the nurse and then the Director took him to the special room. A man and a lady were waiting there. He thought maybe they were the same ones but he couldn't be sure. The lady's hair was short now and the man did not look as tall, but they acted like they knew him. They picked him up, hugged him, and took lots of pictures. Then they put new outdoor clothes on him. The Director told him that he was going to get to go in a car, a train, and an airplane to his new home. He knew he was supposed to be happy but he was scared. He didn't understand anything the new mama and papa were saying. He tried very hard not to cry.

The next days were just a blur. He liked the car and he liked all the food he got (he ate until he was sick). He didn't like the baths. He screamed and screamed until they took him out of the water. There was a lot to explore, new things to try. He ran up and down the halls, pushed buttons on the wall that lit up, flipped switches turning the lights on and off, and flushed the toilet over and over. The new mama and papa didn't yell and didn't hit, but he could tell they were not happy.

The little boy did not like the plane. He wanted to get up and run but this time the parents said "No!" He took the seat belt off but they put it right back on unless he had to go to the toilet—he had to go to the toilet a lot.

Finally the plane stopped and they got off. There were lots and lots of people waiting there for them with balloons and signs and toys. Everybody wanted to hug him and hold him. He did what he did in the children's home and hugged everybody, searching their pockets and bags for treats. They got into another car and drove for a long time. He finally fell asleep. When he woke up, he was in a strange bed in a room all by himself. He'd never been alone before, so he screamed. Mama and papa came right away. After that he screamed every time they put him in that bed alone.

Little by little he started to understand what the mama and papa were saying to him. He figured out the routine—he liked knowing what was next. He learned how to ask for food and to ask what's next. Otherwise he kept to himself most of the time. Sometimes he would ask for food when he wasn't hungry and hide it in his room for later. Sometimes he would find pretty things around the house and hide those too because he wanted them. He had lots of things to play with and could even go outside. The mama and papa were nicer than the nurses at the children's home. Sometimes they got mad at him and made him sit, but he didn't mind that—unless they left him alone. He didn't like being alone and when he was left alone he would scream until they came back. Most of the time America was OK. But the little boy didn't know how to be part of a family yet. He still had a lot to learn.

> Depending on the child's attention span, this story could be broken up into short stories or chapters. Subsequent stories could describe further the difficulty the character faced adjusting to family life. The character might have to learn to share, to ask instead of help himself, to wake his parents up if he had a bad dream or was sick, and that it was OK to cry if he got hurt. Most of all, he would have to learn to trust that his parents were going to take care of him.

Developmental narrative example: How children learn secure base behaviors

> Developmental narratives are designed to teach behavior typical of children at each age and stage of development. It is assumed that the child is not naughty or bad, but instead has not yet mastered the skill being described.

Remember when we told you what it would have been like if you had been born in this family? Well, this is a story about all the things you would have learned if you had been in our family from the beginning. Did you know that when babies are born they know the sound of their parents' voices? When they hear their parents they will turn to look even though they can't see very well. When we were feeding you, you would stare up into our eyes like you were memorizing what our faces looked like. When you got a little older, if you were sitting in an infant seat, you would watch me as I was cooking or cleaning. And if I looked at you or talked to you—you would smile and get so excited you would wave your little hands and feet. If you fussed because you were hungry, all I would have to do is talk to you and tell you that I was coming, that the bottle was almost ready, and you would quiet right down. You would have been learning to trust me.

When you got a little older and started to crawl you would crawl a little and then look back over your shoulder to make sure I was watching. Sometimes you might pick up a toy and bring it back to show me. About that time, you would be a mama's girl. You wouldn't let anyone else hold you—even grandma and grandpa. You'd wriggle and fuss until they passed you back to me and, as soon as you got in my arms, you'd settle down and be a smiley little girl again. If a stranger talked to you at church or the grocery store you would bury your face in my shoulder—you wouldn't even look at them. If they tried to hand you a cookie or some candy you wouldn't take it. I would have to take it and then hand it to you.

When you were a toddler you would hide behind my legs and peek out at strangers. You wouldn't talk to them unless I told you it was OK to say "Hi." You liked playing with the other kids at daycare or in the church nursery, but you didn't like it much when I left. You'd cry for a little while and then you would play. But when I returned, you would yell "Mommy!" and run to jump into my arms. At home, you could play by yourself for a little while but then you would come looking for me to show me something or because you needed something—just checking in.

Even when you were old enough for school you would check in once in a while. If you were outside you would come in and get a drink or snack. Then out the door you would go again. And I would put little notes in your lunch box to let you know I was thinking of you during the day. If you had been born in this family you would have always known that I'd be there.

Developmental narrative example: How children learn to regulate anger and frustration

Developmental narratives teach children appropriate behavior for their age. The stories are used to encourage a child. When a child is having a hard time acting his age, empathetic parents commiserate with the child. They acknowledge that on some days it is very hard to be four, seven, or twelve. They offer help. Developmental narratives are less effective when used to point out that the child is acting like a two-year-old. Most of the time, children are very aware that they are different from their peers.

They want to fit in. By using the third person perspective, parents avoid triggering a sensitive child's shame and defensiveness.

When babies are little, like baby Andrew, they can't talk—you remember baby Andrew? When they need something they fuss, and if no one answers right away, what do they do? That's right, they cry. Crying isn't naughty; it's just how babies speak. When a baby gets frustrated or mad they cry to let their mom and dad know that something isn't right. It's up to the mom and dad to figure out what the baby is saying, what they need. When babies get a little older they can motor around, crawling or walking but they still can't talk very well. Sometimes they can say "mama" or "dada" or "baba." Sometimes they grunt "uh, uh" and point at what they want. If someone doesn't understand what they need, they get mad. They might even plop down on their bottom and cry until someone comes to help them.

Two-year-olds have a lot more words. They can say: "Me do it," "Mine!" "No!" "More," "Please," and "Thank you." But when a two-year-old gets mad because their mom or dad says "No," what do they do? Yep, you're right—they have a big tantrum. They fall on the floor screaming, crying, and kicking their legs. They might even hit or bite. They just don't have enough words and they don't know how to calm themselves down. Three- and four-year-olds have lots of words. They know how to ask for what they need. They can say "I'm mad" or "I don't like you!" Sometimes they whine or plead. But when the final answer is "No" they still might have a meltdown and cry. They might even hit or kick someone, or throw something. They just can't stop the mad from coming out.

Five- and six-year-olds are pretty good at arguing and trying to get their way. Sometimes when they are really mad, though, they might still cry. Seven- and eight-year-olds like things to be fair and they want everyone to follow the rules. They are learning to be patient. When Mom and Dad have to say "No" they might make a face or grumble under their breath, even stomp up the stairs and slam the door. But after they calm down they come back downstairs, do whatever it was that their mom or dad asked, and then they play again. Nine-, ten-, and eleven-year-olds still get mad. After all, everyone gets mad now and then. Sometimes they don't like what their mom or dad say. They might argue and yell a little, and turn the music up in their bedroom to annoy their parents. But after a while they calm down too. If you had grown up with us from the beginning, you would have learned how to calm yourself down as you got older. Oh, you still might not like the rules, the chores, or hearing us say "No", but you would trust deep inside your heart that we loved you, wanted to keep you safe, and weren't just making up rules to be mean.

Successful child narrative example

Successful child narratives are used to teach new, more adaptive ways of behaving. The third person perspective is commonly used to avoid embarrassing the child. When a child feels ashamed, he may get angry and no learning takes place. Instead of just talking about the behavior and telling the child what to do, stories allow the child to listen, laugh, and, it is hoped, apply the lesson to him- or herself.

Once upon a time there lived a creature, an alien really, named Fizzik. He lived on a pink planet that you can only see on very clear nights in July. As aliens go, he wasn't so scary to look at. Basically, he and all the others of his kind looked like gigantic blue soap bubbles with one little eye sticking out on the top of the bubble. No hands and no feet—they didn't need them on the low gravity pink planet. They just floated along to wherever they wanted to go. They didn't have mouths either because they didn't talk, at least not out loud.

On this planet everyone could hear everyone else's thoughts. Now that was pretty convenient in some ways, but pretty annoying too. Sometimes you would think something that you really didn't want anyone to know and the whole town would know in an instant. Some of the aliens had the ability to control their thoughts so no one else knew what they were thinking, but not Fizzik. He had no self-control. His thoughts just popped out no matter how hard he tried not to think them. He had tried everything.

He tried squeezing his eye shut, figuring that if he couldn't see anyone or anything, he couldn't think anything that would get him into trouble. But then he kept running into things. On the pink planet when your bubble ran into something, it popped, covering everything around it in a very stinky blue slime. It was bad enough when he ran into a building or a tree, but it was horrible when he ran into someone else and they both got slimed.

Now the pink planet aliens didn't have mouths or ears but they did have NOSES! The slime smelled worse than a putrefied purple pufferbergen (that would be a dead fish on earth). And, of course, without self-control he thought unkind thoughts and that made the other alien even angrier.

When a bubble popped the pink planet creatures had to go to a special clinic where they could blow air into the slime and inflate the bubble again. It was a very time-consuming, uncomfortable process. Imagine sitting all day with a strong wind blowing in your face—that's what it felt like. And if they had to spend the day at the bubble clinic kids missed school, grownups missed work, and everyone missed meals. Obviously going around with his eye shut did not make Fizzik a popular alien. It was worse than the trouble he got into when he couldn't control his unkind thoughts from popping out!

The next idea Fizzik tried was doomed to fail from the start. He thought if he stayed away from everyone, no unkind thoughts would pop out and he wouldn't get into trouble. But he got into trouble when he missed school. And he got into trouble when he didn't come down for dinner when his mother called. And he got into trouble when he didn't answer the door. His best friend in the whole world came over to play. He was out of ideas.

[Aside] "Do you have any ideas that Fizzik could try?" If the child comes up with an idea, incorporate it into the story, asking additional questions about how the idea worked out. But resume the story if she does not offer an idea.

Fizzik envied his friends who could control their thoughts and stay out of trouble. He thought it was hopeless. He watched them float through the day with nothing but kind thoughts popping out of their head and wondered why he couldn't do that. Wait…why couldn't he do that? Of course! That was the answer. He'd just fill his head with happy and kind thoughts, and not leave room for any of those angry, mean, unkind words. Just thinking of this idea made his bubble swell with happy feelings and happy thoughts. Why, it was so easy—he should have thought of this a long time ago!

But you know what Fizzik found out? It wasn't so easy after all. He tried. He tried really, really hard to think happy thoughts, but how do you think happy thoughts when your mom asks you to take out the garbage and the garbage is full of smelly pufferbergens? Or when your teacher gives back your math test and there is a big red D on it for everyone to see? It was impossible! Sometimes he couldn't help but think something angry and unkind.

But Fizzik kept on trying. If he thought an unkind thought, he quickly thought, "Sorry, I didn't mean that." If he thought an angry thought, he quickly added, "Sorry, I need a minute to calm down." And he quickly filled his head with kind happy thoughts like: "That's OK, I'll do better next time." Or he'd think, "I'll ask Mom for help studying." The funny thing was that when he thought happy thoughts, even when he felt upset, he soon started to feel happy. This self-control stuff was hard, but Fizzik started to get better at it. He still got in trouble sometimes, but not as much. He could float through some days without getting in trouble even once!

> Self-control is a common issue. Kids are sometimes challenged to control what comes out of their mouth, and what their hands and feet do. Depending on the emphasis, this story can easily be modified to fit an individual child's problem with impulsivity, respect, or negative thinking. Expanding on the stinky slime concept would enable this story be used to address personal hygiene issues. It could also be modified and used to address interpersonal boundaries.

Successful child narrative: Telling the truth

Once upon a time there was a little boy named Freddie. He lived with his mom and dad and two very annoying twin sisters. His mom and dad told him that it would be so fun to have a baby brother or sister. What a joke! They couldn't do anything except eat and sleep. His mom and dad were always busy taking care of them. Wherever they went, everyone went gaga over them. They got mountains of presents. Nobody even noticed him anymore; he might as well be invisible. He figured that when they got older, everybody would get used to them and life would go back to normal. As the months passed, however, not much changed. The twins still took all of his parents' time. Even when they went to his baseball games, all the parents would crowd around his sisters to see the cute little girls. He didn't even think his parents saw him hit that double.

The first time he did it—lied—it just kind of popped out. He didn't mean to do it. He was mad. So when his parents asked who had made the mess in the toy room he told them his sisters did it. And it worked—they believed him and made his sisters put all the toys away. It was great; maybe he felt a little guilty, but he thought that they deserved it anyway. He was always picking up after them. He wouldn't do it again, so it was not a big deal, right? Well, before he knew it, he was telling lies every day: tattling, exaggerating, and blaming. He got pretty good at it too. He'd look the other person right in the eye, tell them some wild story and they believed him! For the first time in a long time his parents were actually paying attention to him. He knew it was wrong, but there was no way he was going to stop now.

[*Aside*] Parent: Well what do you think happened next?

Child: He got caught?

Parent: You bet he did.

If it hadn't been for school conferences he might never have been caught lying this time. He knew he was in big trouble as soon as his parents walked in the door. He could see it in their eyes. He squirmed all through supper, even offered to clear the table and took the garbage out without being asked. And when they didn't say anything after dinner he thought that maybe he'd gotten away with it after all. But after his sisters went to bed, he heard his dad call him downstairs and he knew he was busted. At first he tried to blame the teacher, that maybe she had just misunderstood or got him mixed up with another kid. Even though he looked them right in the eye, he didn't think they were buying it this time. The hardest part was that they weren't yelling at him, they just looked sad and disappointed. He couldn't even give them a good reason. He just wanted someone to pay attention to him for a change. "You don't know what it's like." he mumbled. "It's always the twins this and the twins that. I just wanted to feel special; I wanted someone to pay attention to me for a change."

To his surprise, his mom and dad apologized and said he was right, they needed to make sure they spent time with him no matter how busy they were. "Why didn't you tell us?" "Why didn't you just ask to do something with us?" He didn't have an answer to that one.

He got grounded. Worst of all, every time he opened his mouth he could tell that his parents didn't believe him anymore. They didn't trust him. Even when he told the truth and said he'd swear on a stack of bibles, they didn't believe him. How could he ever show them he had learned his lesson? The problem was he couldn't. Even if he promised to never lie again, it was just going to take time. And if he slipped up and fibbed, even a little one, he would have to start all over again. He wished harder than he had ever wished for anything before—even harder than he had wished for his new skateboard last Christmas—that he hadn't told that first lie.

Trauma/successful child narrative: How to move forward

"Rosebud," by Gaye Guyton

Once upon a time there lived a man and wife who wanted a baby. The day came when a darling baby girl was born to them. She had pink cheeks, a pink little rosebud of a mouth and that wonderful baby smell that all babies have. To them, she smelled as good as a rose too, and so they named her Rosebud. Rosebud was held and rocked and cuddled and soon she grew into a curious toddler. It was about this time her parents began giving her garbage to hold. "Here, Rosebud, take care of this," her dad would say, handing her an empty sauerkraut can. Or "Hold these," her mom would say, tossing her the potato peelings as she prepared dinner. Some days Rosebud had several things to hold at once. That was difficult because her hands were so small.

As Rosebud grew, her parents trained her to hold more of the household garbage. "You're a big girl now; you have to carry more," they'd say, "We're doing this for your own good." If Rosebud's hands grew too full, she soon learned to use other parts of her body to balance things. Her parents would tuck used Kleenexes under her arm, and old newspapers under her chin, and drape worn-out socks over her head. She didn't really like this at all, but wanted to show them how good she was.

If she said she was uncomfortable, her daddy would say, "Don't complain! Other kids have it much worse than you." And her mommy would add, "I know you can handle this. Just try, Rosebud."

Because Rosebud wanted to please her parents, she began thinking of ways she could carry more garbage. When her parents gave her a shopping bag one day, with only a small rip in the bottom, she cleverly repaired it with some chewed gum and found that it would hold quite a lot.

When she was five, Rosebud began kindergarten. Her mommy took her shopping to buy a brand-new backpack, new crayons, and a brand-new special first-day-of-school outfit. On the first day of school her proud mommy and daddy took her picture wearing her new outfit and her backpack filled with her new school supplies, and holding her bag of garbage. She was so excited to be starting school that she didn't even care about the banana peel around her neck.

At school, Rosebud noticed that it was hard to take care of her family's junk and learn at the same time. Sometimes she'd accidentally drop some garbage when she needed to hold her pencil or swing on the playground. She realized that she was going to have to manage the family trash better, so she asked her parents to buy her an enormous backpack. By packing all the rubbish in the backpack, she freed her hands for other things. She could participate in art class more easily and gym class became a breeze, since she didn't have to balance things on her head anymore. She could even play tag at recess.

It was about this time that Rosebud began to worry. Other people liked her but she kept them away because she didn't want them to notice her garbage. She couldn't quite figure out how the other kids handled their families' garbage and wondered if she was the only one carrying stuff to school each day. She worried that she was weird or dumb or something. She especially wondered if she might smell bad, so she didn't let the other kids get near her. If she saw some children heading her way, she'd scoot off to hide under the slide. She learned to do everything herself, never asking for help.

She'd pretend the garbage wasn't there, sometimes. "Garbage? What garbage?" she'd say. (The teachers sometimes dropped the subject because they saw she was sensitive about it, but the kids thought she was a little strange. "How can Rosebud not notice she has chicken bones riding on her shoulder and dead flowers tucked in her shirt?" they wondered.) She also tried to be perfect. She worked really hard at school and at home, trying to please everyone. Of course, that is impossible in real life, as well as fairy tales.

When her parents took her shopping for new clothes, they helped her choose things with lots of big pockets. "Dark colors look best on you, dear," her mother would say. "They don't show the dirt." Her parents began holding their noses when she walked by. "You don't smell like our sweet Rosebud anymore," they'd say, but *still* they'd give her garbage to hold. "Take care of this garbage," they'd say, and because she was a good girl, she would.

First, second, and third grade went by and as Rosebud grew, her parents relied on her to take care of more and more of their garbage. Already, her closet was jammed completely full of their stuff and she was beginning to think about sacrificing her dresser as well. By this time, Rosebud had a little brother and he too would sometimes give her garbage to hold. Before things got completely out of hand, Rosebud asked for bins and put them in her room. She began organizing the garbage by type: food scraps in one bin, paper in another, plastics in a different container. She felt proud about how she was able to handle everything her family gave her. Before the year went by, she had lined the walls of her room with bins. The bins kept most of the smells to a minimum, but she still didn't want to have any friends over. That idea made her feel a little uneasy. Of course, she didn't actually have any friends yet, but she dreamed that some day she might.

One day at lunch she had tried asking Marcy, a neighbor and one of the nicest girls in her class, about what she did with her garbage and whether she sorted it or not. The girl looked confused and said that her family thought recycling was important, then hurried off when one of her friends called her. From her reaction, Rosebud decided that though her parents had never mentioned it, this must be one of those topics that weren't polite to mention in public, and thought she'd better not bring it up again.

Though family garbage wasn't a popular topic, she'd watched closely and discovered that other families gave junk to their children too. She remembered the day she made that discovery because she'd gone with her family to see a movie when she was about seven. They were leaving the movie theater when she'd noticed some candy wrappers on the floor.

She was used to rubbish by now so she stooped to add them to her collection. At that moment, she heard a family behind her giving their old popcorn boxes, empty cups, and sticky nacho container to their son. He was smaller than she was and didn't seem to have developed a system yet, because he kept dropping things. Rosebud wanted to give him a few pointers but thought that might not be polite and hurried to catch up with her parents instead.

By this time, Rosebud had grown used to the smell in her room from the household trash. It was the smell of home. When she was away, she missed it. She began carrying a small sack of her favorite garbage to school with her. On the days she became anxious, she'd take a whiff of that comforting scent. It made her feel better. There was only one other place she knew of with those familiar smells of decay: that was the waste processing plant and recycling center her class had visited once on a field trip. Rosebud enjoyed that day very much and came home with some new ideas for how to make her storage system even better. Of course, she didn't dare open her closet. There was an avalanche of her family's oldest garbage inside waiting to tumble out. Still her family gave her more garbage.

One day, Rosebud became quite ill. She had to stay home from school for more than a week. When she was beginning to feel better, there came a knock on the door. "May I come in?" said the voice. Rosebud was so taken aback she didn't know what to do. No one had ever come into her room before, but she was tired of being alone, and so she opened the door. Marcy was standing there with an armload of books.

"Hi, I heard you were sick and thought you might like to work on the stuff you missed. I hate to get behind, don't you?"

"Umm, yeah, I guess. I've never really missed school before," said Rosebud.

"Is it OK if I come in?" said Marcy. "That way I can explain everything to you."

"Well, I don't know. I've never had anyone in my room before," said Rosebud.

"Never?! Weird. I have friends over all the time," exclaimed Marcy.

"Well, I haven't." Rosebud didn't want to be rude, so she decided that like it or not, she'd better invite Marcy in. "Sure. Come on in."

Marcy set the schoolwork down on the bed and looked around. She'd never seen a room like this. There were bins from floor to ceiling around every wall.

"What's in the bins?" she asked.

"It's all the garbage my family has given me," Rosebud answered.

"Wow. Why are you saving all this trash?" said Marcy.

"Because my parents told me I have to keep it for them. I take care of it. It's important."

"Why? Are they garbage collectors?" asked Marcy.

"No, of course not!" answered Rosebud. "I'd rather not talk about it, if you don't mind. Just tell me what I need to do and then you can go."

"Sorry," apologized Marcy. "I didn't mean to pry; it's just that I've never seen anything like this before. Doesn't the smell bother you?"

"No! Now can we get to work?" insisted Rosebud, who was growing more anxious by the moment. Who did this girl think she was anyway—barging in here and asking questions about a topic that was unmentionable? What did Marcy mean about never seeing anything like this before? Was her system of keeping the garbage tightly shut away in bins —the system she'd worked so hard on—really a bad system?

"Rosebud, listen to me. You can keep all this garbage in your room if you really want to, but you'd sure have a lot more space to do things if you got rid of all this junk. No wonder you've been sick; anyone would living with all this trash."

Rosebud stared at Marcy. "What do you mean?"

"No other kids I know have to take care of stuff like this. My parents *never* expect me to carry rubbish around. You may have a great system for keeping the garbage locked away, but it's *still* garbage."

In a very small voice, Rosebud asked, "What do you do when someone gives you garbage?"

"I throw it in a trash can, of course. That *is* what they are for. You know, Rosebud, your room could be really cool if you cleaned all this stuff out; you could even decorate it! Not to mention, it would sure smell a lot better. You don't have to live like this."

Marcy explained the homework and left, closing the door behind her. Rosebud flopped onto her bed to do some thinking. Then she got up and started pacing.

"Really? What if I did get rid of some of this old stuff? It might be nice to see the windows again or have a place to stretch out and read." She decided to ask her parents.

"Mom, Dad, please may I get rid of some of the garbage you gave to me?"

"Absolutely not!" her mom said. "That's special garbage. We gave it to you! How can you even think of discarding it?! Why, you've had some of those things since you were small!"

"But I need a place to play and read. My room is completely full, and I've never been able to have anyone over. Other kids at school have friends over to play." said Rosebud. "Besides, it smells. *I* smell. You've told me so often enough."

"We love you, Rosebud," her dad said. "We know what's best for you. You smell like yourself, and we don't want you to change. How would we know where you are if we couldn't smell you? Besides, if you changed, what would we do with our garbage?"

Rosebud ran downstairs crying. She didn't know what to do.

As the days went by she began having nightmares about being smothered. She dreamt of skyscrapers made of garbage towering above her, threatening to collapse, and she would wake up shaking uncontrollably. Rosebud had tried to do everything perfectly, even with all the garbage her parents had given to her, yet where was it getting her? She didn't have a single friend and handling all the garbage was getting to be a full-time job. What would happen when she went to college? What then? Could she take all her bins with her?—Just then the thought struck her: "College! That is still years away! How many more bins will I have by then? And where on earth am I going to put them all? There's scarcely room in here for me now! Where will I even sleep?!" And Rosebud began to cry. That made her feel much better, and when she'd calmed down, she knew what she had to do.

The next morning, she began hauling the bins out to the curb. It was hard work. Her muscles ached, and so did her ears from the shouting her parents did. At first that slowed her down and made her cry, but she was determined to be healthy and with two old cotton balls, pulled from the bin that held fabric items, things improved. With one in each ear, she didn't mind the shouting as much. In fact, it confirmed that she had made the right decision. Loving parents wouldn't shout at kids for throwing out stinky, disgusting, rotting things that were making them sick.

In some ways the garbage was harder to get rid of than she had thought. She'd been collecting junk for so long that she'd forgotten some of the places she'd put things in the early days. She found a bunch of rubbish under her dresser and more tucked into corners. The day after she thought she had finally finished the main part of her room, she found more tucked between her bed and the wall. Some days it was frustrating; she thought she'd never be done!

As Rosebud emptied the bins and moved them out, the space became roomier and she became more anxious. She dreaded what would happen on the day she finally had to tackle her closet. She vividly remembered when she'd forced those doors shut and knew that she would not be able to re-open them without an avalanche of garbage pouring down upon her. She didn't want to be buried alive, but if she asked for help, it would mean letting people know about her garbage, and that would be *so* embarrassing. What would they think? It took her several weeks of worrying to realize that while she didn't have a choice about asking for help, she could control who knew about her garbage. Who better than a professional waste management team? She remembered her field trip to the garbage processing plant and made a phone call. Within an hour, a big shiny truck pulled up to the curb and people with white suits jumped out, carrying exactly the equipment she needed. "You'll need to open the doors, Rosebud," the manager said. "We'll be able to help with the rest."

When they were through, Rosebud threw open the windows and let the fresh air and sunshine in. The smells of rotting fish, stinky chemicals, moldy lettuce and stale sauerkraut began to fade. She took a deep breath of that good clean air…and coughed. It was going to take time to get used to this. What she needed was a long, relaxing, warm bath after all her hard work. Rosebud pulled a bag out of her dresser and smiled. Inside was a beautiful bottle of perfumed bubble bath. She unscrewed the top and sniffed. It smelled just like roses.

That's not quite the end of the story. Rosebud felt lonely without the garbage at first. It felt strange to have such a clean room. She missed the bins and even the sorting. As long as she'd had all the trash to sort, she had felt she was doing something worthwhile, and it had kept her occupied. She didn't have to think about the things that bothered her, like her parents or her life. Once she'd made the decision to change though, other things changed too, for the better. She made lots of friends at school and they came over to visit. Marcy helped her decorate her room. Her body felt freer and lighter than it had since she was a toddler and so she treated herself to a wardrobe of new clothes—in beautiful colors and without a single big pocket. Now and then, out of habit, or when she was stressed, she would still pick up some trash, but she never held onto it too long. There was always a trash can nearby to remind her where garbage belonged. And once in a while, she would walk by the garbage processing plant to smell the old familiar smell of home, but she was healthy and happy in her new life and knew she would never live that way again.

Trauma/successful child narrative: Lying and stealing

> In this example, lying and taking what you needed was the way to survive in an abusive, neglectful situation. The problem behaviors were adaptive, enabling the child to endure deprivation and violence. Survival skills are hard to change. By combining trauma and successful child stories, parents convey that they understand the meaning of the behavior.

When Mike was little, before he came to live with his new mom and dad, he lived with his birth mother and her boyfriend. The boyfriend was mean. Mean to his mom and mean to him. He got yelled at and hit all the time, even if he didn't do anything wrong. He tried to be good. He did whatever he was asked to do right away. He stayed quiet when the TV was on. He stayed in his room when they were having a party. But no matter how hard he tried, he messed up. He'd forget to put the cap on the toothpaste, he'd leave his towel on the floor, or he'd eat something he wasn't supposed to. He learned pretty quickly that sometimes if he lied, and said he didn't do it, it worked. Oh, he still got hit sometimes, but he didn't get hit all the time. The more he lied, the easier it got and the better he got at it. Sometimes he even started to believe the lies himself.

But now he was in a foster home. No one hit him—ever. Sometimes he got a time out. Big deal he thought, this is nothing. Lying worked there too. Talk about stupid, that mom and dad believed everything. He could pretty much do as he pleased. He'd sneak snacks and just blame some other kid living there. If he made a mess or broke something, he'd lie and one of the other foster kids would have to clean it up. It was easy.

The trouble started when he got a little too confident. Usually he waited until everyone was in bed before he snuck into the kitchen. But one night, his foster mom was in the basement doing laundry and the other kids were watching a movie when he got hungry. He grabbed some chips and ran up to his room to scarf them down. Wouldn't you know his foster brother walked in on him! His foster brother ran to tell Mom. What a tattle tale. He had even offered to share if he would keep it secret. He tried telling his foster mom that he had found them in his room and that someone else must have stolen them, but he didn't think she bought it.

Of course, he didn't stop sneaking food, he just had to be more careful. Now, every time something went missing they came straight to him—like he was the only kid who ever stole! Worse, they were making him go to *therapy*! No way was he talking to anyone about anything. If he could just figure out how to make this problem go away…

> Not all stories must have a happy ending. Some parents leave the problem unsolved, letting the child think about what he might do. Cliffhangers like this also work with oppositional children who are likely to argue with every possible solution and ending you suggest.

Developmental/successful child narrative: Learning how to be a friend

> Combining developmental and successful child narratives is useful when parents know the child's difficulties are not deliberate and purposeful. The child wants friends but simply does not know how to make or keep a friend. Without a safe, supportive environment at this sensitive period of development, he missed out on key lessons about social relationships.

This is a story about me, when I was little, just two years old. My mom— your Grandma Nelson—told me that I used to go up to kids on the playground and push them away from the slide or swing. If I wanted to do something, I just did it. I didn't know how to talk well enough to ask for something, so I would just grab it. She had to teach me how to take turns and share, and ask for something if I wanted it. It was hard! I got into trouble all the time. When I was three or four she would invite someone over from the neighborhood for a play date, but she would play with us. I had to learn to share my snacks and toys, let my friends go first, and let them pick what they wanted to do. But I didn't always want to share my stuff.

When I was five and six I had lots of friends. We used to play in the backyard or down in the basement. It was easier to share and take turns. But she said that I still hated losing. If I lost a game, I got mad and threw a fit. Sometimes I even cheated or changed the rules. I figured that if they didn't like it, they could go play with someone else. My house, my rules, right? If they didn't want to do it my way, they weren't going to be my friend anymore. Sounds silly I guess, but I was just a little kid and was still learning.

When I got to be seven and eight, I had a best friend. We did everything together and told each other everything. Sure, we got into fights sometimes, but we always made up. I would say "I'm sorry," or she would pass me a note in class asking me to come to her house after school and we would be friends again. She is still my friend. We stayed friends all the way through high school and still get together once in a while. We don't always agree on everything, but we are still friends no matter what.

When I got to be your age, almost a teenager, my best friend and I used to whisper and giggle together all the time. Once we even got sent to the principal's office for laughing in class! Pretty soon the teachers figured out that they had to put us on opposite sides of the room.

The most important thing I had to learn that year was how to keep a secret. You know how girls like to talk and spread rumors? Well, my best friend told me something she didn't want anyone else to know—it was a big secret. But one day at recess, one of the really popular girls asked me to play. I guess I thought I was pretty cool that day. She and her friends were laughing and talking about the other girls, and then they all looked at me like I was supposed to say something. And my best friend's secret just popped out. I really didn't mean to tell; I just wanted them to like me and ask me to hang out with them again. Well, it didn't take long before the whole school knew her secret. She was so embarrassed and mad! She didn't talk to me for weeks. Eventually we made up, but I learned that lesson the hard way.

Kids love to hear about the trouble their parents got into when they were kids. This story could be altered to focus on one particular social skill such as sharing, taking turns, playing fair, or apologizing. It is important to stress that the character is not "bad" but just learning new skills as he grows up.

Successful child narrative: Learning to trust

"Mistfire," by Donna Oehrig

Newly knighted Sir Bruce hopped off his horse and, leading it by the reins, strode confidently through the darkening forest. It would soon be totally dark, but he was sure he would find the camping spot before then. If not, he would simply wait till the moon came out, and then continue on to the clearing.

The whinny from his horse was his only warning. He swiftly reached for his sword, intending to pull it out and swing around in one fluid motion, something he had practiced so much he could do it in his sleep. But as his fingertips brushed the hilt, the evening calm was rent with a dreadful howl and an odor most foul wrapped around him. Even though the roar and smell chilled him to his core with terror, he continued pivoting on his feet, eyes searching wildly through the thick undergrowth.

Bam! Something hit his shoulder and he slammed into a tree. As he righted himself, noting that his right ankle was in pain, he was hit again. His superb reflexes took over and he twisted away, just missing another painful collision with the tree. But as he landed at the edge of the path, his right foot folded underneath him and he tumbled into the ravine below.

Sir Bruce woke in a cottage. He was in so much pain, he dared not move. Quick footsteps hurried over to him.

"There, there, now. No need to move. Those broken bones need to knit." An old woman in peasant garb leaned over him, studying him with kindly brown eyes. "Garrells hauled you in here a couple of days ago, said he found you in a heap on the rocks by the river." She gave a quick nod and said, "Yep, it's good to see you're gonna live." Then she bustled out of sight to her cooking fire. Since his body felt as if a large boulder had rolled over him, Sir Bruce sincerely doubted he *would* live. But live he did, in that simple cottage with Garrells and Francine. During his convalescence, he and Garrells would sit by the fire and talk. Garrells eventually told Sir Bruce that he thought that he had been attacked by the dread dragon Mistfire. After the attack, he found no horse—only a few large bones scattered in the bushes. He found Sir Bruce's gear untouched.

"Mistfire…" Garrells said, shaking his head, "We haven't heard from that wily old beast in a very long time."

Garrells told Sir Bruce stories about Mistfire—about how he used to terrorize the villages around there, and how hunting parties would surround him and see him just disappear in smoke while their companions were slaughtered in a trice. "Some even say that Mistfire is magical and can take on the shape of anything or anyone," Garrells said one evening.

On the day Sir Bruce gathered up his gear to leave, Garrells pointed to the armor and said, "I'd keep that close by if I were you. You have been marked by the dragon, and you will never be safe from him till he is dead." Sir Bruce thanked his hosts one last time and set out on the footpath. At the bend in the trail, he turned back for one last look at the cottage with wispy smoke curling from its chimney. At least, that is what Sir Bruce expected to see. But what he saw turned his blood cold: there was no wispy smoke, no chimney, and no cottage at all. *The dragon is magical. It can take any shape…you are marked…* Sir Bruce ran from the forest. He sat down to catch his breath and think. Carefully, he took his armor out of its sack and put it on piece by piece. The armor was bulky and hot and cumbersome. But at least he was safe. Maybe the dragon Mistfire would not know it was him in that armor and would leave him alone.

Sir Bruce trudged along the dusty road with the rest of his belongings slung in a sack over his shoulder. If he had not seen that Garrells and Francine were the dragon, how would he ever know when he encountered the dragon again? How could he know who or what to trust, or what was real and unreal? The sun shone brighter and hotter and Sir Bruce chose the shady sides of the road as he plodded along. Every time a cart, horse or peasants on foot passed by, he would pause at the side of the road, his back against a tree and his hand on the hilt of his sword. Several times passersby offered a ride in one of those carts, and a lift would have been welcome indeed. But then Sir Bruce would remember that the driver of the cart could be Mistfire and the gesture of friendliness could be a trick to get him alone. So reluctantly he declined the offers and kept walking. He listened to the birds twitter in the tress, the insects foraging in the bushes for food. There was an especially loud bzz, bzz, bzz nearby. Sir Bruce, resting under a tree, opened one eye to locate the bee and discovered it was hovering right in front of him. He was quite sure he did not smell like a flower. Well—maybe a dead one, but surely not one with sweet nectar that would attract a bee. He closed his eyes and wondered why the bee was interested in him. It seemed ridiculous, unless...unless...Mistfire!

Sir Bruce lurched to his feet, grabbed his sword and swung at the bee. The insect dodged and darted over the bushes. Sir Bruce reached for his helmet. He hated to put it back on, but it seemed to be the only way to guarantee Mistfire could not identify him.

Eventually, Sir Bruce settled in a small town. He built a house of stone with no windows, only slits between the stones, and one door, cleverly crafted to open only from the inside. A spiral staircase led to a lookout from which he could observe the land and town through his spyglass. He was looking, always looking for signs of Mistfire. At first he tried to warn the townsfolk about the dragon but they mostly laughed at him. He was angry they could be so free and unafraid. Sometimes one or another of the townsfolk would come by and invite him to join them for a picnic at the lake. Oh, how he wanted to go. But there was Mistfire. What if, when he let his guard down, Mistfire came roaring out of the forest? What if one of those neighbors was really Mistfire in disguise? He couldn't take the chance.

Every so often a neighbor would get too close and Sir Bruce would jab a spear or sword through one of those slits to scare them away. If they got too close they got hurt. One day after jabbing at an old woman, he heard a leathery voice say, "Well, guess you showed her who's boss." Peering through the slits he saw an old man leaning on a cane, white hair fluttering from under a peasant's cap.

"Who are you?" Sir Bruce demanded, readying his sword. The old man tilted his head, eyeing the slit through which Sir Bruce spoke.

"Everyone calls me Gramps."

"I've never seen you before." The old man just shrugged his shoulder.

"You're not a man. You're Mistfire, I know it."

"Ah, Mistfire. You've seen him?" the man asked.

"I don't have to tell you about yourself!" Sir Bruce shouted back. The old man shrugged again and shuffled off to town. Sir Bruce clanked up the stairs to his lookout tower searching in every direction. Nothing. He wanted to take off his helmet to wipe the sweat but he dare not.

The old man came back every few days to talk. Sir Bruce always responded by jabbing his sword through the slit. Still the old man came and Sir Bruce became glad for Gramps' company. Months passed, a year, then two. Gramps and Sir Bruce often talked through the slits. Gradually, without Sir Bruce noticing, Gramps would stand closer and closer to his house. One day, Sir Bruce finally told him of Mistfire's attack so many years ago. The old man nodded, with a far-off look in his eyes.

Then he said, "But are you sure Mistfire is real?"

Sir Bruce shouted, "But he attacked me! I have the scars to prove it." And he jabbed a spear at the old man, drawing blood. "Go away and don't come back again *ever!*"

His armor too rusty to even climb the stairs to his lookout, he waited for an attack from the townsfolk. But no one came. Total silence engulfed him. And he was lonelier than he'd ever felt before. "Well, at least I'm safe here. At least I'm safe." Sir Bruce patrolled his house examining the protective stone walls. No one had ever breached those walls in all the years he had lived there. Not that anyone had taken the chance to, what with all the swords and spears. Not even a dragon could attack through those walls. A dragon. What if Mistfire truly did not exist? No, no, no, impossible. He had been attacked by an evil-smelling, invisible foe; he must be real. "But if it's not true," he said to the silence in his sparsely furnished home, "then I've wasted my life behind these walls. No, Mistfire has to be real, or my life, all of this, has no meaning!"

Sir Bruce walked his patrol slower and slower as his armor was so rusty and creaky that it took a great deal of effort just to take a step. And Sir Bruce did not feel all that well. He went to lie down. It was so hot inside the armor, but he dared not take it off. He awoke to hear Gramps calling his name.

"What do you want, old man?"

"You, Sir Bruce. I want to see you. Open the door."

"So you can kill me?"

"No, so I can take care of you. You are a brave knight and I fear that you are rotting inside that armor. It is no longer protecting you, but killing you."

Sir Bruce reached his door and with great effort pulled the latch up. The door swung out against his weight and Sir Bruce fell out of his house onto his face. Sir Bruce lay helplessly as villagers swarmed his yard, his house, his body as they snipped and oiled and tugged. It was an invasion of the scariest and sweetest kind. Someone bathed him and dressed him in clothes—real, soft, sweet-smelling clothes. Gramps directed most of the action, finally ordering them to carry him back into his house. A woman leaned over Sir Bruce and said, "Dragons aren't real. You know that, right?"

Alarm ran through Sir Bruce. She was going to go all aggressive on him, he knew it. He grabbed at his side for his sword but it wasn't there, and he missed it terribly. *You are a brave knight* echoed in his brain. Sir Bruce took a steadying breath and braced himself. If this woman was Mistfire, so be it. He'd had enough of hiding.

"I can live with it even if they are," he replied daringly, staring straight into her eyes.

Summary

Many parents might be thinking, "I can't make up a story like this." We would argue that anyone can. We have found that the quality of the story is less important than the connections formed during the telling—emotional and mental connections between the parent and child.

We would like to acknowledge the contributions of many parents we have worked with over the years. These stories are their stories. Our special thanks to Gaye Guyton, author of "Rosebud," and Donna Oehrig, author of "Mistfire."

Conclusion

Once there were two women who never knew each other.
One you do not remember, the other you call mother.

Life is about connections: connections between people, between people and their community, between communities and the world. We believe that humans are designed to be in relationship with others. We also believe that early life interactions are critical to development, because they form the foundation for an internal model of the self and of relationships with other people. Whether positive or negative, that model guides and directs behavior. The importance of a healthy attachment or connection between an infant and caregiver cannot be overstated. It is the basis for the internal model and for the child's future relationships and behavior in society.

Heredity, environment, and experience interact to create a unique individual. Development is a lifelong process (Sroufe *et al.* 2009). Each and every experience we have changes the brain. As a baby struggles to cope with life circumstances the successive adaptations he or she makes alter the developmental pathway. For a developing infant, toxic stress changes the structure and the function of the brain. The damaging effects of stress may persist despite dramatic interventions such as removing the child from the harmful situation and placing him in a nurturing adoptive home. Although the past can never be erased, the story of who we are can be reassessed and rewritten. Discovering their internal working model is the key to helping children heal from traumatic life events. Attunement, regulation, and therapeutic narratives challenge maladaptive working models and may shift the child back to a more normal pathway for growth and development. Regulating children requires parents to assess the meaning of behavior and consider sensory, nutrition, neuro-chemical, and developmental issues. Attunement is possible when parents and children spend time together. It is a process. Kids need both quantity and quality time.

The words of a story, when combined with appropriate non verbal messages (e.g., gestures, understanding the other, etc.), have a powerful impact on both the conscious and subconscious level, bypassing defenses normally triggered by talking about "the problem." Emerging research suggests that narrative is essential to brain development and integration. Narratives organize and shape our experiences—change the story, change the mind.

When first relationships do not provide the kind of emotional and physical care that is required for healthy growth and development, the individual may face multiple challenges throughout her life. Fortunately, the importance of early life experience is gaining increased acceptance, and strategies are being developed to ameliorate the effects of less-than-optimal early life interactions. Still, there are far too many children who suffer maltreatment and inadequate parental care when young. This sad fact is evidenced by the increasing case loads of social workers in social service departments around the world. Change must occur in families and in our society as a whole to prevent the disaster of wounded children. We need to fully support the parents and families who welcome these children into their homes. This support needs to be in terms of adequate financial, educational, and other resources—regardless of the legal status of the relationship. The loving home of a family offers the best hope for correcting the damage from inadequate early life attachment relationships. The bond between parent and child must be recognized and nurtured by our society.

A final word

We hope this book has been useful for parents who are searching for a way to connect or reconnect with a troubled child. We want to emphasize once again that we believe parents are in the best position to reach and to help their children. But occasionally parents need additional help from professionals. The tremendous stress of rearing a child with a history of trauma and disruptions in attachment relationships may have temporarily frustrated their capacity for attunement. Parents should seek professionals who listen and honor the knowledge they have about their child. The role of the parents must be supported, even elevated, in order to reactivate their attunement capacity. Professionals who take on the role of "guru" may undercut the parents and render them powerless to help their child resolve attachment issues.

It is not lack of effort or knowledge that leads parents to us, but rather a realization that techniques to merely manage behavior are not enough. Narratives work to bond, heal, and teach. The individualized stories address underlying mistaken beliefs and the negative internal working model that drive challenging behaviors. Daily story times build bonds between parents and children. Sensitive narratives about early life experiences help children resolve trauma and losses. Captivating characters model new behaviors that the child can choose to use when ready.

We believe that parents should not only be included in the therapy process but be considered the primary healing agent. Parents have an innate ability to understand and respond to their child's cues. Looking beyond the behavior to discover the child's internal working model may not come naturally at first. However, focusing on the "why" of behavior effectively changes day-to-day parenting and leads to construction of narratives that can shift the internal working model. Intimate knowledge of the child's thoughts and feelings permits parents to construct a one-of-a-kind narrative. Instead of a "one size fits all" story, parents insert their own idiosyncrasies into every created narrative. It's a bestseller for an audience of one.

EMDR

Trauma narratives told by parents may provide a coherent life story for the child. During the telling, the events may become desensitized. The parents' presence and availability provide a secure base so that the child does not become dysregulated during the story. Eventually, the child becomes bored with it. Parents may see a reduction in anxiety and behaviors related to the trauma. Narratives also seem to shift the negative meaning the child attributed to the event and to himself. A child who believed that he was bad and deserved abuse and abandonment may begin to accept the possibility that, like all babies, he deserved attention and love. He may question the conclusion that what happened was his fault. But in some cases the extent and severity of the trauma may be beyond what parents feel comfortable handling within a narrative.

Seeking out professionals trained in Eye Movement Desensitization and Reprocessing (EMDR) to assist in helping the child heal from past abuse, neglect, and losses may be advisable. Eye Movement Desensitization and Reprocessing was discovered and developed by Francine Shapiro in 1987. It is postulated that EMDR provides a mechanism for healing on neurological, physiological, emotional, and cognitive levels. Shapiro (1995) asserts that trauma obstructs a natural information processing system. The event remains in memory in its anxiety-producing form. Images, strong feelings, and physical sensations are then triggered by a multitude of stimuli encountered in everyday life. The bilateral stimulation of EMDR (eye movement, hand taps, auditory or tactile stimuli) seems to reactivate the information processing system. Unobstructed, the memory is processed and loses its emotional and physical impact. The child is enabled to consider new conclusions about the event. For more information on EMDR visit the website www.EMDR.com.

Appendix B

Story Construction Guide

- What would you like to work on with your child?

- What is the message you would like the story to convey?

- What perspective (first or third person) seems most appropriate for your situation and message?

- In the first person perspective, you may use your own experience or a story that your child may identify with to communicate the message to your child. Describe the events of the experience...

- Think about the emotional content. How can you convey the emotions both verbally and nonverbally?

- If you are considering using the third person perspective, with what character might your child identify?

  ○ Describe the appearance of the character…

  ○ Describe the setting in which the story takes place…

- Referring back to the message you would like to convey, what plot would capture your child's interest while communicating the message?

- What are the character's thoughts, feelings, and actions as the plot unfolds?

- Would any story aids be helpful? If so, what?

References

Achenbach, T.M., and Rescorla, L.A. (2001) *Manual for the ASEBA School-Age Forms and Profiles*. Burlington, VT: University of Vermont Research Center for Children, Youth and Families.

Ainsworth, M.D.S. (1967) *Infancy in Uganda: Infant Care and the Growth of Attachment.* Baltimore, MD: Johns Hopkins Press.

Ainsworth, M.D.S., Blehar, M., Waters, E., and Wall, S. (1978) *Patterns of Attachment.* Hillsdale, NJ: Erlbaum.

Beck, A.T., and Weishaar, M.E. (1989) "Cognitive Therapy." In R.J. Corsini and D. Wedding (eds) *Current Psychotherapies* (4th edn). Itasca, IL: F.E. Peacock Publishers.

Becker-Weidman, A. (2005) "Dyadic Developmental Psychotherapy: The Theory." In A. Becker-Weidman and D. Shell (eds) *Creating Capacity for Attachment.* Oklahoma City, OK: Wood 'N' Barnes Publishing.

Belsky, J., and Cassidy, J. (1994) "Attachment: Theory and Evidence." In M.L. Rutter, D.F. Hay, and S. Baron-Cohen (eds) *Development Through Life: A Handbook for Clinicians.* Oxford: Blackwell.

Booth, P.B., and Jernberg, A.M. (2009) *Theraplay: Helping Parents and Children Build Better Relationships Through Attachment Based Play* (2nd edn) San Francisco, CA: Jossey-Bass Publishers.

Bowlby, J. (1969/1982) *Attachment and Loss, Vol. 1. Attachment.* New York, NY: Basic Books.

Bowlby, J. (1973) *Attachment and Loss, Vol. 2. Separation.* New York, NY: Basic Books.

Bowlby, J. (1980) *Attachment and Loss, Vol. 3. Loss.* New York, NY: Basic Books.

Bowlby, J. (1988) *A Secure Base.* New York, NY: Basic Books.

Bretherton, I. (1985) "Attachment Theory: Retrospect and Prospect." In I. Bretherton and E. Waters (eds) "Growing Points of Attachment Theory and Research," *Monographs of the Society for Research in Child Development, 50* (1–2, Serial No. 209).

Bretherton, I. (1987) "New Perspectives on Attachment Relations: Security, Communication, and Internal Working Models." In J. Osofsky (ed.) *Handbook of Infant Development.* New York, NY: Wiley.

Bretherton, I. (2006) "In Pursuit of the Internal Working Model Construct and Its Relevance to Attachment Relationships." In K.E. Grossmann, E. Waters, and K. Grossmann (eds) *Attachment from Infancy to Adulthood: The Major Longitudinal Studies*. New York, NY: Guilford. (Original work published in 2005).

Bretherton, I., and Munholland, K.A. (1999) "Internal Working Models in Attachment Relationships: A Construct Revisited." In J. Cassidy and P.R. Shaver (eds) *Handbook of Attachment: Theory, Research and Clinical Applications*. New York, NY: Guilford Press.

Bretherton, I., Oppenheim, D., Buchsbaum, H., Emde, R.N., and The MacArthur Narrative Group (1990) *MacArthur Story Stem Battery*. Unpublished manuscript.

Bretherton, I., Ridgeway, D., and Cassidy, J. (1990) "Assessing Internal Working Models of the Attachment Relationship: An Attachment Story Completion Task for 3-Year-Olds." In M. Greenberg, D. Cicchetti, and M. Cummings (eds) *Attachment in the Preschool Years: Theory, Research and Intervention*. Chicago, IL: University of Chicago Press.

Briere, J. (1996) *Trauma Symptom Checklist for Children: Professional Manual*. Odessa, FL: Psychological Assessment Resources, Inc.

Bruner, J. (1987) "Life as narrative." *Social Research 4*, 1, 11–32.

Burack, J.A., Flanagan, T., Peled, T., and Sutton, H.M. (2006) "Social perspective-taking skills in maltreated children and adolescents." *Developmental Psychology 42*, 2, 207–217.

Caplan, F. (1973) *The First Twelve Months of Life: Your Baby's Growth Month by Month*. New York, NY: Perigree Putnam.

Carlson, E.A., and Sroufe, L.A. (1995) "Contributions of Attachment Theory to Developmental Psychopathology." In D. Cicchetti and C.J. Cohen (eds) *Developmental Psychopathology* (Vol. 1). New York, NY: Wiley.

Cohen, J.A., Mannarino, A.P., and Deblinger, E. (2006) *Treating Trauma and Traumatic Grief in Children and Adolescents*. New York, NY: Guilford.

Collin, P.H. (ed.) (1999) *Webster's Student Dictionary*. New York, NY: Barnes and Noble.

Colvert, E., Rutter, M., Kreppner, J., Beckett, C., *et al.* (2008) "Do theory of mind and executive function deficits underlie the adverse outcomes associated with profound early deprivation? Findings from the English and Romanian adoptees study." *Journal of Abnormal Child Psychology 36*, 7, 1057–1068.

Cozolino, L.J. (2002) *The Neuroscience of Psychotherapy: Building and Rebuilding the Human Brain*. New York, NY: W.W. Norton.

Crockenberg, S.B. (1981) "Infant irritability, mother responsiveness, and social support influences on security of infant–mother attachment." *Child Development 52*, 857–865.

Delaney, T. (2008) *Sensory Processing Disorder Answer Book*. Chicago, IL: Sourcebooks.

Dozier, M., Manni, M., and Lindheim, O. (2006) "Lessons from the Longitudinal Studies of Attachment." In K.E. Grossmann, E. Waters, and K. Grossmann (eds) *Attachment From Infancy to Adulthood: The Major Longitudinal Studies.* New York, NY: Guilford. (Original work published in 2005).

Dreikurs, R. with Soltz, V. (1990) *Children: The Challenge.* New York, NY: Plume Penguin.

Egeland, B., Yates, T., Appleyard, K., and van Dulmen, M. (2002) "The long-term consequences of maltreatment in the early years: a developmental pathway model to antisocial behavior." *Children's Services: Social Policy, Research, and Practice* 5, 4, 249–260.

Elicker, J., Englund, M., and Sroufe, L.A. (1992) "Predicting Peer Competence and Peer Relationships from Early Parent–Child Relationships." In R.D. Parke and G.W. Ladd (eds) *Family–Peer Relationships: Modes of Linkage.* Hillsdale, NJ: Erlbaum.

Engert, V., Efanor, S.I., Dedovic, K., Duchesne, A., Dagher, A., and Pruessner, J. (2010) "Perceived early-life maternal care and cortisol response to repeated psychosocial stress." *Journal of Psychiatry Neuroscience 35,* 6, 370–377.

Erickson, M.F., Sroufe, L.A., and Egeland, B. (1985) "The Relationship Between Quality of Attachment And Behavior Problems in Preschool in a High-Risk Sample." In I. Bretherton and E. Waters (eds) "Growing Points of Attachment Theory and Research," *Monographs of the Society for Research in Child Development 50* (1–2, Serial No. 209).

Finzi, R., Ram, A., Har-Even, D., Schnit, D., and Weizman, A. (2001) "Attachment styles and aggression in physically abused children." *Journal of Youth and Adolescence 30,* 6, 769–786.

Fonagy, P. (1999) *Transgenerational Consistencies of Attachment: A New Theory.* Paper presented to the Developmental and Psychoanalytic Discussion Group, American Psychoanalytic Association Meeting, Washington DC.

Fonagy, P. (2000) *Attachment in Infancy and the Problem of Conduct Disorders in Adolescence: The Role of Reflective Function.* Plenary address to the International Association of Adolescent Psychiatry, San Francisco.

Fonagy, P., Steele, H., Moran, G., Steele, M., and Higgitt, A. (1991) "The capacity for understanding mental states: the reflective self in parent and child and its significance for security of attachment." *Infant Mental Health Journal 13,* 3, 201–218.

Fonagy, P., and Target, M. (1997) "Attachment and reflective function: their role in self-organization." *Development and Psychopathology 9,* 4, 679–700.

Fraiberg, S.H. (1996) *The Magic Years: Understanding and Handling the Problems of Early Childhood.* New York, NY: Scribner. (Original work published in 1959).

George, C., and Solomon, J. (1999) "Attachment and Caregiving: The Caregiving Behavioral System." In J. Cassidy and P. Shaver (eds) *Handbook of Attachment: Theory, Research and Clinical Applications.* New York, NY: Guilford Press.

Granqvist, P., and Dickie, J. (2006) "Attachment and Spiritual Development in Childhood and Adolescence." In E. Roehlkepartain, P. King, L. Wagener, and P. Benson (eds) *The Handbook of Spiritual Development in Childhood and Adolescence.* Thousand Oaks, CA: Sage.

Green, J., Stanley, C., Smith, V., and Goldwyn, R. (2000) "A new method of evaluating attachment representation in young school age children: the Manchester Child Attachment Story Task (MCAST)." *Attachment and Human Development 2*, 1, 48–70.

Gurganus, S. (2002) *A Reliability and Validity Study of the May-Nichols Child Behavior Rating Scale.* Unpublished doctoral dissertation, Minnesota School of Professional Psychology.

Hodges, J, Steele, M., Hillman, S., and Henderson, K. (2003) "Mental Representation and Defenses in Severely Maltreated Children: A Story Stem Battery and Rating System for Clinical Assessment and Research Application." In R.N. Emde, D.P. Wolfe, and D. Oppenheim (eds) *Revealing the Inner Worlds of Young Children: The MacArthur Story Stem Battery and Parent–Child Narratives.* Oxford: Oxford University Press.

IJzendoorn, M.H., and Juffer, F. (2006) "The Emanuel Miller Memorial Lecture 2006: Adoption as intervention. Meta-analytic evidence for massive catch-up and plasticity in physical, socio-emotional, and cognitive development." *Journal of Child Psychology and Psychiatry 47*, 12, 1228–1245.

Jacobvitz, D., and Hazen, N. (1999) "Developmental Pathways from Infant Disorganization to Childhood Peer Relationships." In J. Solomon and C. George (eds) *Attachment Disorganization.* New York, NY: Guilford Press.

Keck, G.C., and Kupecky, R.M. (2009) *Adopting the Hurt Child: Hope for Families with Special-Needs Kids.* Colorado Springs, CO: Piñon Press. (Original work published in 1995).

Leach, P. (1994) *Children First: What our Society must do—and is not doing—for our Children Today.* New York, NY: Alfred A. Knopf.

Liotti, G. (1999) "Disorganization of attachment as a model for understanding dissociative psychopathology." In J. Solomon and C. George (eds) *Attachment Disorganization.* New York, NY: Guilford Press.

Lyons-Ruth, K. (1996) "Attachment relationships among children with aggressive behavior problems: the role of disorganized early attachment patterns." *Journal of Consulting and Clinical Psychology 64*, 1, 64–73.

Main, M., and Cassidy, J. (1988) "Categories of response to reunion with the parent at age 6: predictable from infant attachment classifications and stable over a 1-month period." *Developmental Psychology 24*, 3, 415–426.

Main, M., Kaplan, N., and Cassidy, J. (1985) "Security in Infancy, Childhood, and Adulthood: a move to the next level of representation." In I. Bretherton and E. Waters (eds) "Growing Points of Attachment Theory and Research," *Monographs of the Society for Research in Child Development 50* (1–2, Serial No. 209).

Main, M., and Solomon, J. (1986) "Discovery of a New, Insecure–Disorganized/ Disoriented Attachment Pattern." In T.B. Brazelton and M. Youngman (eds) *Affective Development in Infancy.* Norwood, NJ: Ablex.

Main, M., and Solomon, J. (1990) "Procedures for Identifying Infants as Disorganized/ Disoriented during the Ainsworth Strange Situation." In M.T. Greenberg, D. Cicchetti, and E.M. Cummings (eds) *Attachment in the Preschool Years.* Chicago, IL: University of Chicago Press.

May, J.C., and Nichols, T. (1997) *Child Behavior Rating Scale.* Deephaven, MN: Family Attachment and Counseling Center.

Mehta, M.A., Golembo, N.I., Nosarti, C., and Colvert, E. *et al.* (2009) "Amygdala, hippocampal and corpus callosum size following severe early institutional deprivation: The English and Romanian adoptees study pilot." *The Journal of Child Psychology and Psychiatry 50,* 8, 943–951.

Miller, L.J. (2007) *Sensational Kids: Hope and Help for Children with Sensory Processing Disorder.* New York, NY: Penguin Books. (Original work published 2006).

National Child Traumatic Stress Network Complex Trauma Task Force. Cook, A., Blaustein, M., Spinazzola, J., and van der Kolk, B. (eds) (2003) *Complex Trauma in Children and Adolescents.* Available at www.nctsnet.org/trauma-types/complex-trauma, accessed on 24 January 2011.

Nichols, M., Lacher, D., and May, J.C. (2002) *Parenting with Stories: Creating a Foundation of Attachment for Parenting Your Child.* Deephaven, MN: Family Attachment and Counseling Center.

Oppenheim, D. (2006) "Child, parent, and parent–child emotion narratives: implications for developmental psychopathology." *Development and Psychopathology 18,* 3, 771–790.

Oppenheim, D., and Waters, H.S. (1995) "Narrative Processes and Attachment Representations: Issues of Development and Assessment." In E. Waters, B. Vaughn, G. Posada, and K. Kondo-Ikemura (eds) "Constructs, Cultures, and Caregiving: New Growing Points in Attachment Theory and Research," *Monographs of the Society for Research in Child Development 60,* 2–3, 197–215.

Palacios, J., and Brodzinsky, D. (2010) "Adoption research: trends, topics, outcomes." *International Journal of Behavioral Development 34,* 3, 270–284.

Parish-Plass, N. (2008) "Animal-assisted therapy with children suffering from insecure attachment due to abuse and neglect: a method to lower the risk of intergenerational transmission of abuse?" *Clinical Child Psychology and Psychiatry 13,* 1, 7–30.

Perry, B. (1997) "Incubated in Terror: Neurodevelopmental Factors in the Cycle of Violence." In J. Osofsky (ed.) *Children in a Violent Society*. New York, NY: Guilford Press.

Perry, B., Pollard, R., Blakely, T., Baker, W., and Vigilante, D. (1995) "Childhood trauma, the neurobiology of adaptation, and use-dependent development of the brain: how states become traits." *Infant Mental Health Journal 16*, 271–291.

Piaget, J., and Inhelder, B. (1969) *The Psychology of the Child*. New York, NY: Basic Books.

Reese, E., Yan, C., Jack, F., and Hayne, H. (2010) "Emerging Identities: Narrative and Self from Early Childhood to Early Adolescence." In K.C. McLean and M. Pasupathi (eds) *Narrative Development in Adolescence: Creating the Storied Self*. Boston, MA: Springer.

Riggs, N., Jahromi, L., Razza, R., Dillworth-Bart, J., and Mueller, U. (2006) "Executive function and the promotion of social–emotional competence." *Journal of Applied Developmental Psychology 27*, 4, 300–309.

Robbins, J. (2000) A *Symphony in the Brain*. New York, NY: Atlantic Monthly.

Rutter, M., Beckett, C., Castle, J., and Colvert, E. *et al.* (2009) "Effects of Profound Early Institutional Deprivation: an overview of findings from a UK longitudinal study of Romanian adoptees." In G.M. Wrobel and E. Neil (eds) *International Advances in Adoption Research for Practice*. New York, NY: Wiley.

Rutter, M., and O'Connor, T.G. (2004) "Are there biological programming effects for psychological development? Findings from a study of Romanian adoptees." *Developmental Psychology 40*, 1, 81–94.

Schoenfield, P. (undated) *Paul Schoenfield: Four Parables, Vaudeville, Klezmer Rondos Compact Disc liner notes*. Argo 440 212–2 (1994).

Schore, A.N. (1994) *Affect Regulation and the Origin of the Self: The Neurobiology of Emotional Development*. Hillsdale, NJ: Erlbaum.

Schore, A.N. (1998) "Early Shame Experiences and Brain Development." In P. Gilbert and B. Andrews (eds) *Shame: Interpersonal Behavior, Psychopathology and Culture*. New York, NY: Oxford University Press.

Schore, A.N. (2001a) "Effects of a secure attachment relationship on right brain development, affect regulation, and infant mental health." *Infant Mental Health Journal 22*, 1–2, 7–66.

Schore, A.N. (2001b) "The effects of early relational trauma on right brain development, affect regulation, and infant mental health." *Infant Mental Health Journal 22*, 1–2, 201–269.

Schore, A.N. (2005) "Attachment, affect regulation, and the developing right brain: linking developmental neuroscience to pediatrics." *Pediatrics in Review 26*, 6, 204–217.

Shapiro, F. (1995) *Eye Movement Desensitization and Reprocessing: Basic Principles, Protocols, and Procedures.* New York, NY: Guilford Press.

Siegel, D.J. (1999) *The Developing Mind: How Relationships and the Brain Interact to Shape Who We Are.* New York, NY: Guilford.

Siegel, D.J. (2001) "Toward an interpersonal neurobiology of the developing mind: attachment relationships, 'mindsight,' and neural integration." *Infant Mental Health Journal 22,* 1–2, 7–66.

Siegel, D.J., and Hartzell, M. (2003) *Parenting from the Inside Out: How a Deeper Self-Understanding Can Help You Raise Children Who Thrive.* New York, NY: Tarcher Putnam.

Sparrow, S.S., Balla, D.A., and Cicchetti, D.V. (2005) *Vineland-II: Vineland Adaptive Behavior Scales, Second Edition. Survey Forms Manual.* Circle Pines, MN: American Guidance Service.

Spock, B. (1945) *The Common Sense Book of Baby and Child Care.* New York, NY: Duell, Sloan, and Pearce.

Sroufe, L.A. (1996) *Emotional Development: The Organization of Emotional Life in the Early Years.* New York, NY: Cambridge University Press.

Sroufe, L.A., Egeland, B., Carlson, E.A., and Collins, W.A. (2009) *The Development of the Person: The Minnesota Study of Risk and Adaptation from Birth to Adulthood.* New York, NY: Guilford. (Original work published in 2005).

Steele, M., Hodges, J., Kaniuk, J., Hillman, S., and Henderson, K. (2003) "Attachment representations and adoption: associations between maternal states of mind and emotion narratives in previously maltreated children." *Journal of Child Psychotherapy 29,* 2, 187–205.

Stern, D.N. (1985) *The Interpersonal World of the Infant.* New York, NY: W.H. Freeman.

Stiles, J. (2008) *The Fundamentals of Brain Development: Integrating Nature and Nurture.* Cambridge, MA: Harvard University Press.

Sunderland, M. (2006) *The Science of Parenting.* New York, NY: DK Publishing.

US Department of Health and Human Services, Administration for Children and Families, Administration on Children, Youth and Families (2010) *Child Maltreatment, 2009.* Available at www.acf.hhs.gov/programs/cb/pubs/cm09/, accessed on 11 September 2011.

van der Kolk, B.A. (1996) "The Complexity of Adaptation to Trauma: Self-Regulation, Stimulus Discrimination, and Characterological Development." In B.A. van der Kolk, A.C. McFarlane, and L. Weisaeth (eds) *Traumatic Stress: The Effects of Overwhelming Experience on Mind, Body, and Society.* New York, NY: Guilford.

van der Kolk, B.A., and Fisler, R.E. (1994) "Childhood abuse and neglect and loss of self-regulation." *Bulletin of the Menninger Clinic 58,* 2, 145–168.

Vermeer, H.J., and van IJzendoorn, M.H. (2006) "Children's elevated cortisol levels at daycare: a review and meta-analysis." *Early Childhood Research Quarterly 21*, 3, 390–401.

White, B.L. (1975) *The First Three Years of Life*. New York, NY: Avon Books.

White, M., and Epston, D. (1990) *Narrative Means to Therapeutic Ends*. New York, NY: W.W. Norton.

Yapko, M.D. (1990) *Trancework: An Introduction to the Practice of Clinical Hypnosis* (2nd edn). New York, NY: Brunner/Mazel, Inc.

Resources and Further Reading

About resources

A wide range of parenting techniques and strategies may all be useful at various times with a particular child. No single parenting methodology is going to work all the time, with all kids. Over the years, we have encountered some parenting resources that contribute to the attachment process and others that seem counter to connecting with kids. Avoid parenting techniques that emphasize controlling the child or rely only on consequences to shape and teach behavior. Instead, search out tools that nurture the child, help the child increase self-awareness and her ability to regulate emotions, and experience success.

We created an instructional DVD and accompanying study guide for parents and professionals who are looking for more information about the therapeutic process of creating narratives. Included on the DVD are five hours of narratives from actual therapy sessions. The DVD, detailed below, is available at our website, www.familyattachment.com.

First Steps for Strengthening Adoptive Families: Tools and Techniques for Meeting the Needs of Your Adopted Child, DVD and accompanying study guide, by the Family Attachment Center. This DVD training program explains attachment theory and offers tools and techniques for parents to help their adopted child learn healthy behaviors, strengthen attachment, and recover from trauma.

For further reading

- *Attaching in Adoption: Practical Tools for Today's Parents,* by Deborah D. Gray. Indianapolis, Indiana: Perspectives Press, 2002. Gray focuses on techniques that nurture while providing consistency and increased structure to help parents form close family relationships with traumatized children. She illustrates the seven stages of attachment and gives ideas for facilitating development.

- *Attachment Parenting: Instinctive Care for Your Baby and Young Child*, by Katie Allison Granju and Betsy Kennedy. New York: Pocket, 1999. The authors provide a thorough guide to the nurturing style of "attachment parenting." They advise parents on how to fully accept and meet their children's dependency needs with consistent awareness and action.

- *Attachment-Focused Parenting: Effective Strategies to Care for Children*, by Daniel A. Hughes. New York: W.W. Norton & Company, 2009. This book portrays behavioral problems as a result of attachment issues between the child and the parents. Hughes advocates refocusing parenting from a method of correction and consequences to one of bonding and attachment as a tool of change.

- *Beyond Consequences, Logic, and Control: a Love-Based Approach to Helping Attachment-Challenged Children with Severe Behaviors*, by Heather T. Forbes and B. Bryan Post. Orlando, Florida: Beyond Consequences Institute, 2006. This book offers parents a new understanding of the body/mind system and how the connection may be affected by stress and trauma. It demonstrates new ways to respond to a child which will create emotional safety. The authors promote love-based parenting as opposed to parenting based on control.

- *Born for Love: Why Empathy Is Essential—and Endangered*, by Maia Szalavitz and Bruce D. Perry. New York: William Morrow, 2010. Empathy is an essential part of an individual's happiness and a functional society. The authors explain how today's world threatens the development of empathy.

- *The Boy Who Was Raised as a Dog: and Other Stories from a Child Psychiatrist's Notebook: What Traumatized Children Can Teach Us about Loss, Love, and Healing*, by Bruce D. Perry and Maia Szalavitz. New York, New York: Basic Books, 2006. Perry and Szalavitz explore the impact and consequences of childhood trauma on the brain, behavior, and development of children and adolescents and discusses possible interventions.

- *The Connected Child: Bring Hope and Healing to Your Adoptive Family*, by Karyn B. Purvis, David R. Cross, and Wendy L. Sunshine. New York: McGraw-Hill, 2007. The authors provide practical techniques to help adoptive parents effectively deal with problem behavior and other psychological disorders, build trust and attachment, and discipline their adopted child.

- *Dissociation in Children and Adolescents: a Developmental Perspective*, by Frank W. Putnam. New York: Guilford Press, 1997. This book explores how dissociation is used by traumatized children to organize their experiences. It will help parents understand their behavior and describes effective treatment options.

- *The Explosive Child: a New Approach for Understanding and Parenting Easily Frustrated, Chronically Inflexible Children*, by Ross W. Greene. New York: HarperCollins, 2005. Dr. Greene outlines behaviors in explosive children and how parents can effectively handle situations both in the home and at school.

- *Filling in the Blanks: a Guided Look at Growing Up Adopted*, by Susan L. Gabel. Fort Wayne, Indiana: Perspectives Press, 1988. This workbook, for 10–14-year-old youths and their helpers, aids in the search for identity and addresses other issues young adoptees encounter as they get older.

- *The Five Love Languages of Children*, by Gary Chapman and Ross Campbell. Chicago, Illonois: Northfield Publications, 1997. The authors assist parents in identifying and learning which of the five methods of communication their child uses to express and receive love.

- *Ghosts from the Nursery: Tracing the Roots of Violence*, by Robin Karr-Morse and Meredith S. Wiley. New York: Atlantic Monthly, 1997. Using case studies, the authors explore the phenomenon of child violence and bear witness to the importance of experiences in a child's development between the ages zero to three.

- *Healing ADD: the Breakthrough Program that Allows You to See and Heal the Six Types of Attention Deficit Disorder*, by Daniel G. Amen. New York: G.P. Putnam's Sons, 2001. Dr. Amen identifies six different varieties of ADD and reveals the most effective treatments for each kind.

- *Healing Anxiety and Depression*, by Daniel G. Amen and Lisa C. Routh. New York: Putnam, 2003. This book identifies specific types of depression and anxiety. It offers information to understand how the brain is affected, as well as how to diagnose and treat different types of anxiety and depression.

- *Hold on to Your Kids: Why Parents Need to Matter More than Peers*, by Gordon Neufeld and Gábor Máté. New York: Ballantine Books, 2005. The authors present various reasons for and methods to reestablish an adult-oriented hierarchy in youth as opposed to a peer-oriented hierarchy.

- *Mind Coach: How to Teach Kids and Teenagers to Think Positive and Feel Good*, by Daniel G. Amen. Newport Beach, California: Mindworks, 1994. The author provides a manual for children and teens to learn "thinking skills" that encourage effectiveness and success in life.

- *The Out-of-Sync Child: Recognizing and Coping with Sensory Processing Disorder*, by Carol Stock Kranowitz. New York: Perigee Books, 2005. This book offers parents comprehensive information about Sensory Processing Disorder and suggests drug-free treatment methods.

- *Parenting from the Inside Out: How a Deeper Self-Understanding Can Help You Raise Children Who Thrive*, by Daniel J. Siegel and Mary Hartzell. New York: J.P. Tarcher/Putnam, 2003. This book explores how the parents' own childhood informs their parenting methods. A better understanding of their own life facilitates raising strong and compassionate children.

- *Parenting the Hurt Child: Helping Adoptive Families Heal and Grow*, by Gregory C. Keck and Regina M. Kupecky. Colorado Springs, Colorado: Piñon, 2009. The authors explore how families can aid adopted children who suffer from attachment issues, through effective parenting techniques.

- *Parenting with Stories: Creating a Foundation of Attachment for Parenting Your Child*, by Melissa Nichols, Denise Lacher, and Joanne C. May. Deephaven, Minnesota: Family Attachment and Counseling Center, 2002. A companion manual to this book; the authors provide a step-by-step way to encourage a strong parent–child attachment with the help of narrative therapy.

- *Positive Discipline: the Classic Guide to Helping Children Develop Self-Discipline, Responsibility, Cooperation, and Problem-Solving Skills*, by Jane Nelsen. New York: Ballantine Books, 2006. This book focuses on parental discipline based on respect, not punishment. It offers solutions for parents which are both firm and kind.

- *Raising a Sensory Smart Child: the Definitive Handbook for Helping Your Child with Sensory Processing Issues*, by Lindsey Biel and Nancy Peske. New York: Penguin, 2009. The authors offer an informational guide to assist parents in meeting the needs of children who have sensory difficulties.

- *Sensational Kids: Hope and Help for Children with Sensory Processing Disorder (SPD)*, by Lucy J. Miller. New York: G.P. Putnam's Sons, 2007. The author of this book answers questions many parents have about Sensory Processing Disorder in children, including how it is diagnosed and treated.

- *The Sensory Processing Disorder Answerbook: Practical Answers to the Top 250 Questions Parents Ask*, by Tara Delaney. Naperville, Illinois: Sourcebooks, Inc., 2008. A reliable reference book, this provides both answers and advice regarding Sensory Processing Disorder.

- *Theraplay: Helping Parents and Children Build Better Relationships Through Attachment-Based Play*, by Phyllis B. Booth and Ann M. Jernberg. San Francisco, California: Jossey-Bass, 2009. The authors explore the methods and benefits of attachment-based play or "Theraplay."

- *Touchpoints: Your Child's Emotional and Behavioral Development*, by T. Berry Brazelton. Reading, Massachusetts: Addison-Welsey, 2006. Brazelton offers a thorough understanding of children's physical, emotional, and behavioral development from ages zero to six.

- *Transforming the Difficult Child: the Nurtured Heart Approach*, by Howard Glasser and Jennifer Easley. Tuscon, Arizona: Center for the Difficult Child Publications, 1999. The authors provide strategies for parents and teachers to convert the behavior of a difficult child into positive and successful patterns of behavior.

- *Twenty Things Adopted Kids Wish Their Adoptive Parents Knew*, by Sherrie Eldridge. New York: Delta Trade Paperbacks, 1999. Informing adoptive parents of various issues adoptees face, Eldridge discusses subjects such as anger, mourning, shame, and the need for acknowledgment. The author uses case studies to demonstrate how parents can better relate to and interact with their adopted child.

- *The Unwritten Rules of Friendship: Simple Strategies to Help Your Child Make Friends*, by Natalie Madorsky Elman and Eileen Kennedy-Moore. Boston, Massachusetts: Little, Brown, 2003. This book will help parents identify which of the nine styles of interaction their child uses so that they may teach the child how to engage in happier relationships with fewer problems.

- *Why Do They Act That Way? A Survival Guide to the Adolescent Brain for You and Your Teen*, by David Allen Walsh. New York: Free Press, 2004. Describing the brain's development from child to teenager, this book explores the scientific reasons for typical teenage behavioral problems. It also offers ways in which to understand and communicate with adolescents constructively.

Websites

American Psychological Association: Magination Press

www.apa.org/pubs/magination/index.aspx
Children's books addressing special topics may be located on this site.

Association for Treatment and Training in the Attachment of Children

www.attach.org
This site offers information about therapy and parenting for children with attachment difficulties.

The Bipolar Child

www.bipolarchild.com

Information and resources regarding the symptoms and treatment of bipolar children.

Brain Place: SPECT Imaging for Your Brain Health

www.brainplace.com

Author Daniel Amen's website provides educational images of the changes in the brain when it has been affected by abuse, chemicals, and various emotional states.

Center on the Developing Child

www.developingchild.harvard.edu

This site contains information regarding the science of early childhood and early brain development.

Child Trauma Academy

www.childtrauma.org

This non-profit organization provides research and education regarding childhood trauma.

Children and Adults with Attention-Deficit/Hyperactivity Disorder

www.chadd.org

This site offers support services and resources for parents and children with ADHD.

Depression and Bipolar Support Alliance

www.dbsalliance.org

This site provides information and support for parents struggling with their child's mental health.

Do 2 Learn: Educational Resources for Special Needs

www.dotolearn.com

A website offering special learning tools and resources for youth with disabilities and special needs.

Fetal Alcohol Spectrum Disorders

www.fasdcenter.samhsa.gov

This site is devoted both to preventing and treating Fetal Alcohol Spectrum Disorder (FASD) by providing information and resources to the public.

Goal for It! Success Made Simple

www.goalforit.com

A website providing parenting tools and behavior charts.

Jessica Kingsley Publishers

www.jkp.com

This site catalogs children's books and books for the parents of special needs children.

Juvenile Bipolar Research Foundation

www.jbrf.org

This site provides educational resources and research regarding early-onset bipolar disorder.

Mind Modulations: Conscious Tools for Conscious Minds

www.mindmodulations.com

This website provides audio and visual entertainment programs and information about DAVE.

National Child Traumatic Stress Network

www.nctsnet.org

This website provides information about complex trauma in childhood and other resources and training materials.

North American Council on Adoptable Children

www.nacac.org

This website is focused on finding placements and meeting the needs of children waiting for adoption and for potential adoptive families.

Pocket Full of Therapy

www.pfot.com

This site provides a catalogue of tools, toys, and products for sensory processing needs.

Really Good Stuff: Fun and Creative Teaching Tools for Today's Classroom

www.reallygoodstuff.com

This site offers a wide range of useful and fun teaching supplies.

Special Needs Children

www.specialchildren.about.com

This site contains occupational therapy tools and toys under the equipment link.

Tapestry Books: Complete Resource for Adoption Books

www.tapestrybooks.com

This site offers a selection of books about and relating to adoption.

University of Minnesota Department of Pediatrics: International Adoption Clinic

www.peds.umn.edu/iac

This site offers research, education, and clinical care resources to improve the health of internationally adopted children.

Subject Index

abandonment fears 156
Achenbach Child Behavior
    Checklist (CBCL) 45–6
adaptive ways of behaving
    150–64
    narrative examples
        190–208
    purposes of narrative
        therapy 150–4
    techniques and narrative
        methods 154–64
adolescence, brain
    development 30–1
adoption
    age and outcomes 25
    importance of "being
        claimed" 96–112
    international 181–7
    older children 178–9
    see also "claiming"
        narratives
aggressive behaviors 157–8
alcohol and drug use,
    prenatal 18, 48
allergies 88–9
alternative therapies 94–5
Animal-Assisted Therapy 95
anxious-avoidant behavior
    patterns 22–3
anxious-resistant behavior
    patterns 21–2
asking questions during
    narratives 106, 107–8
assessment of children's
    internal working
    models 41–56

behavior checklists and
    standardized tests
    45–9
    history-taking 44–5
    observational methods
        49–51
    parental contributions
        51–5
    putting the pieces
        together 55–6
assessment of sensory
    processing abilities
    87–8
assessment tools 45–9
attachment
    as regulatory system 28
    theory of 20
attachment figures 20
attachment relationships
    18–19, 20–7
    development 20–3, 33–5
    importance 24–5
    patterns of behavior 20–3
    transmission 25–7
Attachment Story
    Completion Task
    (Bretherton et al. 1990)
    47–8
attention deficit
    hyperactivity disorder
    (ADHD)
    assessments 48–9
    problems sitting still 130
attunement see emotional
    attunement (parental)
avoidance responses 31

basic life skills 153–4
Behavior Assessment System
    for Children 45
behavior checklists and
    standardized tests 45–9
behavior patterns
    and attachment relations
        20–3
    see also problem behaviors
beliefs about self and others
    see internal working
    models
biofeedback therapies 94
birth order 100
birth parents, and trauma
    narratives 175–8
bonding difficulties 97–8
boundaries, problems with
    disclosures 129
brain development
    impact of trauma 28–9,
        30–1
    lifelong changes and
        developments 29,
        32–3
brain plasticity 29
building relationships, and
    narrative 135–6

"cause and effect" thinking
    35, 151
CBCL see Child Behavior
    Checklist (CBCL)
    (Achenbach and
    Rescorla 2001)

CBRS *see* Child Behavior Rating Scale (CBRS) (May and Nichols 1997)
change processes 33–5, 115
learning to move forward 194–201
checklist assessments *see* behavior checklists and standardized tests
Child Behavior Checklist (CBCL) (Achenbach and Rescorla 2001) 45–6
Child Behavior Rating Scale (CBRS) (May and Nichols 1997) 45–6
child development 33–5
and attachment 18–19
information sources 147
regression 146–7
slowed down or arrested 34–5
"claiming" narratives 96–112, 168–72
aims and purposes 97–104
examples 168–72
methods 104–12
problem-solving tips 109–12
"cliffhangers" and suspense 161
cognitive functions
deficits and arrested development 35
narratives to assist development 132–4
cognitive testing 48
"complex trauma" 29
Connors Rating Scales 45
conscience and remorse 35
consistency in parenting 91
control issues 111–12
coping strategies 151–2
creativity and narratives 166

desensitization to narratives 129–30
"deserving" of love 99–100
The Developing Mind (Siegel 1999) 28
development
impact of emotional attunement and regulation 75–6
as lifelong process 29, 33–5
use of narratives 138
wanting to stay a baby 146–7
see also brain development
developmental delays 157
developmental narratives 131–48
aims and purposes 131–9
examples 187–90
learning secure base behaviors 187–8
learning to regulate emotion 188–90
methods and techniques 139–47
diagnostic labels 41–3
diets 94–5
Digital Audio Visual Entrainment (DAVE) 94
discipline measures 92
disclosure of past
fears of rejection 118–20
inappropriate 129
disorganized attachment patterns
early childhood 23
lifelong patterns 24–5
dissociation responses 31, 129
Dyadic Developmental Psychotherapy 61

early life experiences
discovery and assessment 41–56
impact on children 17–39

see also trauma narratives; traumatic early life experiences
EMDR *see* Eye Movement Desensitization and Reprocessing (EMDR)
emotion regulation 85–90
impact on development 75–6
impact of early trauma 31
influencing factors 86–90
recreating past problems 157–8
techniques and narrative methods 90–5, 188–90
use of movement and touch 93–4
emotional attunement (parental) 73–85
benefits for child development 75–6
developing skills and methods 76–8
influencing factors 81–5
key components 79–81
emotional development
and narrative 134–5
regression and poor expression 157–8
empathy 89–90
deficits 32, 35
lack of remorse feelings 35
understanding through narrative 115–17
environmental influences on brain development 28–9
settings for telling stories 63–5
equine therapy 95
executive function 30–1
extended families 101
Eye Movement Desensitization and Reprocessing (EMDR) 126, 212

Family Attachment
    Narrative Therapy
  concept outline and
    theoretical basis
    36–9, 57–62
  constructing and telling
    stories 63–71
  core beliefs 62
  examples 167–208
  key themes 71
  settings 63–5
  story "heroes" and
    perspectives 65–7
  story messages and
    therapy aims 67–9
  use of props 69–70, 108
  vocabulary and language
    use 70–1
  see also "claiming"
    narratives; trauma
    narratives
family support 85
family traditions 102
fantasy and make–believe
  136–7
fetal alcohol syndrome,
  tests 48
"fight or flight" responses
  31
food intolerance 94–5
foreign language use 69
friends and support
  networks (family) 85
friendship building 89–90,
  202–4

genetic factors,
  intergenerational
  transmission of stress
  28
gluten-free diets 95
grandparents 101
guilt feelings, lack of 35

healing following trauma
  114
"heroes" in stories 66–7

history-taking 44–5
  see also parental narratives
homeopathic medicine 94–5
horses 95
hyperarousal 31
hypervigilance 156

imaginative play 133–4
Individual Education Plan
  (US) 93
infertility 102–3
information sources 223–31
  further reading 223–8
  websites 228–31
insecure attachment patterns
  diagnostic labels 41–3
  early childhood 21–3
  lifelong patterns 24–5
instinctive responses to
  children see emotional
  attunement (parental)
institutional care 25
intergenerational attachment
  patterns 25–7
internal working models
  17–39
  concepts and
    representations
    18–19, 36–7
  development of
    attachment
    relationships 20–3
  discovery and assessment
    41–56
  impact of life events 27–9
  importance of early
    relationships 24–5
  intergenerational
    transmission 25–7
  meanings and beliefs
    36–9
  potential to change and
    develop 33–5
  role of complex trauma
    29–33
  theoretical basis for
    narrative therapies
    36–9

internationally adopted
  children, trauma
  narratives 181–7

language choice for storytelling 70–1
life events 27–9
life skills, teaching the
  basics 153–4
life story books 123–4
lying 136–7, 156
  learning to tell the truth
    192–4, 201–2

MacArthur Story Stem
  Battery (Bretherton et
  al. 1990) 47–8
Manchester Child
  Attachment Story Task
  (Green et al. 2000) 48
meanings in behavior
  155–8
"meltdowns" and tantrums
  31, 54–5
memory, and self-concepts
  37
messages in stories 67–9
metaphor use 58–9
migraines 86
morals and values 150–1
movement techniques 93–4
moving forward 194–201

narrative assessments 47–8
narrative construction guide
  213–14
narrative therapy see
  "claiming" narratives;
  developmental
  narratives; Family
  Attachment Narrative
  Therapy; trauma
  narratives
neuroscience of narratives
  59–60
  see also brain development
nutrition therapies 94–5

object permanence 35, 134, 143
observational assessment methods 49–51
oppositional behavior 158

parental attachment styles and childhood experiences 25–7, 81–3
parental attunement *see* emotional attunement (parental)
parental mental states 83–4
parental narratives 51–5
   see also Family Attachment Narrative Therapy
parenting
   discipline measures 92
   importance of consistency 91
   primary aims and purpose 90
   quantity vs. quality time 84
   resources 223–31
   structuring the environment 92–3
   see also emotional attunement (parental)
"pet" names 102
pets 95
"phony" behaviors 156
plasticity 29
plot development 68–9
   creating suspense 161
   narrative construction guide 213–14
problem behaviors 149
   causes and meanings 33–5, 155–8
   effecting changes 158–61
   purposes and aims of narrative therapy 150–4
   remedial skill building 136–7

teaching appropriate behaviors 161–4
techniques and methods of narrative therapy 154–64
tips and problem-solving 165–6
professional help 125–7
   website information 228–31
projective assessments 47–8
props 69–70, 108
psychodynamic therapies 61

questions during narratives 106, 107–8

refusal to listen 128
regression enactments 144, 146–7
relationship building, and narrative 135–6
relatives 101
religion 102
remorse and conscience 35
representational maps of beliefs *see* internal working models
Rorschach Inkblot Test 47

school environments 92–3
secure attachment patterns
   early childhood 20–1
   lifelong patterns 24
secure base behaviors 187–8
seeking professional help 125–7
self concepts
   impact of trauma 30
   see also internal working models
self soothing 85
   see also emotion regulation
self-confidence 24
sensory processing problems 48–9, 86
   assessment checklist 87–8

use of movement and touch therapies 93–4
   see also emotion regulation
settings for telling stories 63–5
sleep difficulties 88, 95
social cues, problems understanding 89–90
social skill deficits 24, 89–90, 157
   relationship building and narrative 135–6
standardized testing 45–9
Stanford-Binet Intelligence Scales 48
stealing 156, 201–2
story books 123–4
story construction guide 213–14
story telling therapies *see* Family Attachment Narrative Therapy
stress responses, and patterns of behavior 30–1, 155–6
support systems 85
suspense building 161
symbolic functioning 35, 133

tantrums and "meltdowns" 31, 54–5
teaching values 150–1
Thematic Apperception Test (TAT) 47–8
third person narratives 65–6
   for trauma 117–18
time factors, quantity vs quality 84
touch therapies 93–4
trauma narratives 113–30, 172–87
   aims and purposes 113–17
   examples 172–87
   for internationally adopted children 181–7

trauma narratives *cont.*
  for older adopted
    children 178–81
  methods and techniques
    117–30
  problem-solving tips
    128–30
  when to seek professional
    help 125–7
Trauma Symptom Checklist
  (Briere 1996) 45
Trauma-Focused Cognitive
  Behavioral Therapy
  61–2
traumatic early life
  experiences 18, 19
  and brain development
    28–9, 30–1
  effects 30–3
trigger factors 88–9
trust issues 98–9, 204–8
truth telling 192–4, 201–2

values and ideals 150–1
Vineland Adaptive Behavior
  Scales 46–7
vocabulary for story-telling
  70–1

websites information sources
  228–31
Wechsler Intelligence Scale
  for Children 48
working parents 84
written narratives 123

Author Index

Achenbach, T.M. 45
Ainsworth, M.D.S. 20, 50

Balla, D.A. 46–7
Beck, A.T. 61
Becker-Weidman, A. 61
Belsky, J. 24
Booth, P.B. 50
Bowlby, J. 19–20, 25, 34,
    43, 75, 157
Bretherton, I. 24–6, 47,
    60, 75
Briere, J. 45
Brodzinsky, D. 24, 26
Bruner, J. 59
Burack, J.A. 32

Caplan, F. 147
Carlson, E.A. 26
Cassidy, J. 23–4, 47–8, 155
Cicchetti, D.V. 46–7
Cohen, J.A. 61
Colvert, E. 31
Cozolino, L.J. 29, 59, 61,
    114, 131, 149
Crockenberg, S.B. 85

Deblinger, E. 61
Delaney, T. 86
Dickie, J. 76, 90
Dozier, M. 83
Dreikurs, R. 32

Egeland, B. 24, 34
Elicker, J. 24
Engert, V. 76
Englund, M. 24

Epston, D. 61
Erickson, M.F. 24, 34

Finzi, R. 76
Fisler, R.E. 27
Fonagy, P. 25–6, 60, 79,
    82, 89
Fraiberg, S.H. 92

George, C. 81
Granqvist, P. 76, 90
Green, J. 48
Gurganus, S. 42

Hartzell, M. 61
Hazen, N. 155
Hodges, J. 115

Ijzendoorn, M.H. 52, 139
Inhelder, B. 124, 133

Jacobwitz, D. 155
Jernberg, A.M. 50
Juffer, F. 52, 139

Kaplan, N. 24
Keck, G.C. 123
Kupecky, R.M. 123

Lacher, D. 57
Leach, P. 84
Lindheim, O. 83
Liotti, G. 27
Lyons-Ruth, K. 157

Main, M. 23–4, 155
Mannarino, A.P. 61

Manni, M. 83
May, J.C. 45, 57
Mehta, M.A. 29
Miller, L.J. 86, 88
Munholland, K.A. 25

National Child Traumatic
    Stress Network 29–30,
    83
Nichols, M. 57
Nichols, T. 45

O'Connor, T.G. 25
Oppenheim, D. 26–7, 48,
    60

Palacios, J. 24, 26
Parish-Plass, N. 95
Perry, B. 28, 31
Piaget, J. 124, 133

Reese, E. 61
Rescorla, L.A. 45
Ridgeway, D. 47–8
Riggs, N. 30
Robbins, J. 76
Rutter, M. 25

Schoenfield, P. 58
Schore, A.N. 28, 30, 33,
    64–5, 75–6
Siegel, D.J. 21, 28, 32–3,
    37, 59–61, 75–6, 79
Solomon, J. 23, 81
Soltz, V. 32
Sparrow, S.S. 46–7
Spock, B. 147

Sroufe, L.A. 19, 21–2, 24,
    26, 32–4, 42, 53, 58,
    85, 131, 152, 209
Steele, M. 53
Stern, D.N. 65
Stiles, J. 28
Sunderland, M. 76

Target, M. 26, 79, 82, 89

US Department of Health
    and Human Services
    30

van der Kolk, B.A. 27, 30,
    32, 114, 156
van Ijzendoorn, M.H. 84
Vermeer, H.J. 84

Waters, H.S. 48, 60
Weishaar, M.E. 61
White, B.L. 147
White, M. 61

Yapko, M.D. 59